Yule

Anna Franklin

LEAR

www.learbooks.co.uk

This first edition published by:
Lear Books
Windrush House
High Tor West
Earl Shilton
Leics
LE9 7DN
UK

Cover design by Paul Mason
Cover photograph by Anna Franklin

ISBN 978-1-907614-07-1

Printed in England by Booksprint.

CONTENTS

INTRODUCTION

The winter solstice is probably the most ancient festival of all. Evidence for its celebration goes back at least 30, 000 years and is found on every continent.

Sheltered in our warm houses and able to buy food from the supermarket all year round, we find it hard to imagine what winter meant for our ancestors. During the summer, the long hours of light and warmth provided a bountiful harvest of greenery, corn and fruit. Animals had plenty of grazing and reproduced, supplying meat, milk and cheese. But then winter came. Darkness and cold increased daily, causing plants to shrivel and animals expired while struggling to find fodder. Humans died from cold and hunger. Every day, the sun seemed to grow weaker, as if it too were dying. Every day, it rose lower and lower in the sky. Darkness and death threatened to overwhelm the world forever.

And yet, in the very moment of greatest gloom, the sun was reborn. Life and hope were rekindled - the light would grow, warmth would increase, spring, summer and harvest would come. The Wheel of the Year, which had been briefly stilled, would spin on.

At midwinter and midsummer the sun apparently changes its course. In midwinter having reached the lowest point in its path, it turns about and begins to mount the skies; conversely at midsummer, having attained the highest point, the sun seems to turn about once more and descend. Consequently it was often imagined the sun god was born at the winter solstice and grew until midsummer, afterwards declining towards his death at the midwinter solstice, before being reborn and the whole cycle beginning again. Hurs or Hors, for example, was the Slavonic god of the old winter sun who became smaller as the days grew shorter and died on *korochun* (the winter solstice) defeated by the dark powers of Chernobog. The next day Hors was resurrected as the new sun, Koleda. (*Koleda* survives in the modern Slavonic languages as the word for Christmas.) Because of his transformation the Slavs worshipped Hors as the god of healing and the triumph of health, a characteristic shared by most of the sun gods around the world.

We experience changing seasons because the axis of the Earth - an imaginary line between the north and south poles - is tilted from true by 23.5 degrees. As our planet revolves around the sun, this means that part of the earth tilts towards the sun, then away again. Between June and September the Northern Hemisphere is tilted toward the sun and gets more light, experiencing the season of summer. At the same time the Southern Hemisphere experiences winter. Between December and March the Northern Hemisphere is tilted away from the sun and experiences less light and warmth, while the Southern Hemisphere enjoys summer. Just how much sunlight you experience depends on the latitude you occupy. By June 21st there are twenty-four hours of daylight above the Arctic Circle, while below the Antarctic Circle there are twenty-four hours of darkness. During spring and autumn, both hemispheres experience milder weather and the two equinoxes mark the junctures when the Earth's axis is pointing sideways. Without the tilt in the Earth's axis we would have the same degree of light and warmth - or dark and cold - all year round, and have no seasons at all; the sun's rays would always be directly over the Equator. The solstices and equinoxes are the four stations of the sun during the year, represented by an equal armed cross and there is a frequent connection between sun gods and crosses.

The winter solstice is generally considered to be the start of winter, and the three winter months are reckoned as December, January and February. However, the 'solar winter'- the period with the fewest hours of daylight and the weakest sunlight - stretches from November 1st to February 1st with the solstice marking Midwinter. Though the winter solstice is the shortest day of the year, it is not the date of either the earliest sunset or the latest sunrise. The earliest sunset occurs around Little Yule on 13th December, and the latest sunrise around New Year at the beginning of January.

It is impossible to separate the celebrations of the winter solstice and Christmas as all of the myths, symbols and customs of Christmas are Pagan in origin. But while Christians see time as linear and believe that the birth of the Divine Child came but once, two thousand years ago, Pagans view time as cyclical, and know that the Child of Light, and with him the world, is reborn and renewed every year.

Chapter 1
THE DARKEST HOUR

THE SUN SETS THE WORLD IN MOTION

The sun governs the pattern of life on Earth, its cycles dividing the hours, days, months and years, and the round of sowing, growth, harvest and decay. It is only the movement of the sun that makes life possible. The Egyptians called the sun the divine creator of all things, the master of time and the seasons. Its regular daily and seasonal rotations stand as a symbol of cosmic order. From where we stand on earth, each day the sun seems to rise in the east, scattering the powers of darkness and diffusing light and fertility as it climbs to its zenith at noon. Then it declines, descending into the west and eventually sinking below the horizon, only to return with the following dawn.

The word *solstice* is derived from Latin and means 'sun stands still'. The sun usually rises at a different point on the horizon each day (it only rises due east at the spring equinox). It travels north-east to its furthest position at the summer solstice and appears to stand still for three days before heading south-east, reaching its southernmost position at the winter solstice where it seems to rest again for three days before heading north once more.

The Sanskrit root of the word summer means 'half year', suggesting the light and dark halves of the year were marked by the two solstices.[1] This division of the year by the solstices into two halves was common in the ancient world. The Saxon year began at the winter solstice and the summer solstice marked its mid-point.

Ancient man would have realised that we depend on the sun for life - in the summer the long hours of daylight and warmth make the crops grow but in the winter darkness and cold, they shrivel and die. Each day, up to the winter solstice, the sun grows weaker and weaker. Each day it is lower and lower on the horizon, and each day the hours of daylight grow fewer. Darkness is spreading; everything is winding down, threatening to come to a standstill.

---

1   Dr E.C.Krupp, *Beyond the Blue Horizon*, Oxford University Press, Oxford, 1992

8

As the Roman writer Lucan (39-65 CE) described it:

> *"Nature's rhythm stops. The night becomes longer and the day keeps waiting. The ether does not obey its law; and the whirling firmament becomes motionless, as soon as it hears the magic spell. Jupiter – who drives the celestial vault that turns on its fast axis – is surprised by the fact that it does not want to turn."*

If the sun does not regenerate then time will come to an end, life will be extinguished and the world will return to the dark womb of night from which it emerged. And when the sun decays towards its death at Yule, that primal chaos threatens to return.

THE THREAT OF CHAOS

Our ancestors thought that before the sun was set spinning on its course - creating the hours, days and seasons - there was only chaos; it was the beginning of regularised time that brought the cosmos into being

Many ancient cultures believed that the cosmos – the manifest universe as we know it - emerged from a primal chaos. In Greek, chaos (χάος) did not mean 'disorder' as it does today, but primordial emptiness, space and darkness. The word is derived from the Proto-Indo-European root *ghn* or *ghen* meaning 'gape' or 'be wide open', in the sense of a chasm or abyss.

According to Hesiod (8th –7th century BCE) in the *Theogony* ('Origin of the Gods'), Chaos was the original dark void from which everything else appeared. Ovid (1st century BCE) thought of the initial state of the universe as a confused mixture of the four elements, a formless mass without order, but which contained everything in potential: *"…a rude and undeveloped mass, that nothing made except a ponderous weight; and all discordant elements confused, were there congested in a shapeless heap"*. [2] Orphic cosmogony thought of the primal chaos as a 'womb of darkness' in which the cosmic egg was hatched. Indeed, modern Pagans often think of it as the womb of the chthonic goddess from which everything emerges and to which it eventually returns, analogous to the Cauldron of Ceridwen which dissolves and recreates all things.

In many myths, it was the interaction of opposing forces that caused order to emerge.[3] In Norse legend the primal chaos was called Ginnungagap, and existed before heaven and earth. The Northern region of Ginnungagap was an icy region land known as Niflheim. Muspelheim, the southern

---

2   Ovid, *Metamorphoses*

3   The Pagan idea of a primordial state of matter was opposed by the Christian Church from the 2nd century, who posited a creation *ex nihilo* (out of nothing) by an omnipotent god.

region, contained bright sparks and glowing embers. When the two met, the
primordial giant called Ymir was conceived. Later, when Odin, Vili and
Vé killed Ymir they used his body to create Midgard: his flesh became the
earth; his blood the seas and lakes; his bones the mountains; his teeth became
stones and from his hair grew trees. Maggots from his flesh became the race
of dwarfs. The gods set Ymir's skull above Ginnungagap and made the sky,
supported by four dwarfs called East, West, North and South. Odin cast Ymir's
brains into the wind to become the clouds.

Sometimes the primal chaos was thought of as a realm of water. In
Sumero-Akkadian myth, Apsu (*ab* = water, *zu* = far) personified the primeval
chasm of sweet waters underneath the earth, while his consort Tiamat was the
salt waters of chaos. When the two mingled in a kind of sacred marriage, the
first elder gods were created - Lahmu and Lahamu ('Muddy') who became
the parents of Anshar ('Pivot of Heaven') and earth (Kishar) who met at the
horizon and thus created Anu (the heavens) and Ki (the Earth).

Similarly, in Egyptian mythology, the god Nun - called 'Infinity,
Nothingness, Nowhere and Darkness' - was chaos or the primeval waters and
filled the entire cosmos. Shu, the air, separated the sky from the earth and
then the Ogdoad (the eight primal gods) created a mound which rose from the
primordial waters, and on this they formed an egg from which the young sun
god emerged to divide the hours, days, months and years, while Nun guarded
and kept in check the demonic powers of chaos.

While earlier myths saw the primal chaos, often characterized
as female, as unformed potential, later patriarchal myths tended to view
it as threatening, something that had to be defeated and contained by the
chaoskampf, an allegorical or mythological battle between a hero/god and
a monster (such as a dragon) which represented chaos. Tiamat became a
monstrous dragon or sea serpent who made war on the deities she had given
birth to, and who was killed by the storm-god Marduk. The heavens and the
Earth were formed from her divided body, in an echo of the story of Ymir.
Other examples of the *chaoskampf* include Baal's fight against Yamm, Tarhunt
against Illuyanka, Yahweh against Leviathan, Zeus against Typhon and even
George and the dragon and St Michael and the devil.

Pherecydes of Syros (6th century BCE) in his lost work *Pentemychos*
('Five Recesses') [4] proposed that there were three divine principles which
had always existed - Zas ('he who liveth'), Chthonie ('she who underlies
the earth') and Chronos (time). We only know this work as quoted by later
authors, and as Hermias explained "*Pherecydes says the principles are Zen*

---

4   or *Heptamychos* ('Seven Recesses')

and Chthonie and Cronus; Zen is the aither, Chthonie the earth and Cronus is time; the aither is that which acts, the earth is that which is acted upon, time is that in which events come to pass." [5]

In this version of the creation myth, a structure made of five recesses or caves (also called ditches or gates) existed within Chthonie. [6] (These five nooks or recesses may relate to the symbol of the pentacle; in 3000 BCE the pentacle was used, two points up, in Sumerian pictograms which represent the word *UB* meaning a cavity or hole.) The *pentemychos* lay outside of the *aither* (air/space), the domain of Zeus, and was beneath the earth. To the five recesses were assigned the elements. The recesses were inseminated by the seed of Chronos, and from the elements a multitude of additional gods were born. Zas (Zeus) ordered and distributed the creation, making a cloth on which he decorated earth and sea, and which he then presented as a wedding gift to Chthonie, wrapping it around her. [7] Zas seems to have been a personification of masculine sexual creativity. Proclus wrote that *"Pherecydes used to say that Zeus changed into Eros when about to create, for the reason that, having created the world from opposites, he led it into agreement and peace and sowed sameness in all things, and unity that interpenetrates the universe"*. [8]

However, before this could happen, five pre-cosmic beings - dark forces representing disorder - under the leadership of Ophioneus the Snaky One contended against the world-order of Zas. As they were eternal and indestructible, once defeated they had to be confined by Chronos in Tartaros, the underworld (which may be the *pentemychos*) or in an alternative version, hurled into Oceanus (the sea), and bound with locks fashioned in iron (space), by Zeus and in bronze (water) by Poseidon and put under the guard of the Harpies and Thyella, daughters of Boreas. Tartaros was where all the enemies of the cosmic order were locked away, and was thus called the 'prison-house' of Zeus.

Although Chaos was locked away, it still continued to exert an influence; Homer called it 'the subduer of both gods and men'. The *mychos* (recess) is the gateway to the underworld and the passage from it, and through it chaos continues to influence the world. Many Greek heroes passed through

5   Werner Jaeger, The Theology of the Early Greek Philosophers 1936–1937, www.giffordlectures.org

6   It is probable that Chthonie is the *pentemychos* and the prototype of Persephone.

7   In another fragment it is not Chthonie, but "a winged oak" that he wrapped the cloth around.

8   Kirk, G. S., Raven, J. E., & Schofield, M., *The Presocratic Philosophers*, Cambridge Univ. Press 1999

it to seek knowledge from the underworld which was considered the source of all wisdom.[9] It was the domain of the witch goddess Hecate who was called the Lady of Tartaros, Phulada (Guardian), Propulaia (Before the Gates), Kleidophoros (Key-bearer) and Kleidoukhos (Key-holder). In Euripides' play *Medea*, the sorceress Medea calls upon Hecate with the words, *"By that dread queen whom I revere before all others and have chosen to share my task, by Hecate who dwells within my inmost chamber, not one of them shall wound my heart and rue it not."* The inmost chamber is, of course, the heart, but it is also the *mychos*, the source of all being. It was from this that the world got its *psyche* (soul) and its *daimon* (genius). This may be represented by the inmost chamber of the pentagram.

CRONOS

Distinction is usually made between Chronos/Khronos and the Titan Kronos/Cronos/Cronus, though their mythologies became conflated or more likely had a common origin. Chronos was the personification of time. His name in modern Greek means 'year' and he was sometimes depicted with three heads, that of a man, a bull and a lion, representing the tripartite Greek year, or shown in Greco-Roman mosaics as a man turning the Zodiac Wheel and named Aeon/Aion (Eternal Time), giving us our idea of Father Time.

He and his sister Rhea took the throne of the world as king and queen. This was a Golden Age on Earth, as everything ran according to its proper courses and seasons, and people had no need for laws or rules as everyone lived honourably and kindly. There was no need for work, as everything grew in abundance. There was no decay and no death. Hesiod wrote of the Five Ages of Mankind as Gold, Silver, two Ages of Bronze and an Age of Iron, saying that Cronus' Age of Gold was the purest epoch.

However, Cronus learned that there was a prophecy that he was

Cronus, on the other hand, was the leader of the Titans, descendants of Gaia the earth and Uranus the sky. Uranus incurred Gaia's anger when he confined her gigantic youngest children, the hundred-armed Hecatonchires and one-eyed Cyclopes, in Tartaros. She created a great stone sickle and persuaded Cronus to castrate his father, casting his testicles into the sea, from the foam of which Aphrodite was born. From the blood which fell upon the earth the Gigantes, Erinyes (Furies), and Meliae (Ash Nymphs) were produced. However, Cronus ignored his mother and re-imprisoned the Hecatonchires, the Gigantes and the Cyclopes in Tartaros and set the dragon Campe to guard them.

---

9   http://www.experiencefestival.com/a/Pentagram_-_History/id/597436

destined to be deposed by his son, just as he had overthrown his own father. Consequently as Rhea gave birth to their children Demeter, Hera, Hades, Hestia and Poseidon, he seized each child in turn and devoured it. When the sixth child was due Rhea was determined to save it, travelling to Crete where she secretly gave birth to Zeus in the Dictean Caves. When Cronus demanded the child, she deceived him by giving him a stone wrapped in swaddling clothes, which he promptly wallowed. Rhea kept Zeus safely hidden in a cave on Mount Ida. According to some versions of the story, he was raised by a goat nymph named Amalthea, while a company of Kouretes or Korybantes,[10] armoured male dancers, shouted and clapped their hands to make enough noise to mask the baby's cries.

When he reached adulthood, Zeus sought the help of his grandmother Gaia, who produced a poison that caused Cronus to disgorge the contents of his belly (or some say Zeus slit open the stomach). First to be vomited was the stone. This was set down at Pytho near Mount Parnassus as the *omphalos* ('navel') stone, the centre of the world. Then followed Zeus's five siblings. A great war followed called the *Titanomachy*, in which Zeus enlisted the help of the Gigantes, the Hecatonchires and the Cyclopes, who forged his thunderbolts. They were able to overcome Cronus and the other Titans, and Zeus confined many of them in Tartaros.

THE WHEEL STOPS TURNING

As the sun winds down and darkness increases, our ancestors believed that the immortal spirits of chaos are released from the underworld and try to overtake the world. At the solstice, the sun is still for three days as though time itself is frozen. Everything stands in suspension, waiting for the rebirth of the sun to chase the chaotic spirits back to the Otherworld and set time spinning on its course once again.

In reflection of this, the Lapps forbade the turning of any kind of wheel, including cartwheels and churns. In many countries across Europe all forms of spinning and weaving were also prohibited. In Shropshire no spinning was done during the Twelve Days of Yule, for if any flax were to be left on the distaff the Devil would cut it.

In other places fairies or hag goddesses were said to destroy any

---

10   There is some confusion between the Korybantes and the Kouretes in Greek literature. Both were ecstatic dancers associated with elder earth goddesses, Cybele and Rhea respectively. The Kouretes danced in armour (a Pyrrhic dance) which is thought to have been a male coming of age ritual or initiation. The Kouretes also presided over the infancy of Dionysus and Zagreus. They were magicians and seers, and were metal workers, a magical art in itself.

spinning left at Yule. In central Germany and in parts of Austria the hag was called Frau Holle or Holda, in southern Germany and Tyrol she was Frau Berchta or Perchta, and in the north down to the Harz Mountains she was called Frau Freen or Frick (linking her to Frigg), or Fru Gode or Fru Harke. The same function was performed by the Mittwinterfrau in Slovenia and Croatia, and by Luca in Hungary. In Scotland the Gyre Carline would steal any flax left on women's distaffs at the year's end.[11]

In Bavaria Perchta burned the hand of lazy spinners and ruined the flax they didn't finish off. At the very least, she sent the tardy spinners bad luck. In the Orlagau, on the night before Twelfth Day, Perchta examined the spinning-rooms and presented the spinners with empty reels which they had to fill within a short time.[12]

At Yule, Austrian women would spin some flax especially for the shaggy 'wood-woman' and throw it on the fire as an offering to her, and women in Vicentina would make the same offering to the holzweibel, a similar wood fairy. [13] In Switzerland the Sträggele ('Little Witches') was abroad on the Embernight, checking to see if girls had finished their spinning, and punishing them if they had not. [14] In the Alps, spinners made sure that they had finished spinning by Christmas Eve and then hid their distaffs behind the chimney until the New Year to conceal them from the Tsaôthe Vidhe, a witch who would travel around on a blind horse searching for any unfinished work, and tangle up the threads. This tradition was carried on into the early 1800s. [15]

In the myths of both Uranus and Cronus and then Cronus and Zeus, younger gods overthrow a set of elder gods and imprison them in the underworld. The worn-out age (or year) is defeated and imprisoned with the other forces of chaos, and the new age (or year) begins. Even today we have the familiar image of Father Time, usually depicted as an elderly bearded man carrying a scythe, who is the personification of the Old Year who passes the duty of time on to the New Year baby. At Yule, the old year, the old cycle of existence and time, dissolves back into the primordial chaos. The sun reborn and the new year represent the world rejuvenated and reality renewed.

---

11   Max Dashu http://www.suppressedhistories.net/secrethistory/witchtregenda.html

12   Clement A. Miles, *Christmas in Ritual and Tradition*, Christian and Pagan, T. Fisher Unwin, 1912

13   Max Dashu http://www.suppressedhistories.net/secrethistory/witchtregenda.html

14   *ibid*

15   *ibid*

THE SPIRITS OF CHAOS

The threat of the longest night and dangerous Twelve Days that follow is reflected in the folk tales of ghosts and fairies temporarily freed from the underworld. In the Orkneys the evil trow fairies leave their mounds and dance. In Guernsey the powers of darkness are supposed to be especially active between St. Thomas's Day (21st December) and New Year's Eve, and it is dangerous to be out after nightfall. People may be led astray then by Will o' the Wisp, ominous black dogs appear to them, or folk find mysterious white rabbits hopping along just under their feet.

In England people prepared for supernatural visitors during the Twelve Days. The house and its contents were cleaned with extra care. In Shropshire, the pewter and bronze vessels had to be polished to the point that that the maids could see to put their caps on in them, otherwise the fairies would pinch them. If the fairies were satisfied, the maid would find a coin in her shoe. In Shropshire special care was taken to put away any washing suds.

In the Orkneys, because it was the dark time of year, precautions had to be taken against supernatural visitors, especially from the influence of the trows, the ugly and malicious fairies of the Northern Isles who leave the underworld at Yule. [16] To protect the cows, a hair was taken from the tail of each beast and plaited and hung over the barn door. People protected themselves by *sainin'* or making the sign of the cross. [17] The house had to be especially clean and tidy, or the trows would be offended. Everyone had to wash themselves well on Yule Eve, dropping three live coals into the washing water "*less the trows take the power o' the feet or hands*". [18] An iron blade was placed before each door and a candle left burning through the night. The hogboon, a mound dwelling spirit, had to be offered food and drink at Yule.

In the Scandinavian countries peasants sensed the nearness of the uncanny on Christmas Eve and stayed indoors so as not to meet the spirits, especially between cock-crow and dawn. In Sweden the trolls were believed to be abroad, celebrating the dark time with dancing and revelry or flying to assemblies in the mountains in the company of witches, mounted on wolves, shovels or broomsticks. Passersby might hear their laughter and music.

In Iceland the thirteen Yule Lads or *Jolasveinar* appear. Though today they have become cuddly gift bringers leaving presents for good children and potatoes for naughty ones, originally they were terrifying characters, the

---

16   Anna Franklin, *The Illustrated Encyclopaedia of Fairies*, Vega, London,

17   http://www.orkneyjar.com/tradition/yule/index.html

18   *ibid*

sons of two undead trolls, Gryla and Leppaludi, who stole and ate naughty children. The Yule boys start arriving during the days before Christmas to cause mischief. On December 13th comes Giljagaur (Gully Imp), followed on December 14th by Stúfur (Itty Bitty), December 15th Þvörusleikir (Pot Scraper Licker), December 16th Pottasleikir (Pot Licker), December 17th Askasleikir (Bowl Licker), December 18th Hurðaskellir (Door Slammer), December 19th Skyrgámur (Curd Gobbler), December 20th Bjúgnakrækir (Sausage Snatcher), December 21st Gluggagægir (Window Peeper), December 22nd Gáttaþefur (Doorway Sniffer), December 23rd Ketkrókur (Meat Hooker), and lastly on December 24th comes Kertasníkir (Candle Beggar).

Kallikantzaroi

More frightening and closer to their original characters are the Greek *Kallikantzaroi* who appear during the Twelve Days. In Greek folk tradition it is believed that when Christ is born, so too are these winter spirits. They are half-animal, half-human monsters, black, hairy, with huge heads, red eyes, goats' or asses' ears, lolling red tongues, ferocious tusks, long curved claws and animals' feet. Though they normally live in the underworld, at this time they attempt to climb up the World Tree to emerge on earth. In the Macedonian plain of Saraghiol, the *Kallikantzaroi* emerge from a stone named Kiatra Schuligan, beneath which an abyss opens, black and deep, and the sound of laughter, sobs and screams can be heard issuing from it, along with the sounds of pipes and beating drums.[19]

The *Kallikantzaroi* hide in dark places during the day but come out at night, led by the Great Kallikantzaros riding a cock. They lurk around lakes and crossroads in particular. People who meet them are challenged with the riddle "hemp or lead?" and if they answer "lead" they are attacked and half torn apart.

The *Kallikantzaroi* enter houses by swarming down the chimneys to smash the place up and eat all the Christmas pork, urinate on all the water and wine and whatever food which remains, leaving the occupants half dead with fright or violence. They will disappear at the third cock crow each morning when the light of the sun sends them back to their dark holes.

To scare them away, the Greeks kept their Christmas log burning. They also burned old shoes, believing the smell would repel the creatures.

---

19   This Macedonian lore of the *kallikantzaroi* connects high rock formations with the dead, especially infants who died without baptism. Similar associations were made by the Scots, who used to have a custom of burying unbaptised babies among inaccessible rocks. The child's spirit entered into the rocks and became the echo (called 'child of the rock' in Gaelic).

Houses had to be protected from these onslaughts by marking the front door with a black cross on Christmas Eve (though even then, the demons can trick householders into opening it by imitating the voice of a family member), the burning of incense and the invocation of the Trinity, the lighting of the Yule log, the burning of something that smells strong, and the hanging of pork-bones, sweetmeats or sausages in the chimney.

The signal for their final departure does not come until Twelfth Night with the *Kalanda* festival, when the 'Blessing of the Waters' ceremony takes place. Some of the holy water is put into vessels and with these and with incense the priests sometimes make a round of the village, sprinkling the people and their houses to which the Winter Spirits react:

"Quick, begone! we must begone,
Here comes the pot-bellied priest,
With his censer in his hand
And his sprinkling-vessel too;
He has purified the streams
And he has polluted us."[20]

Like other such creatures elsewhere, they are often said to be spirits of the dead. Children born at Christmas are susceptible to becoming *Kallikantzaroi*, as are people with inept guardian angels. In some places they are thought to be transformed humans placed under a spell after being born with a caul during the Twelve Nights.

Werewolves

This is a characteristic they share with the werewolf, a man who is supposed to change into a ravening wolf - 'man-wolves' is the name given to the *Kallikantzaroi* in southern Greece. The connection between Christmas and werewolves is not confined to Greece. According to a belief in the north and east of Germany, children born during the Twelve Nights become werewolves, while in Livonia and Poland that period is the special season for the werewolf's rapacity.[21]

The French historian Simon Goulart (1607) said that when Christmas day is past, a lame boy goes into the countryside and calls the devil's slaves together in great numbers, and a great man comes with a whip made of iron chains, and they are changed into wolves.[22] In Poland, an excitable drunk is

---

20   *Christmas in Ritual and Tradition, Christian and Pagan,* by Clement A. Miles, London: T. Fisher Unwin

21   *ibid*

22   Nigel Jackson, Compleat Vampire, Capall Bann, Chieveley

said to be like one 'who runs amok at Christmas in a wolfskin'. In Campania, those born on Christmas night turn periodically into werewolves. In Naples, those born on Christmas day have tails and turn into werewolves. Reginald Scott wrote in *Discoverie of Witchcraft* (1584) that every year at the end of December a knave or devil summons witches to a certain place and leads them through a pool of water, when they change into wolves. To change back they have to go back through the water (possibly the boundary river between the worlds).[23] Witches are thought to change into wolves by Romany gipsies.

There are many stories of werewolf transformations at Christmas. The wolf is associated both with the wild side of nature and the time of chaos and boundaries. In France, the twilight is called 'between the dog and the wolf'.[24] In Norse myth the Fenris wolf embodies the forces of night and chaos and will bring about Ragnorok, when those forces will overwhelm the world.

The Dead Return
In many parts of the world it is believed that the dead return at Christmas. In Hungary, troops of the dead returned at the Epiphany, accompanied by witches. [25] In Scandinavia Christmas was the time when the dead revisited their old homes and had to be made welcome. Before people went to bed, they made sure the house was left tidy with a fire burning in the hearth. Food and ale were left out on the table. If earth was found on the chairs in the morning, it was known that a kinsman, fresh from the grave, had sat there. Sometimes a warm bath was left for the dead visitors so that they might wash before their meal. [26] In Poland, the dead were invited inside to warm themselves and funeral foods were eaten including pork.

In Portugal the souls of the dead, the *alminhas a penar*, are welcomed on Christmas. Crumbs are scattered for them on the hearth. In ancient times, seeds were left out for the dead so they could return with fruits and grains from the Otherworld at harvest time. At the *consoada* in the early morning of Christmas Day people set out extra plates for the dead among them to celebrate as well.[27]

In Lithuania a special dish called *kûèia* was prepared for the souls of

23   *ibid*

24   *ibid*

25   Éva Pócs, *Between the Living and the Dead*, Central European University Press, Budapest, 2000

26   http://www.abcog.org/xmas2.htm

27   http://christmas-world.freeservers.com/portugal.html

dead ancestors. It was made of stewed wheat, peas and beans, and sweetened with honey. [28] Oat puddings were also considered to be suitable food for the dead, and a spell was chanted while they were being made. In the region of Merkinë, *kûèia* was a special loaf of bread which was carried three times around the house by the master of the household. He would knock on the door saying "God together with *kûèia* asks to be in your house". [29] In other regions, baskets of *kûèia* foods or Christmas wafers were carried around in the same manner. Supper was eaten by the living when the stars rose in the sky, and if a family member had died during the year, a place was laid for them. The eldest family member went outside to invite the souls of the ancestors, the cold, the wind and bees to eat together. [30] Food would be left on the table as it was believed that once the family was asleep, the dead would come in and feast. The tradition of feeding the souls of the dead continued into the twentieth century in Lithuania.

MISRULE - THE WORLD TURNED UPSIDE DOWN
Only the sun's rebirth can send the spirits of chaos back and restore time and order to their proper courses. Until then the world is turned upside down, and the Kingdom of Misrule is established.

The Saturnalia
The customs of the Lord of Misrule, along with most of our other Christmas traditions, seem to derive directly from the ancient Roman Saturnalia.

Saturn (the Latin equivalent of the Greek Cronos) was the original king of the Golden Age which was temporarily regained at the Saturnalia. It was an annual period of license, when the customary restraints of law and morality were thrown aside and everyone gave themselves up to excessive mirth and jollity. [31] Catullus called it 'the best of days'. Masters changed places with their servants, and the slave might dine with his master or even be waiting on by him. Every house had its *Saturnalicius Princeps* (Master of the Saturnalia), the Lord of Misrule, chosen by lot, who had to act as foolishly as possible and was free to order others to do his bidding. His command was law, whether it was to dance naked, to sing, suffer a dunking in icy water, or carry

28   *Lithuanian Customs and Traditions*, http://ausis.gf.vu.lt/eka/customs/tradc.html

29   *ibid*

30   *ibid*

31   James Frazer, *The Golden Bough*, Macmillan Press, London, 1976

a flute girl round the house. This mock king may have represented Saturn. [32]
Seneca the Younger described the Saturnalia around 50 CE in the *Epistolae*:

> *"It is now the month of December, when the greatest part of the city is
> in a bustle. Loose reins are given to public dissipation; everywhere you
> may hear the sound of great preparations, as if there were some real
> difference between the days devoted to Saturn and those for transacting
> business....Were you here, I would willingly confer with you as to the
> plan of our conduct; whether we should eve in our usual way, or, to
> avoid singularity, both take a better supper and throw off the toga."*

Pliny even built himself a sound-proof room so he could work during the
Saturnalia.[33] In *Epistles* (early second century CE) he wrote:

> *"...especially during the Saturnalia when the rest of the house is noisy
> with the licence of the holiday and festive cries. This way I don't hamper
> the games of my people and they don't hinder my work or studies."*

Originally a single feast day on December 17th, the festival grew
into a week long celebration ending on the 23rd despite the efforts of several
emperors to shorten it, which only resulted in public protests and open
revolt.

It was a time for feasting, drinking and merry making. Trees were
decorated and houses hung with holly and other greenery. Slaves wore the
badge of freedom known as the *pillius* and were exempt from punishment;
there was a school holiday and a special market (*sigillaria*). Senators left
aside their togas for more informal clothes, and people greeted each other with
"Io Saturnalia" ('Hail/praise Saturn') rather in the manner we say "Merry
Christmas". The Greek Sophist Libanius (fourth century) wrote:

> *"Everywhere may be seen carousals and well-laden tables; luxurious
> abundance is found in the houses of the rich, but also in the houses
> of the poor better food than usual is put upon the table. The impulse
> to spend seizes everyone. He who the whole year through has taken
> pleasure in saving and piling up his pence, becomes suddenly
> extravagant. He who erstwhile was accustomed and preferred to live
> poorly, now at this feast enjoys himself as much as his means will
> allow.... People are not only generous towards themselves, but also
> towards their fellow-men. A stream of presents pours itself out on all
> sides...Another great quality of the festival is that it teaches men not to
> hold too fast to their money, but to part with it and let it pass into other
> hands."*[34]

---

32   *ibid*
33   John Matthews, *The Winter Solstice*, Godsfield Press, Arlesford, 2003
34   Quoted in *Christmas in Ritual and Tradition, Christian and Pagan*, by Clement A. Miles

On the last day it was the custom to exchange small gifts, especially *sigillaria* (small pottery dolls) for the children and *cerei* (candles) for adults, though *Martial Epigrams Book 14* (circa 84 or 85 CE) also describes writing tablets, dice, knuckle bones, moneyboxes, combs, toothpicks, hunting knives, balls, perfumes, pipes, items of clothing, statues, masks, books and pets.

Though the festival was celebrated privately in every home, it also involved public rituals. It began with a formal public sacrifice of a young pig at the temple of Saturn in the forum. The woollen bonds were untied from the statue of Saturn.

The Saturnalia incorporated the festivals of Consus, the god of the corn store, on December 15th and his consort Ops on December 17th (see Appendix 1, the Calendar of Yule). It ended with the Juvenalia, which was a festival of children, games, fools and misrule and merged into the Kalends of January and the New Year.

The Lord of Misrule

The Kalends of January were celebrated with singing and dancing all night long in the streets, the giving of money to the poor and men wearing women's clothes and people wearing masks and disguises, a custom which prevails in places to the present day. This was condemned by various Christian writers. Caesarius of Arles (sixth century CE) wrote that

"...the heathen put on counterfeit forms and monstrous faces....
Some are clothes in the hides of cattle, others put on the heads of
beasts...furthermore those who have been born men are clothed in
women's dress...blushing not to clothe their warlike arms in women's
garments..." [35]

Asterius, bishop of Amasea in Pontus (c.375-405 CE) noted that the feast was

"...full of annoyance; since going out-of-doors is burdensome, and
staying within doors is not undisturbed. For the common vagrants and
the jugglers of the stage, dividing themselves into squads and hordes,
hang about every house. The gates of public officials they besiege with
especial persistence, actually shouting and clapping their hands until
he that is beleaguered within, exhausted, throws out to them whatever
money he has and even what is not his own. And these mendicants
going from door to door follow one after another, and, until late in
the evening, there is no relief from this nuisance. For crowd succeeds

---

35   Quoted in John Matthews, *The Winter Solstice*, Godsfield Press, Arelsford, 2003

crowd, and shout, shout, and loss, loss." [36]

He railed against the principle of the world turned upside down:

"For the soldiers… appoint pretended lictors and publicly act like buffoons. This is the nobler part of their ribaldry…Does not the champion, the lion-hearted man, the man who when armed is the admiration of his friends and the terror of his foes, loose his tunic to his ankles, twine a girdle about his breast, use a woman's sandal, put a roll of hair on his head in feminine fashion, and ply the distaff full of wool, and with that right hand which once bore the trophy, draw out the thread, and changing the tone of his voice utter his words in the sharper feminine treble?"

The *Sayings of Saint Pirmin* in the eighth century condemned as demonical the celebration of the Vulcanales and the Kalends:

"You, men, adorn yourselves not in the clothing of women, nor you, women, in the garb of men, on the occasion of the calends or of certain holidays." [37]

The customs of the Saturnalia and Kalends seem to have prevailed for centuries. Even Christian priests were roundly accused of wearing masks, dressing as women and singing lewd songs. At Bourges and Sens, at the Feast of the Ass the usual mass was substituted with a bawdy ritual in which the participants were invited to approach the altar of Bacchus:

"Let us drink: take from us Bacchus, all our clothes that we may be worthy…to enter into the tavern. Unto us all, drink without end!" [38]

The mediaeval festivities were presided over by the Lord of Misrule in England or the Abbot of Unreason in Scotland, a peasant chosen by lot or an elected fellow of the company to preside over the Christmas revelries, thus reversing the 'natural' order. The celebrations got so rowdy that they were outlawed by the Council of Basel in 1431, though they survived in Britain and other places into the seventeenth century. At the Inns of Court, for example, a master of the revels was elected and called the Christmas Prince or the King of Christmas. [39] The Puritans frowned on the practice as early as the reign of Elizabeth I, as shown by Stubs' *The Anatomie of Abuses* in 1585:

"…all the wilde heades of the parishe…chuse them a grande Capitaine

36   *Asterius of Amasia, Sermons*, http://www.ccel.org/ccel/pearse/morefathers/files/asterius_00_intro.htm

37   Quoted in Philippe Walter, *Christianity, The Origins of a Pagan Region*, Inner Traditions, Vermont, 2003

38   Quoted in John Matthews, *The Winter Solstice*, Godsfield Press, Arelsford, 2003

39   Thomas K. Hervey, *The Book of Christmas*, The Folklore Society, 1888

(of mischief) whom the innoble with the title of my Lorde of Misserule, and hym they crown with great solemnitie, and adopt for their kyng (who) chuseth for himself for the twentie, fourtie, three score, or a hundred lustie guttes like to himself...the heathen companie towards the church yard...their handkercchefes swyngyng about their heades like madmen, their hobbie horses and other monsters skyrmishyng amongst the throng...like devilles incarnate."

A related figure was the King of the Bean, chosen by finding a bean hidden in a cake on Twelfth Night. This was once a common feature of the festivities at the English and Scottish courts, as well as some universities and many private parties. In France, it was also customary to hide a bean in a cake, and the boy who got the bean in his slice was the Bean King, to whom the guests showed mock reverence. [40] Sometimes a pea was included for the choosing of a queen too. Samuel Pepys recorded a Twelfth Night Party in 1659:

"...to my cousin Stradwick, where, after a good supper, there being there my father, mothers, brothers, and sister, my cousin Scott and his wife, Mr. Drawwater and his wife, and her brother, Mr. Stradwick, we had a brave cake brought us, and in the choosing, Pall was Queen and Mr. Stradwick was King. After that my wife and I bid adieu and came home, it being still a great frost." [41]

The Midwinter guising customs survive in the mumming plays that are performed all over Britain at this time of year. They usually involve the death and resurrection of a particular character, often St George, which presumably represents the death and rebirth of the year.

---

40   *Brewers Dictionary of Phrase and Fable*, Blitz Editions, Leicester, 1990

41   http://www.pepysdiary.com

Chapter 2
THE REBIRTH OF THE SUN

"...the winter solstice was the turning point of time and the birthday of the sun, the moment of new beginnings. All of nature was poised to step over the border of the year.
Krupps, Beyond the Blue Horizon

The year has declined and languishes in the season of its old age, standing on the edge of its grave. The rich and fruitful days of summer have given way to the dreary days before the winter solstice, and flowers have given way to naked branches. Each day grows a little shorter. The great source of life is failing, overcome by the powers of darkness and chaos. The sun god is dying. Will he be overwhelmed, or will he fight and overcome? The fate of the whole world rests with him.

Then, on the shortest day, in the time of greatest darkness, the sun is reborn.

SUN GODS
Each sunrise, the sun demonstrates the victory of life over the forces of death and darkness; it is a metaphor for human spiritual and physical life, reflecting our own experiences of birth, growth, decay and death, as well as our hope of rebirth, our struggles against negativity and the triumph of spirit. For our ancestors the eternal cycle of the sun was the central paradigm of their spiritual beliefs. Sun gods were:

"...the types and models of the divine potentiality...they were the mirror held up to men, in which could be seen the possibilities locked up in man's own nature. They were type figures, delineating the divine life that was an ever possible realization for any devoted man. They were the symbols of an ever coming deity, a deity that came not once historically in Judea, but that came to ever fuller expression and liberation in the inner heart of every son of man. The solar deities

were the gods that ever came, that were described as coming not once upon a time, but continuously and regularly. Their radiant divinity might be consummated by an earnest person at any time or achieved piecemeal."[42]

There are thousands of sun gods and goddesses with remarkably similar characteristics: they battle the forces of darkness and dispel evil; they illuminate the sky; see everything on their path and uncover those secrets hidden by darkness (often in the form of prophecy); they represent truth, justice and enlightenment and they bring healing.

THE SUN TURNS BACK

At midwinter and midsummer the sun apparently changes its course. In midwinter, having reached the lowest point in its path, it turns about and begins to mount the skies; conversely at midsummer, having attained the highest point it reaches, the sun seems to turn about once more and descend.

THE SUN'S BIRTHDAY

The sun god is born at the winter solstice and grows until midsummer, afterwards declining towards his death at the midwinter solstice, where he languishes for three days in his grave before rising from his tomb, reborn. Sun gods born at the winter solstice include Zeus, Dionysus, Bacchus, Osiris/ Horus, Adonis, Zeus, Chris of Chaldea, Mithras, Sakia of India, Chang-ti of China, Jesus and Krishna. These gods have several things in common:

- They are usually counted as the saviours of mankind (because the sun saves the world from chaos, darkness and death).
- Many were thought to have incarnated upon the earth, in order to help humankind.
- They are born of a virgin mother, the Queen of Heaven.
- They are born in a cave or underground chamber.
- They are born on 25th December (which stands for the solstice).
- There is a star in the east.
- There is a flight into a distant country (while the sun is still too weak to finally triumph over darkness).
- They are sacrificed to benefit mankind.
- They descend into the underworld and rise again on the third day.

---

42   Alvin Boyd Kuhn, *The Great Myth of the Sun-Gods,*
http://www.mountainman.com.au/ab_kuhn.html

It is only at the vernal equinox in March that the sun is strong enough to complete its final triumph over darkness, when the daylight hours become longer than the hours of night. Until then, the sun god is seen as a youth who has not come into his full power.

The Roman Emperor Aurelian (270 to 275 CE) blended a number of Pagan solstice celebrations of the nativity of such saviours into a single festival called *Dies Natalis Invicti Solis*, the 'Birthday of the Unconquered Sun' on *Bruma*, the winter solstice or December 25th. Roman women would parade in the streets crying "unto us a child is born!" The god Sol Invictus had been introduced into the Roman pantheon from Syria during the first century CE by Roman legionaries stationed there. The cult grew more influential by the reign of Commodus (180-192 CE) and in 272 CE it became the chief imperial cult of the Roman Empire, until it was replaced by Christianity.

December 25th was the day of the winter solstice in the calendar established by Julius Caesar in Rome in 46 BCE. Actually, the solstice usually falls on 21st December, and the difference is due to an error in the Julian calendar which calculated the year on 365 ¼ days, which meant a discrepancy of one day in the Julian calendar in 128 years. By 274 CE the Emperor Aurelian established the sun cult as the Roman state religion with the traditional birthday of Sol Invictus as 25th December, though by then the actual solstice had happened two and a half days earlier.[43]

NURTURED BY THE GOAT

The constellation of Capricorn ('horned goat' or 'goat-horn'), in which the winter solstice theoretically takes place, was called 'the House of Death', as in winter all life in the Northern Hemisphere is at its lowest ebb.

Capricorn is the second faintest constellation after Cancer. It is generally represented as a mythical creature, half goat, half fish, an association that goes back to the Bronze Age and recorded in the Babylonian star catalogues. For the Babylonians it represented Ea (Enki in Sumer) the god of water and magic. Ea was adopted by the Greeks as Oannes, an exceptionally wise creature, half-fish and half-human, who was said to have emerged from the ocean on four occasions to bring culture and civilisation to mankind. Ea and Oannes are both described as articulate, patient, tolerant and serene. In the ancient Egyptian zodiacs of Denderah and Esna, Capricorn is also as a goat-fish and is called *Hu-penius*, meaning 'the place of sacrifice', i.e. the sacrifice of the sun.

The constellation is sometimes identified as Amalthea (though she is

---

43   Dr E.C.Krupp, *Beyond the Blue Horizon*, Oxford University Press, Oxford, 1991

also identified with Capra) the goat or goat-nymph that suckled the infant Zeus after his mother Rhea saved him from being devoured by his father Cronos. The goat's broken horn was transformed into the cornucopia or horn of plenty. Some ancient sources claim that this derives from the sun 'taking nourishment' while in the constellation in preparation for its climb back northward.

Manilius also saw Capricorn as the source of metal-workers' talents because Capricorn, as the sign of winter, related to the year's (and therefore the earth's) depths. He associated Capricorn with that which needs a 'renewal of flame' because its season brought back a renewal of the sun's light following the winter solstice. [44] Deep in the earth the solar forge created life through the agencies of the smith gods such as Hephaestus, Agni, Vulcan and Wayland.[45]

Since the sun ascends and travels north after leaving the sign of Capricorn at the winter solstice, the Romans called that month *Januanus*, or January, from *janua* meaning 'a gate' leading to the New Year.

THE GATE OF THE GODS

The constellation of Cancer became known to the Chaldean and Platonist philosophers as the 'Gate of Men' though which they said the souls of people came down from heaven and were incarnated at the summer solstice, as opposed to Capricorn which was the Gate of the Gods where departed souls returned to the heavens at the winter solstice, and though which the sun god was reborn:

"In Babylonian tradition there were actually two entrances to the underworld, each of which is associated with one of the solstices. The winter time entrance is used by discarnate souls journeying to the afterlife, but the summer entrance, located in the region of the crab, is used by the spirits of the ancestors when they return to earth to visit their family homes for the great ancestral festival celebrated in month five. It is also the route that the souls of newborn babies use to enter in the world of men." [46]

Macrobius wrote that souls descended to earth through the gate of Cancer, the Gate of Men, but Capricorn was called the Gate of the Gods, because through

---

44   Manilius, *Astronomica*, (c. 10 AD) trans. G.P. Goold, Harvard Heinemann, London. 1997

45   Adrian Bailey, Caves of the Sun, Jonathan Cape, London, 1997

46   Gavin White, *Babylonian Star Lore*, Solaria Publications, London, 2008

it, men ascended to their seats of immortality and became gods. [47] Certainly, many gods were said to be born at this time. Sometimes the old god had to die so that the new god, his reincarnated self, could be born, as when Osiris was reborn as the babe Horus.

In Hermetic Philosophy, the sphere of the Moon (the planetary ruler of Cancer) is the final realm in which incarnating souls acquire shape and form in birth, while the sphere of Saturn (the planetary ruler of Capricorn) is the final realm in which ascending souls free themselves from earthly trappings upon death. The Sun's ingress into Cancer marked its greatest elevation and Capricorn marked its nadir. Early philosophers looked upon water as the element from which all life emerged, so the symbolism of an aquatic nature is prevalent in the constellations linked to these points.

THE POLARITY OF THE SOLSTICES

In ancient China the two solstices were celebrated as polar opposites, with *chi* energy flowing in different directions right after the summer and winter solstices. *Yin* was born (began) at the summer solstice and *yang* was born (began) at the winter solstice. *Yin* is the moon, dark, passive, downward, cold, contracting and weak, while *yang* is the sun, bright, active, upward, hot, expanding and strong. In rituals that took place at the Forbidden City, the summer solstice was celebrated on the square altar of the earth, while the winter solstice ritual utilised the round mound. Both featured a sacrifice, but while the summer victim was buried the winter one was burned.

Some cultures, such as the Celts, believed that there were two suns – the summer sun and the winter sun. The summer sun was born at the winter solstice and increased in strength until the summer solstice, the longest day of the year. The dark winter sun began his reign at the summer solstice and increased his powers of darkness until the point of the winter solstice, the shortest day of the year. From this we get the idea of a battle between light and darkness in an endless cycle. Modern Pagans often re-enact this as the battle of the Oak and Holly Kings – often erroneously described as an ancient ritual, though it is a mediaeval concept - at the solstices, with the Oak King (the summer sun) slaying the Holly King (the winter sun) at the winter solstice, and vice versa at the summer solstice, a motif suggested by Robert Graves in *The White Goddess*, based on the Arthurian legend of Sir Gawain and the Green Knight. The idea of twin sun gods, or the sun god having twin sons as his heirs, is common. Other examples are Gwyn and Gwythyr, Baldur and Hoder,

---

47   In the same way, the sun is responsible for the birth of each New Age every 2000 years. Because of precession, the Gate of the Gods moves to Sagittarius.

Lugh and Balor, Balan and Balin, Romulus and Remus, Prometheus and Epimetheus, Merodach and Haman, Krishna and Balarama, Esau and Jacob, and Jesus and John the Baptist.

These two lords – often twins or even hero and dragon/snake – fight for rulership of the land, summer and winter. [48] The Greek sun god Apollo killed the Python at Delphi with his sun-ray arrows. The Egyptian god Ra, as the solar cat, fought the serpent of darkness, Set.

Modern Pagans accept these polarities as a necessary part of the whole. Winter comes but summer will return. The sun sets, travels though the underworld at night, and emerges with the dawn. The king dies, returns to the underworld womb of the Earth Goddess and is reborn. The slain god will rise again every year, and the light and dark rule in balance. Later myths see death as a final ending and the light and dark as in opposition. The gods of the light half of the year became dragon slaying gods and saints; the dark became evil and the fruitful underworld womb of the Goddess became the Christian hell.

REBIRTH FROM THE ROCK

It was a common belief that the sun spent each night or each winter in a cave. Most solar deities are said to have been born from a cave: Zeus was born in the Dictean Caves on Crete; the god Krishna was born in a dark dungeon; Apollo was born under Delos, where no rays of sunlight could penetrate; the Phoenician god Melkarth woke from his winter sleep in his sacred cave at the winter solstice and the Japanese sun goddess Amaterasu lived in a cave for a time. In early Christian stories, Jesus was born in a cave (the Greek text of the Gospel of St Luke uses the word *katalemna*, meaning cave, not stable) and in Bethlehem the Church of the Nativity is built over a cave. The sun god was reborn from the chthonic realm, bringing order out of chaos and light out of darkness.

For our distant ancestors, the cave was a place of mystery, its depths linking us to the underworld from which life – and the life-giving sun – emerged. Thirty thousand years ago, at the end of the last Ice Age, people explored deep limestone caves, probably believing the down-sloping vanes led to the underworld. They didn't live in these particular caves; they were reserved solely for religious use. Human bodies were not buried in the caves either - they were the realm of spirit animals - human dead were buried at the entrances to the caves or in large rock shelters, i.e. on the threshold of the underworld. [49]

---

48   In some case the solstices, in others the equinoxes, in others still, Beltane and
       Samhain.

49   David Lewis Williams & David Pearce, *The Neolithic Mind*, Thames and Hudson

Cave paintings of animals, human figures in animal costume and statuettes of female figures began to appear at this time. We know that these ancient artists did not portray all of the animals they saw and hunted, while certain animals appeared more frequently than others. By their arrangement, the pictures seem to have been thought effective only in certain caves, and only in specific places within the caves. [50] The paintings do not represent animals in their natural state, but they are rather spirit animals, floating within the natural features of the rock, reflecting not a realist depiction of the mundane plane, but the inner reality that the artist *saw.* Blood and fat were mixed with the painting pigments as a ritual act of restitution, the paintings thus uniting the spiritual and material planes. Furthermore, they were not painted and left, but continually renewed. With the painting and the blood, the animal spirit was returned to the earth (cave) womb, with the animals sometimes shown entering or leaving the rock itself through natural fissures, suggesting that the rock itself is the membrane between the human world and the world of spirits.

Though in the early Palaeolithic Age the entrance to the spirit realms was through the caves, by the Neolithic it was through structures built above ground to reflect the make-up of the cosmos, mirroring its structure in the ordinary realm, with heaven above and the underworld below. It may have been thought that in this way people could gain greater control of the cosmos (an idea reflected in the sacred architecture of much later periods). Selected dead were buried under the floors of living areas, and were sometimes exhumed, the bones dealt with in certain ways before being re-buried with the object of gaining greater control over the dead - who were obviously part of the spirit realm - and keeping them active longer so the shaman could commune with them.

In Brugh-na-Boyne, County Meath, Ireland, Newgrange was designed to funnel a shaft of sunlight deep into its central chamber at dawn on the day of the winter solstice. It has an entrance passage that is almost sixty feet long. Above the entrance way is a stone box that allows the light from the sun to penetrate to the back of the cairn at sunrise on the winter solstice. It has been dated at about 3,300 BCE and is one of the oldest structures in the world. Its older name was *An Liamh Greine* 'the Cave of the Sun'. The sun shines through the passageway to a series of carved spirals and solar discs on the wall. It is theorized that the triple spiral was drawn to celebrate the arrival of the sun on winter solstice morning (the sun's yearly path is a spiral one).

Ltd, London, 2005

50   Joseph Campbell, *The Way of Animal Powers,* Harper and Row, New York, 1988

Dowth (from *Dubad* or 'Darkness') is another of the great passage graves at Bru na Boinne said to have been built by King Bressail Bodibal ('Bressal the Cow Destroyer'). Built around 5000 years ago, it is sometimes referred to as the Fairy Mound of Darkness, and has two passages, one of which is aligned to the winter solstice sunset.

Maeshowe, a chambered cairn in the Orkneys, has a winter solstice alignment with the last rays of the setting sun shining through the entrance passage to pierce the darkness, possibly to bring rebirth to those who lay within the tomb, carrying their souls to the afterlife. The central axis of the inner entrance passage is directly aligned with the centre of the Barnhouse Stone, a nearby monolith. On the day of the winter solstice, the sun sets over the top of the Barnhouse Stone, the last rays going on to illuminate Maeshowe's inner chamber. The line then travels out to strike Hoy's Ward Hill, at a place where the sun set twenty two days before - and after - the midwinter solstice. This three-week period is referred to by archeastronomers as a megalithic month (a sixteenth of a year). [51]

Goseck Circle in Germany is believed to have been built in 4900 BCE. At the winter solstice, the centre of the circles sees the winter's sun rise and set through the southern gates.

In Egypt, the Temple at Karnak (the temple of Atum) and Abydos (Osiris) focus the rays of the midwinter sun into the heart of the temple enclosures.

The Mayan Palenque is aligned with the sun and its movements - as the sun travels through the day the rays seem to descend the staircase leading to the tomb. At winter solstice, the sun sets in early afternoon behind a large ridge directly aligned with the temple roof's centre; the final rays of light land at the foot of a wall on relief of the God of the Underworld.

At Machu Picchu, located in Peru's Torreon, there is a window through which the rising sun casts a shadow on the central altar of carved rock. When this occurred the Inca knew that winter solstice in the southern hemisphere had occurred and the dry season had begun. The *Intihuatana* ('the hitching post of the sun') Stone was used to attach a line to the sun to prevent it from disappearing completely.

Discoveries in the ritual landscape around Stonehenge made during a six year excavation lead by Mike Parker Pearson, which ended in 2009, indicate that while Stonehenge was a stone-built site where the summer solstice was celebrated, Durrington Walls, two miles northeast of the stone circle, was a henge (about 1400 feet in diameter, enclosing a series of

51   http://www.orkneyjar.com/history/maeshowe/solstice.htm

concentric rings of huge timber posts) where people celebrated the winter solstice. While Stonehenge is aligned with sunrise at the summer solstice, the henge at Durrington Walls is aligned with sunrise at the winter solstice and sunset at the summer solstice.

While Stonehenge was a monument to the ancestors with cremation burials, the complex at Durrington was very much a place for the living, where people lived and held ceremonies and feasts (which included pork) before sending the dead on the voyage to the afterlife, though excarnation, pouring their ashes into the River Avon or burying the ashes of a select few at Stonehenge. (In this it echoes Egypt, where permanent stone constructions were for the gods and the dead on the West Bank of the Nile, and impermanent mud and timber buildings on the East Bank were for the living.) Pearson had worked in Madagascar where the dead were buried in stone and their spirits thought to inhabit the stone.

Both monuments have avenues connecting them to the Avon River, indicating a pattern of movement between the sites. Parker Pearson's research has shown that this site attracted people in droves as far back as Neolithic times, and considerable quantities of pig and cattle bones, pottery, flint arrowheads and lithic debris indicated that occupation and consumption were intense. He believes that the intense human activity was linked to feasting during the solstices, and that there was no permanent occupation at the site, only seasonal activity linked to the solstices.

Chapter 3
THE ONCE AND FUTURE KING

Modern druids refer to the winter solstice as *Alban Arthur*, or Arthur's Time. Several things point us in the direction of Arthur being a sun god or at least a solar hero in the manner of Herakles, whose twelve labours describe the sun's journey through the twelve signs of the zodiac during the year. Like other sun gods, Arthur died and rests in a cave (or under a hill) until he shall return as the 'once and future king'. He is associated with the Wild Hunt - as king of the dead he rides out during the winter months to collect souls. There was a battle between the forces of light and darkness, and Arthur died, though his return is promised. According to Nennius, he fought twelve battles against the Saxons, which may relate to the sun's journey through the twelve signs of the zodiac. He was defeated in the final battle, wounded in the head, which may characterise the failing sun and dying old year before the winter solstice. [52] His sword, which may be seen as a phallic symbol of his virility, was thrown into the lake (which in Celtic myth is the entrance to the Otherworld) and returned to the goddess. A hand came from the lake, took the sword and waved it three times before disappearing with it into the water, saving the sun's virility from destruction before renewing it with the new sun. [53] Arthur was taken away in a barge by three queens, or according to legend, was borne to the heavens on a celestial barge, alternately called Arthur's Chariot and Arthur's Wain (Wagon), corresponding to the Plough stars, or the barque of the sun as it sails into the underworld before returning with the dawn as the reborn sun:

> "...*another symbol of Ced* (the Celtic mother goddess) *is a naked ship or ark, or coracle, called y Llong Voel* (Naked Ship) *in Druidism... often the earth is represented as the middle of Ced's body—floating in the sea of the elements, the Annwn of the Druids, and on the afternoon of each December 20th eagerly receiving the sun back into herself... the*

---

52   Owen Morgan, *The Light of Britannia*, 1892

53   *Ibid*

earth—which is symbolised as an ark-ship navigating the Sea of the Elements, otherwise as a heap or tumulus, otherwise belly of Ced, as the grave of the sun each December 20th . Britain and the Island of Delos, each symbolising the round earth, were said to float. The earth, as a conical heap, the belly of Ced, was set forth as resting on the surface of the ocean. " [54]

Arthur is said to still appear in the form of various birds and this association may account for the many wren customs of Yule. In ancient times, the soul of the king was said to leave his body in the form of an eagle (in Rome), a hawk (in Egypt) or a dove (in Greece). The druids probably used the wren as a symbol of the sun and the soul of Arthur at the winter solstice. (In Welsh the wren is to this day *Derw, Drew* or *Dryw*, meaning 'Druid'.) This is probably because the nest of the wren is round, like the belly of the earth goddess or like a burial mound, with a hole in its centre (a common symbol of the sun, or perhaps representing the navel). From this nest-grave, the eggs hatch and life issues, just as a human may be reborn from the tomb, or the sun from the underworld. The wren is a tiny and feeble bird, perhaps symbolising the weakness of the sun at the winter solstice.

THE GREAT BEAR

Arthur's name means 'Bear-Man' or 'Great Bear' or perhaps even 'Wonderful Bear'. He was associated with the constellation of the Great Bear which was called Arthur's Wain (wagon), or sometimes Arthur's Plough. As Sir Walter Scott wrote:

Arthur's slow wain his course doth roll,
In utter darkness round the pole;
The Northern Bear lowers black and grim;
Orion's studded belt is dim;
Twinkling faint, and distant far,
Shimmers through mist each planet star,
Ill may I read their high decree! [55]

The constellation of the Great Bear circles around the unmoving Pole Star during the course of the year. To this day the Welsh refer to the circumpolar region of the stars as the *Bwrdd Arthur* ('Arthur's Table'), described as round. Following the Great Bear is the constellation of Boötes, the herdsman, with its brightest star Arcturus or 'Bear Keeper'. When it first rises over the eastern

---

54   Owen Morgan, *The Light of Britannia*, 1892

55   Sir Walter Scott, *The Lay of the Last Minstrel*, 1805

34

horizon, not long after the winter solstice each year, it means that spring is on its way as the sun gains strength. Arcturus is known as 'The One who Comes', and just as Arthur is known as the 'Once and Future King.'

The bear hibernates in the winter, entering a cave or some quiet, secluded place. It emerges in the spring with the female often having given birth in the meantime and appearing with cubs in tow. This led to the bear being associated with regeneration and rebirth, adopted as a solar symbol.

THE UNDYING BEARS

The pattern of the night sky changes hour by hour and season by season as it whirls around the still hub, Polaris the Pole Star. [56] This was readily taken by many cultures to mean that the polar region of the stars was the centre of the cosmos, the point in the heavens where the central pole - the cosmic axis - connected. It was called the *Nowl* in Norse lore, which means the 'navel' or the 'nail' which holds the sky in position.

The circumpolar stars never sink below the horizon and were called the undying or imperishable ones, the eternal ones which never enter the underworld as all other constellations do. This gave them a special role in stellar mythology, making them the place of eternity and the everlasting. For the Greeks, the three stars in the tail of the Bear were the three apples of immortality which Herakles, for his eleventh labour, stole from the garden of the Hesperides (identified with the stars of Ursa Minor) which contained the World Tree. [57] For these reasons, the North is the most sacred direction in modern Paganism. In Celtic tradition, the Spiral Castle of Arianrhod (the Corona Borealis) surrounds the North Star, and this is the place that souls travel to at death or for initiation.

Circling the Pole Star are the two bears, Ursa Major and Ursa Minor (which actually contains the Pole Star), which also never set. [58] In Finland, the cosmos was believed to be a great world tree, in the upper branches of which perched a great bear. Ancient Finnish depictions often show a pine tree with seven stars near the top (the seven major stars or Ursa Major), or a picture of a bear nestled in its uppermost branches.

The constellation of Ursa Major, the Great Bear, can be seen from

---

56   This is the current Pole Star, though previously it was Draco and in 14,000 years time it will be Vega

57   The three stars in the tail of Ursa Major are called 'pointer stars' as they point the way to the Pole Star.

58   The bears now set except in high latitudes, but in Homer's day and before, these stars did not sink below the horizon.

nearly everywhere in the world, but is most prominent in the northern hemisphere. In ancient Greece, Babylon, India, China and in North America, it was imagined as a she-bear. Some have even suggested that its identification as a bear could date back to the Ice Age 50,000 years ago when a Palaeolithic bear cult existed. [59]

The Great Bear is probably the most widely recognized because of its distinctive asterism (a group of stars within a constellation) which forms the Plough. The shape of the asterism

Ursa Major

resembles an old-fashioned plough, which gives it its English name, or some say a ladle or saucepan, which gives the constellation its American name, the Big Dipper. The right hand side of the Plough has two stars that point to the Pole Star, the last star in the tail of the Little Bear, and these are called 'the Pointers'. The stars were used as an aid to navigation by travellers on both sea and land as they indicate the way north. Greek sailors judged their courses by the Great Bear, while the Phoenicians steered by the Small Bear because, they said, though it was not as bright as Ursa Major, it turned in a smaller circuit.[60] Homer described Odysseus sailing eastwards by keeping the Bear (and the north) on his left. The far north is now called the Arctic, the word derived from the Greek *arktos*, or 'bear'. Ptolemy (second century CE) described the northernmost lands as being 'towards the Bears'.

The orientation of the Bear figures changes dramatically through the course of the night. The movement of the Plough around the Pole Star, and its changing position, charts the passage of time. As the seasons turn, it moves around the sky, rotating a quarter of a circle each season. After a year, it is back at the same point in the sky. Many cultures used it to pinpoint the calendar, or as a marker for various ceremonies. [61] Its continual circling of the

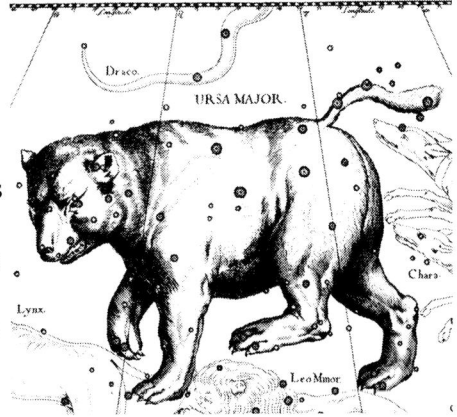

---

59   http://www.aavso.org/myths-uma

60   Dr E.C.Krupp, *Beyond the Blue Horizon*, Oxford University Press, Oxford, 1991

61   It may be that the Greeks saw the Plough as the wheel of Ixion spinning around the North Star, Polaris. Ixion (possibly 'Axle'), King of Lapiths, was the first man to murder a kinsman. Hermes chained him by hands and feet to a wheel which constantly revolves around the sky.

axis stands for eternity, cosmic order, ordered change, cyclical change, and in some cultures, the authority of the king. [62]

Some have suggested that the four seasonal points of the Plough is the origin of the swastika, an ancient symbol of movement and change. In China the Great Bear was originally called the Bushel. As it turns around the centre of the sky, the handle of the Bushel shows successively the four divisions of the day and the four seasons of the year. It was seen as the ruler's chariot, governing the four corners of the Earth, separating *yin* from *yang*, determining the four seasons, balancing the elements and fixing the division of time and space. This was the role of the emperor.

For the Egyptians the constellation was *Meskhetiu,* the Bull's Thigh, which represented immortality because it never went into the underworld. *Meskhetiu* was also the name of the instrument used in the Ceremony of the Opening the Mouth, when the soul was returned to a prepared mummy with an Ursa Major shaped tool. [63] It was also the name of the Leg of Set, won by Horus, the god of the sun, kingship and divine order, in his battles with Set, the god of chaos. As a symbol of the circumpolar stars, it has the power to bring Osiris back to life. [64] (The Chinese painted seven stars on coffins for the same reason.)

"The sky is clear, Sothis lives, because I am a living one, the son of
Sothis, and the Two Enneads have cleansed themselves for me in Ursa
Major, the imperishable. My house in the sky will not perish." [65]

The Plough seems to have been associated with the primal mound from which life emerged and was sometimes called the Cart of Osiris.

The Greeks explained that the constellations were bears with the tale of Callisto ('the Most Beautiful'), a devotee of the goddess Artemis. She was ravished by Zeus who disguised himself as Artemis to get close to her. When the real Artemis discovered the pregnant state of her so-called virgin companion, she exiled her from the company of nymphs, and Callisto later gave birth to a son called Arcas. Zeus's jealous wife Hera transformed Callisto into a bear (or some say it was Artemis who effected the transformation). Years later, Arcas was hunting in the forest when he came across a bear - his mother if he but knew it - and aimed his spear to kill it. Zeus took pity and

62   Dr E.C.Krupp, *Beyond the Blue Horizon,* Oxford University Press, Oxford, 1991

63   *Ibid*

64   *Ibid*

65   *The Egyptian Book of the Dead,* Commentaries by Evelyn Rossiter, Liber, Fribourg, 1979

whirled them both into the sky where they continue to circle the pole star as the Great Bear and Little Bear who never dip a paw into the ocean (i.e. the constellations never set at higher latitudes), though some say that Arcas is Arcturus, the Bear Keeper. Callisto may be an aspect of Artemis herself, who appears

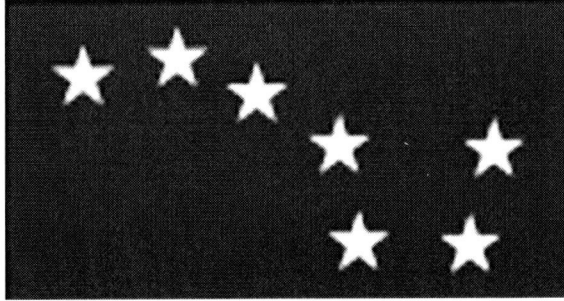

The Plough

in some ancient tales as a bear: wild nature renewed through seasonal death. Young girls in the service of Artemis were called 'she-bears', and it has even been suggested by scholars that the origin of the Greek 'round dances' were done to imitate the motion of the stars around the pole.

THE WISE MEN

A common name for the seven major stars of the Great Bear is 'the Wise Men'. In Hindu tradition they are *sapta-riksha*, or Seven Sages or Seven Poets. In China, the seven stars correspond to the Seven Rulers. In Siberia the seven stars are the Seven Blacksmiths or Seven Watchmen. It may be that this is the origin of the wise men who greet the new born Son of Light (the Bible mentions a visit by wise men, not kings, and does not number them as three).

THE WAGON

The most common name for the constellation is the Wagon. Homer and Hesiod both give the Great Bear the secondary appellation of the wagon. As far back as the seventh century BCE, the Mesopotamians called it *Ma-Gid-Da* or 'wagon'. For the Anglo-Saxons it was Irmin's Wagon, for the Norse Odin's Wagon and for the Teutons it was Woden's Wagon, or Karl's Wagon, which later became Charles' Wagon in England. The Italians called it *Carro* (wagon). In Britain it was known as Arthur's Wagon.

This wagon is a bier or funeral wagon of the sun. The Arabic *Banat Na'ash al Kubra*, 'the Daughters of the Great Bier' or 'the Mourners' are a funeral procession identified with the Bear. Arabic Christians identified them as 'the Bier of Lazarus' and it was thought that the tradition possibly arose from the slow and solemn motion of the Bear around the Pole. The Skidi Pawnees saw it as a stretcher with a sick man on it. The ancient Babylonian Wagon was particularly associated with the dead and funeral processions and

38

was used in astrology to predict forthcoming eclipses which generally forecast the death of the king.

ARCTURUS RISING

When from the Tropic, or the winter's sun,
Thrice twenty days and nights their course have run;
And when Arcturus leaves the main, to rise
A star bright shining in the evening skies;
Then prune the vine.
Hesiod

Following the Great Bear is the constellation of Boötes, the herdsman who rules the spring and summer skies, with its brightest star Arcturus ('Bear Keeper'). When it first rises over the eastern horizon in January, it is a sign that spring is on its way. Arcturus is known as 'The One who Comes', rising not long after the winter solstice each year, just as Arthur is known as the 'Once and Future King' who sleeps until the day of his promised return.[66] In Ancient Egypt Arcturus was Smat 'The One Who Rules' and Bau, 'The Coming One'. The Celtic goddess Brighid was styled 'daughter of the bear', because her early spring festival of Imbolc follows the rebirth of the sun and the rising of Arcturus. The three constellations of the Great and Little Bear and Boötes, together with the star Arcturus, seem to have become inextricably interwoven in myth.

There are certainly bear customs associated with the rising of Arcturus following the winter solstice, which marks the coming of spring. The festival of the Straw Bear or 'Strawbower' is an old custom known in the Fenlands of England, and in other parts of Europe, notably Germany. On Plough Tuesday, (the day after Plough Monday) a man or boy was covered from head to foot in straw and led from house to house where he would dance in exchange for gifts of money, food or beer. Farmers would often reserve their best straw for the making of the Bear. Today, in a restored festival, the Bear processes around the streets with its attendant 'keeper' and musicians, followed by numerous morris dancers, molly dancers, mummers, sword and clog dancers.

66   Madeleine Johnson, *Arcturus Rising*,
      http://www.yewgrove.demon.co.uk/starsong/arcturus.htm, ©1997

Chapter 4
PUNISHMENT AND REWARD

At Yule, the old year dissolves back into the chaos and darkness from which it emerged as the world is reborn and a new cycle begins. At such a time, the pattern for the future could be set by sympathetic magic and the future divined.

It was considered very important to complete the old year's work before the new year began: a magical act of leaving behind the past and being ready to embrace the future. In the same vein, there was also a sense that Yule was a time for settling moral accounts: bad behaviour in the previous year would be punished and good behaviour rewarded. Today's Christmas celebrations still retain an element of this whereby children are told that if they are good, Father Christmas will bring them presents. Less common is the injunction that naughty children will be deprived of their goodies or left pieces of coal instead. In the past bad children were promised severe punishment and whipping by the Winter Spirits, and adults were just as likely to reap penalties ranging from bad luck to dismemberment and death.

THE WILD HUNT
Because this was the time spirits were freed from the underworld as the gate of the Otherworld stood open, and also because this was the time of settling accounts, Yule was the time when the souls of the dead were collected, or returned in ghostly companies accompanying the Winter Hag or Wild Hunter.

In legend, the Wild Hunt, a terrifying spectral host of hounds and hunters, rides out to capture human souls during the Twelve Nights of Yule. Tales of such hunts appear all over Western Europe, led variously by Charlemagne, King Arthur, Herne the Hunter and the Devil amongst others. Various localities have their own version of the Wild Huntsman.

The Scandinavian Wild Hunt the *Jolerei* ('Yuletide Host') is led by the old god Odin and it is death for a Christian to see it, reflecting the life and death power of the old deities. The windows of sick rooms were once opened so that if the soul was ready to depart it could join the hoards. In Germany Woden hunts the spirits of the dead, mounted on a white horse and accompanied by a pack of ghostly black dogs. The Norwegian *Oskorei* are the host of the unforgiven dead who appear in the guise of a hunter and hounds riding out at Yule.

Elsewhere the leader was called Hellekin or Harlekin who led a procession which included a cart full of the souls of unbaptised babies. A priest called Wachin saw him in the vicinity of St Aubin in Anjou in 1901.[67] He was accompanied by a troop of noble ladies, churchmen and men, all in black on black horses carrying black banners. Wachin recognised many of them as people he had known who were dead. Hellekin evolved into the character of Harlequin on the Italian and English stage.

In Windsor Great Park in Berkshire, sightings of Herne the Hunter were usually reported during the winter months, especially around the Twelve Days of Misrule from Yule to Twelfth Night, when he rides out with the Wild Hunt. Although he is often identified with the Gaulish stag god Cernunnos, others think he may be a folk memory of Woden who may have been worshipped in Windsor Forest in Anglo-Saxon times.[68] According to his legend, like may leaders of the Hunt, he was a suicide who killed himself at a blasted oak. He is described as a mighty, bearded figure with a huge pair of stag's horns on his head. He wears chains, carries a hunting horn and rides out on a black horse with a pack of ferocious hunting hounds.

In Germany a wild hunter called Hans von Hackelberg rides in storms and during the Twelve Nights. First the baying of hounds is heard, then the night-owl Tutosel flies in the vanguard (one story makes her a nun who joined the Wild Hunt.) Hackelnberg refused the last rites after an accident in 1521 but prayed that he might hunt forever and this became his doom. In Westphalia he is Hackelbärend who, while alive, hunted even on Sundays and so was cursed in death to hunt forever.

The Spanish called the nocturnal procession of suffering souls 'the ancient host' or simply *la hueste*, an army of spirits.

A wild huntsman called Le Grand Veneur haunts the forest of Fontainebleau when the wind blows through the trees. Another tale involves a prince of Saxony who punished his subjects for breaking forest laws. When a boy stripped the bark from a willow to make a whistle the prince had the boy cut open and his entrails twined round the tree (an ancient punishment for

67   Ordericus Vitalis, 1619

68   Michael Howard, 'The Wild Hunt Rides Out', *Silver Wheel Annual 2*, Lear Books , Earl Shilton, 2010

destroying a sacred tree). When a peasant shot a stag he had the unfortunate serf riveted to the stag. At last the prince broke his own neck by dashing it against a beech tree while hunting and is now doomed to hunt forever. He rides a white horse and is followed by hounds, haunting lonely forests and heaths hunting witches, thieves, murderers and other criminals. He falls down at crossroads and avoids the highways.

The wild huntsman is also found in Carinthia, riding on the wind. To propitiate the wind peasants would place a wooden bowl full of meat in a tree in front of their houses.

A similar figure ranges the Malay forests, and travels with a pack of ghostly dogs, and whenever he is seen sickness and death follow. Certain night flying birds are believed to be his attendants. When their cry is heard the peasants run out with a knife on a wooden platter and cry 'Great grandfather, bring us their hearts'. The huntsman is fooled into thinking they are his own followers asking for a share of his bag and passes them unharmed.

The Iroquois of North America know a comparable figure. He is called Heno the Thunder who rides on the clouds and splits trees with his thunderbolts.

The Carinthians said that the Wild Host circled the world three times on the Twelfth Night, perhaps for a last look before being banished back to the underworld until next winter. Their divine nature is reflected in German proverbs predicting that when the Wild Hunt passed, it would be a good year, or that all would be green.

THE WINTER HAG

As well as ghostly hordes led by a Wild Huntsman, there are legends of similar throngs led by a hag. In some Norse myths the riders are women, *túnridur* or 'hag riders', or *gandreid* 'witch ride'. In ancient Greece, the witch goddess Hecate led the procession of those who had died before their time, accompanied by her underworld hounds. Ancient goddesses were often accompanied by dogs. Gaulish statues and altars often depicted a beneficent goddess, such as Nehalennia of Walcheren, with a dog and basket of fruit. The dog is a psychopomp, and the fruit the gift of the goddess from her underworld womb. Nehalennia might be identified with the Mothers or *matrones* who were worshiped widely among both the Celts and Germanic groups.

The *Disablot* which was held at Winter Nights is identified as being similar to Mother's Night of Germanic customs. The goddesses of fate – the fairy godmothers of later legend - appeared at the birth of a child to bring gifts and set its future.

The Hag Goddess comes into her power during the Twelve Nights and flies through the midnight skies, accompanied by wild women, ghosts and other spirits, collecting the souls of the dead, especially those unbaptised at the time of their death. Usually described as a spinner, she is a crone with long nose, or perhaps a nose made of iron, or she has iron teeth.[69] She sometimes carried a pitcher of live coals or a cauldron to burn the distaffs of lazy spinners.[70] However, though she was severe in her punishments, she rewarded those who pleased her, and her passing blessed the land with fertility. It was she who gave newborns their destiny.

Sometimes she rode in a cart; Harz peasants used to remark on stormy nights, "It's Frau Hulli going in her cart with the devil." In Obersteiermark, damned women drove a boat-shaped sledge across the skies, which bore a narrow flame shaped like a ploughshare, which blessed the fields. If a person should meet the Hag at a crossroads, she might present gifts that possessed hidden magical potency. The cart recalls the ancient wagons of the earth goddess Nerthus or Cybele.

Tyroleans recounted how the Perchtas dismembered those who got in the way of their Twelfth Night Wild Hunt. Sometimes people woke up miraculously restored after this. The Rumanian Iele took a bone from the intruder's leg to replace a broken wheel spoke and returned it a year later. Originally, such tales may have related a shamanic initiation at the hands of the Hag Goddess, but as time passed and cultures shifted, the goddess and her spirits were demonised. While German commoners said that the Furious Host rode with Frau Holle or Percht, courtly poets referred to Venus or the *valantinne* ('she-devil') Herodias. Or, in German and Dutch poetry of the 1200s, the goddess appeared as Frau Aventure, Lady Fortune or Chance.

Frau Gauden

Frau Gauden and her twenty-four daughters were so keen on hunting that they declared they would rather hunt forever than go to heaven. God consequently condemned Frau Gauden to hunt till the Last Judgement and turned her daughters into dogs that pulled her cart, or ran behind it. They were often seen during the Twelve Nights, especially at crossroads, where Frau Gauden might be encountered with her broken cart. In one tale she offered a man dog turds to repair it, and though he fixed the cart, he understandably declined to take more than a few turds in return. However, in the morning, they had turned to gold.

---

69   The Russian witch goddess Baba Yaga had iron teeth and flew with witches
      at the summer solstice.

70   Max Dashu http://www.suppressedhistories.net/secrethistory/witchtregenda.html

A north German proverb declared that when Frau Gauden passed by with her dogs, the harvest would be good. Folk songs remember Fru Gauden as a giver of auspicious gifts to children.

German lore of the 1800s warned that one of her dogs would haunt families who left their doors open during the Winter Nights. Wherever she finds a street-door open she sends a little dog in. Next morning he wags his tail at the inmates and whines, and will not be driven away. If killed, he turns into a stone by day. This, though it may be thrown away, always returns and is a dog again by night. All through the year he whines and brings ill luck upon the house so people are careful to keep their street-doors shut during the Twelve Nights.

Dame Aventure

Dame Aventure originated in France, where manuscript illuminators painted her in a courtly style, often drawing on ancient Roman myths. She is shown with a wheel, like the goddess Fortuna, or she is pictured as a threefold goddess who assigns destiny to infants floating by in the stream of life.

Percht or Berthe

In the southern regions of Germany the Hag Goddess was called Percht or Berthe. In Tyrol, it was often said that the Perchtl was Pontius Pilate's wife, Procula. In the Italian dialects of south Tyrol the she is *la donna Berta*. Berchta ('Shining') is the north German goddess of winter and witchcraft, associated with Eisenberta ('Iron Berta'). She journeys through the clouds with her followers, the Wild Hunt, and descends to earth. Humans must lay a table of food and drink for her in the open air. In southern Germany, Berhta was preceded by her muffled servant, variously called Rupper, Ruprecht, Hersche, Harsche or Hescheklas.

In lower Austria, Iron Perchta and the *Gvozdenzuba* pass over the earth, and descend into it during the winter nights. The Slovenes said that Perchta Baba was accompanied by eagles and snakes, symbols of the upper and lower worlds. Tyroleans said that whoever got in Wild Berchta's way on this night would sink into trance and upon awakening, be able to predict how the next harvest would be. In many places, Perchta was later replaced by Nicholas who assumed her role and appropriated her attendants. Perchta, too, once solicited help in repairing her cart axle and rewarded the man with some wood chips. Disdaining the gift, he only took a few, only to discover later on that they had turned to gold.

In the Orlagau, on the night before Twelfth Day, Perchta examined the spinning-rooms and presented the spinners with empty reels which they

44

had to fill within a short time. She also made sure that people fasted. If they had eaten anything but *zemmede* (fasting fare made of flour, milk and water) that day, she would cut open the perpetrator's stomach, take out any other food they have had and fill the empty space with straw and bricks, before sewing them up again. She would reward those who had served her, and in Styria was the gift giver who presented good children with nuts and apples, symbols of fertility. [71] To placate her, houses were decorated with evergreens and food left out for her on Twelfth Night. If she was pleased, she would leave small presents and treats for the children. In Carinthia the Epiphany was called *Berchtentag.*[72] Medieval documents refer to Yule as *perchtentag* ('bright day') or *perhtennaht* ('bright night').

Perchten Runners

At one midnight on Epiphany Eve in the Tyrol, a drunken peasant suddenly heard the sound of many voices behind him, which came on nearer and nearer. Then the Berchtl in her white clothing, her broken ploughshare in her hand, with all her train of little people, swept clattering and chattering close past him. At the end of the procession was a small child, wearing a long shirt much too big for it, so that it kept tripping over the hem. The peasant felt sorry for it, so he took off his garter and used it to make a belt for the infant, and set it on its way. When the Berchtl saw what he had done she turned back and thanked him and told him that in return for his compassion his children should never come to want.

The German Perchta keeps little ones who died before baptism. She

---

71   Clement A. Miles, *Christmas in Ritual and Tradition*, Christian and Pagan, T. Fisher Unwin, 1912

72   *Ibid*

is ferried across the river with them, recalling Greek and Scandinavian myths of crossing the underworld river of death. Another version says that Perchta, queen of the *heimchen* (possibly a diminutive of *heim*, 'home', an affectionate term for the dead babies) lived in the fertile Saale valley. She fructified the land by ploughing it underground, while her *heimchen* watered the fields. But the people of the place were ungrateful, and she resolved to leave their land. One night a ferryman beheld a tall, stately lady with a crowd of weeping children. She demanded to be ferried across, and the children dragged a plough into the boat, crying bitterly.

The Danish huldra (fairies) received infants who died unchristened, and were seen travelling with multitudes of them on Twelfth Night. Slovenians called the goddess leading the souls of the dead Quaternica, Pehtra Baba or Zlata Baba ('Golden Crone').

In the spirit of Yuletide misrule, guisers dress up as Perchta's host in horned wooden masks with snouts and beaks, black sheepskins or hoods of badger or bear fur. They take part on in processions and ecstatic dances, blowing horns, clashing symbols and bells, thrashing bad children and rewarding good ones. The Perchten run through the streets with glowing embers in their mouths, as if breathing fire. They rush into houses to 'clean' them, and chase the shrieking children, threatening to put them in sacks. The mummers claim the offerings which have been set out for Perchta.[73]

The Perchten Run still continues in German speaking regions, when people wear frightening masks and take to the street with a great deal of noise to drive out the winter spirits. They appear alone or in groups, especially on three specific winter nights, called the 'rough nights' (the Eve of St. Nicholas, the Eve of the solstice and before Epiphany). They carry bells and other loud instruments to dispel the winter. The Perchten Run takes place on January 6th from Badgastein to Böckstein and on January 7th from Badgastein to Hofgastein. They all run in single file. It is believed that the quality and abundance of the next harvest, as well as the well-being of the people, are dependent on the performances of the Perchten.

Elsewhere, there is a ritual battle between the forces of growth, life, summer and good luck, and the forces of decay, death, winter and ill fortune. Masked as the beautiful Perchtas and the ugly Perchtas, the mummers enacted the triumph of the life force over the power of the underworld. In Lötschental, Switzerland, the terrible Perchten sprinkle spectators with liquid manure. The Bavarian and Austrian Perchten give a 'blow with the life-wand'.

---

73   Max Dashu http://www.suppressedhistories.net/secrethistory/witchtregenda.html

Frau Faste

The Germanic Frau Faste is said to tear out the bowels of bad children to teach them a lesson.

Reisarova or Gurorysse

In Norway, the goddess Reisarova or Gurorysse led the *aaskereida* ('lightning and thunder'); a spectral host who rode black horses with eyes like embers. They travel during storms, and to hear them pass was an omen of death. To meet them was even worse, as they would catch up the unfortunate person and carry them away. Max Dashu sees a connection with the Eddic witch-goddess of winter storms Hyrrokin, who rode the heavens on a wolf bridled with snakes. [74]

Frau Holle or Frau Holda

In northern Germany the Hag was Frau Holle or Frau Holt. To placate the goddess and her host, people would leave out offerings. In Germany the *Hollenzopf* ('Hölle's braid') plaited loaf was left out. Her southern German counterpart Frau Holda rides about in a wagon at Yule. Holda, whose name means 'the kindly one' brought rewards for diligent spinners, and on every New Year's Eve, between nine and ten o'clock, she drove in a carriage full of presents through villages where respect had been shown to her. At the crack of her whip the people would come out to receive her gifts. In Hesse and Thuringia she was imagined as a beautiful woman clad in white with long golden hair, and, when it snows hard, people said "Frau Holle is shaking her featherbed." She is derived from the Germanic sky goddess Holda or Hulda, who was also a goddess of fertility, the hearth and spinning.[75]

Befana

In Italy, the hag goddess of the Twelve Nights is Befana, her name a corruption of *Epiphania,* since she is connected with the Feast of the Epiphany or Twelfth Night, January 6th. According to one legend, Befana was an old woman who refused to give food to the Three Wise Men. She regretted her decision almost immediately and went off to find them, but they were gone. She still wanders the earth looking for them, dispensing gifts as she goes to make up for her earlier lack of charity.

Though her role has largely been taken over by Santa Claus in modern

---

74   *Ibid*

75   Anna Franklin, *The Illustrated Fairy Encyclopaedia*, Vega, London 2002

Italy, she was once the yuletide gift bringer. Sicilians especially honoured Befana, also called *la Strega* ('the witch') or *la Vecchia* ('the old woman').

Befana descended from the mountains, riding on her broom, and entered houses through the chimney, leaving presents for children on Twelfth Night. Children left notes for her in the chimney. For those children who had been naughty, she left only coal (shops sold *carbone,* a sweet that looks like coal) or a birch rod (to be spanked with). Mothers would

The Visit of Lucia

sometimes warn their children that if they were naughty the Befana would take them away and eat them.

Formerly images of Befana were placed in the windows of houses, and there were processions through the streets. Singers serenaded houses where cloth images of Befana were placed in the windows, or carried her image from house to house while carolling. Families welcomed the visiting crone with tambourines, horns and drums. Children sang '*la Befanata'* asking her favours. In some places oranges and sweets were put into the Befana doll, which was then broken open and the treats distributed.

The Befana dolls were afterwards burned, probably in token of the passing of the old year and beginning of the new. Omens were taken from the fire. If the smoke blew towards the east, it was an omen that the harvest would be good. If the smoke blew towards the west, it would be poor. Befana herself is sometimes depicted with grain, fruit and nuts. The rites of the Epiphany signal that the dark time has ended.

One of Befana's titles was Marantega (*mater antiga*, 'old mother') or she sometimes appeared as part of a triad with Rododsa and Maratega to weave the destinies of humankind, obviously a version of the Fates. She is associated with spinning and her symbol is the woven stocking. Children hung these from the hearth at the Epiphany for her to fill with gifts. She appeared in Renaissance witch trials as the goddess of the witches. Into modern times, people appealed to her for good fortune on the Epiphany, a night charged with magic, when people can divine the future, animals can speak and even

48

prophesy, the dead return to earth and strange and marvellous things can happen. [76]

Sträggele

In Switzerland, the Sträggele ('witches') are amongst the winter spirits. They are said to steal bad children and rip them to pieces in the air.

Babushka

In Russia Babushka ('Grandmother') visited sleeping children on Christmas Eve putting toys under their pillows. The same story is attributed to her as Befana - the Three Kings invited her along to see the Christ Child, but she refused and regretted it, and spent every Christmas Eve examining every child for him.

Luca or Lucia

For the Hungarians, Czechs, Slovaks, Croats, Slovenians and east Austrians, the witch goddess known as Luca or Lucia went about making sure no one span or baked on her feast day. A woman holding a white-veiled sieve like a mask over her face impersonated Luca during the celebration, giving gifts to children. For all these peoples, Luca fits the eastern European image of the witch with an iron nose. She sometimes took the form of a pig.[77]

Lussi

In Sweden, *Lussinatta*, the Lussi Night, is December 13th. Between Lussi Night and Yule, trolls, evil spirits and the spirits of the dead were especially active. Lussi, a witch, flew through the air with her followers, the *Lussiferda*. She would descend the chimneys to take away naughty children. If people had not finished their work before Yule, she would punish the household.

In other Scandinavian areas, St Lussi is a man dressed in goat skins (like Julbok, the Christmas goat) with a devil mask and horns. Lussi threatens to disembowel children who have been naughty.

There was a *Lussevaka* ('Lucy Wake') vigil, staying awake through the *Lussinatt* to guard the household against evil. To fall asleep before St Lucy's dawn would mean that the devil could come and take you. This is still carried out today, mostly by the younger population having night-long parties.[78]

76   Max Dashu http://www.suppressedhistories.net/secrethistory/witchtregenda.html
77   Clement A. Miles, *Christmas in Ritual and Tradition*, Christian and Pagan, T. Fisher Unwin, 1912
78   http://stephanielevy.blogspot.com/2009/12/artist-advent-calendar-camilla-engman.html

At dawn on the 13th, groups of young people, dressed in white and carrying candles, used to go from door to door singing, and getting treats or money in return. Nowadays, this tradition is kept alive in schools and universities with early morning choir performances, and with children singing to their parents, and taking them breakfast. Lucia's assistants are the Star Boys, who were originally, like the Wildman, dressed in furs with blackened faces. They now wear pointed wizards' hats and wave magic wands with a star on the end.

St Lucy's Eve was a mysterious and dangerous time in many parts of Europe, a time when witches were thought to be especially powerful. In Britain, witches and fairies would kidnap anyone who went to bed without any supper. In Lower Austria witchcraft was feared and had to be averted by prayer and incense. A procession was made through each house to cense every room. On this evening, too, girls were afraid to spin lest in the morning they should find their distaffs twisted, the threads broken, and the yarn in confusion. On St Lucy's Eve, candles were lit and all electrical lights turned off, and on the Sunday closest to December 13th Danes traditionally attend church.

It was also a time when the future could be divined. In Austria a mysterious light called *Luzieschein* ('the Lucy-shining') was observed by boys outdoors at midnight, and the future could be foretold from its appearance. Meanwhile, at midnight the girls would go to a willow-bordered brook, cut the bark of a tree partly away, without detaching it, make with a knife a cross on the inner side of the cut bark, moisten it with water, and carefully close up the opening. On New Year's Day the cutting would be opened, and the future augured from the markings found. Danish maids prayed "Sweet St. Lucy let me know: whose cloth I shall lay, whose bed I shall make, whose child I shall bear, whose darling I shall be, whose arms I shall sleep in."

Whether an actual person called Lucia ever existed or not, the saint seems to have taken her mythology and characteristics from local Pagan deities, and is such is seen differently in different regions. It is likely that she is derived from the Roman goddess Juno Lucina or Lucetia, the Mother of Light who also carried a tray and a lamp, bestowing the gifts of light, enlightenment and sight, who as also known as the opener of the eyes of newborn children. [79] In Scandinavia she seems to have taken on attributes of the goddess Freya who was known as the *Vanadis*, or the shining bride of the gods. [80] The *lussikatter* (Lucy cats) or the golden saffron rolls that are served

79   Susan Granquist, 1995, http://www.irminsul.org/arc/001sg.html
80   *Ibid*

by the Lucia Bride are said to be the devil's cats which Lucia subdued, and the cats were pictured at her feet. Cats were also associated with Freya. Freya's special season was Yule when she dispensed wealth and plenty. The traditional shape of the rolls is a crossed shape where the arms are rolled inward and in the curve are bright pieces of fruit or small candles in the form of a solar wheel. [81] Lucia may also have some aspects of the Norse sun-goddess Sunna, whose emblem is the fiery wheel.

Saelde

In the southern German-speaking lands, from Switzerland to Austria, Saelde possessed a wheel and an abundance-bearing horn, the *Saeldenhorn*. She seems to have been a fate goddess, often described as blind, who visited newborns to endow them with gifts. This is reflected in several mediaeval folk sayings such as 'travel in Saelde's keeping', 'Saelde is the staff you shall lean on', 'Saelde smiled on her' and 'Vrou Saelde turns her neck' i.e., her looking away signalled misfortune. [82] A night vigil called 'waking the Saelde' was held to await her coming, a night when omens could be drawn.

According to several witch trial transcripts, she leads the witches and spirits who roamed the skies on the Ember Nights. Tyroleans said that Frau Selga could be seen riding at the head of the nightly host.

Cailleach

In Scotland was the ceremonial burning of winter and the old year as the Cailleach ('Hag'). A piece of wood was carved roughly to represent the face of an old woman, and then named as the Spirit of Winter, the Cailleach. This was placed onto a good fire to burn away, and all the family gathered had to watch to the end. The burning symbolised the ending of all the bad luck and enmities of the old year, with a fresh start.

THOR AND ODIN

Modern gift-giving spirits have their origin in much older Pagan legends. Some of Santa's characteristics are undoubtedly borrowed from Norse and Germanic lore. The god Odin rode on a white eight legged horse called Sleipnir and delivered either gifts or punishments at the winter solstice. Like Santa, Odin had a long white beard, and a sheaf of grain was left in the fields for his horse. He lived in Valhalla, the Far North. Even after the

---

81   *Ibid*

82   Max Dashu http://www.suppressedhistories.net/secrethistory/witchtregenda.html

Norman invasion in 1066, oaths were commonly sworn 'by God and by Odin'.

Grim or Grimr was a title of Odin, meaning 'hooded' or 'disguised'. Sometimes Odin visited human hearths disguised in a long hooded cloak, and if he were kindly received would leave a gift. In myth the hood often conceals the identity of the supernatural being so that he/she might go amongst mankind undetected. There are a variety of hooded spirits, including Carl Hood, Robin Hood and the Romano-Celtic *Genii Cucullati* ('Hooded Spirits'). Images of triads of hooded and cloaked dwarfs or giants appear all over Celtic Europe during the Roman period carrying eggs or displaying phalluses, obviously marking them as fertility spirits. An obvious association is the 'hood' of the phallus, the foreskin. This is further compounded by the fact that 'Robin' (as in Robin Hood) was once a nickname for the phallus.

Old Christmas

In furry pall yclad,
His brows enwreathed with holly never sere.
Old Christmas comes to close the wained year.
BAMPFYLDE

According to Robert Graves *hood* or *hod* also means a 'log', especially the Yule log perhaps referring us back to tree spirits and renewal at the winter solstice. There is plenty of hood symbolism around at Yule. For humans wearing a hood, mask or disguise often has a sacred or ritual purpose, relinquishing the old identity with the old clothes. Disguising or 'guising' is still a feature of the Yuletide celebrations, with participants blackening their faces, wearing hoods or masks and so on.

Along with Odin, many attributes of the god Thor were transferred to Santa: Thor was often portrayed as a large, elderly man with a long white beard; he rode through the air in a chariot drawn by two white goats called Cracker and Gnasher; he dressed in red; his palace was in the northland; he was friendly and cheerful. Thor was the god of the peasants and the common people and always helped and protected them. The rumble and roar of thunder was said to be caused by the rolling of his chariot. He fought the giants of ice and snow (i.e., the powers of winter). The fireplace in every home was especially sacred to him, and he was said to come down through the chimney into his element, fire. Swedish children wait eagerly for *Jultomten*, a gnome

whose sleigh is drawn by the *Julbocker*, the goats of the thunder god Thor.[83]
Thor's helpers were elves and like Santa's elves, Thor's elves were skilled
craftsman. It was the elves who created Thor's magic hammer. It was Thor
who, in the last days of Heathenism, was regarded as the chief antagonist of
Christ.[84]

THE CHRISTMAS FAIRIES
There are lots of Christmas fairies, probably derived from much older legends
of gods and spirits. The Scandinavian Tomte Gubbe is a kind of brownie, for
whom porridge and new milk must be left on Christmas Eve to win his good
will for the coming year.

The Icelandic Julbuk ('Yule-Buck') is a horned fairy lives in the
woods in summer, the fields in autumn and visits human houses at Christmas.
The Norwegian and Danish Julenisse ('Yule Nisse') delivers Christmas gifts.
Julnissen live in dark corners or under the stairs and creep out at night to
eat the porridge that children are careful to leave out for them. They were
probably originally hearth spirits or household gods. In Sweden the Jultomte
('Yule Tomte') is the king of the fairies who delivers presents.

FATHER CHRISTMAS
The English Father Christmas was a very different figure to the American
Santa Claus until the mid twentieth century. Before then, he personified the
good will and cheer of the season, depicted in a variety of clothes, and never
climbed down chimneys, had reindeer or filled stockings.

He was banned by the Puritans, along with mince pies and games.
Occasionally secret publishers would print broadsheets with a verse about
'Old Christmas'. In *An Hue and Cry after Christmas* (1645), which described
the imprisonment of Christmas on St Thomas' Day, he was portrayed as

*"This hoary headed man was of great years, and as white as snow. He
entered the Romish Kallendar, time out of mind, as old, or very near, as
Father Mathusalem was – one that looked fresh in the Bishops' time,
though their fall made him pine away ever since. He was full and fat...
just like Bacchus upon a tunne of wine, when the grapes hang shaking
about his ears"*

In the *Vindication of Christmas* (1652), 'Old Christmas' complained about
the way he was used in the city and found small comfort in any house,

---

83   Edna Barth, *Holly, Reindeer, and Colored Lights, The Story of the Christmas
      Symbols.* Clarion Books, New York, 1971

84   H.R. Ellis.Davidson, *Scandinavian Mythology*, Peter Bedrick Books, New York 1982

announcing "Welcome or not, I am come." Another periodical (*Mercurius Democritus*) published the verses:

Old Christmas now is come to town,
Though few do him regard;
He laughs to see them going down,
That have put down his Lord.
And
A gallant crew, stir up the fire,
The other winter tale,
Welcome, Christmas, 'tis our desire
To give thee more spic'd ale.

He became the personification of everything the British people held dear about Christmas.

In 1616 CE Ben Jonson presented his play *Christmas, his Masque* at the Court of King James. In this the Season of Christmas was represented by an actor, and his entourage were the attributes of the season personified.

In the eighteenth century, Father Christmas began to appear in the Christmas plays of itinerant players. In the middle of the play, he would appear, heavily disguised, shouting his challenge, "In comes I, Old Father Christmas. Be I welcome or be I not - I hope that old Christmas will never be forgot!" He and appeared regularly in *Punch*. [85] He was used as a symbol of good living and gaiety in the eighteenth century in order to ridicule the Puritan objections to Christmas.

Charles Dickens, in *A Christmas Carol*, described the Spirit of Christmas as a jolly character clad in a green robe and wreathed with holly, and Victorian illustrators usually depicted him as a very Pagan character with icicles or ivy round his head in robes of various colours.

As more influence came to Britain from America after World War II, Father Christmas was presented as a fat and jolly character who filled stockings, and occasionally gave guest appearances at civic and public places. By the twentieth century, he was a common figure in most Department Stores the length and breadth of the British Isles. He was often austere looking and would ask children questions about their prayers, their reading, writing and arithmetic. If they had been naughty, he would tell them they must improve or he would not visit them at Christmas. Most older people still refer to him as 'Father Christmas' rather than Santa Claus.

---

85   http://www.intotruth.org/misc/xmas2.html

SAINT NICHOLAS

St Nicholas was allegedly a fourth century bishop who was imprisoned during
the Roman emperor Diocletian's persecution of Christians, but later released
by Constantine the Great. His historical validity, however, is in some question,
as he does not appear on any contemporary list of bishops, and doesn't appear
as one of the bishops visiting the Council of Nicea.

He is associated with many miracles, both before and after his death.
His most famous legend concerns three poor girls whose father could not
afford to supply them with dowries, which meant that they would be unable
to marry and would be forced to turn to prostitution. Nicholas secretly
went to their house and threw three purses of gold through their window. In
some versions he threw in purses for three nights, in others over a period of
three years. Learning that the father lay in wait to find out the identity of the
mysterious benefactor, St Nicholas dropped the last purse down the chimney,
where it landed in a stocking left hanging by the hearth to dry. In his honour,
medieval nuns are said to have gone about on St Nicholas' Eve leaving baskets
of food and clothes at the doorsteps of the needy. [86]

He had a great reputation for gift-giving, and took over the legends
and functions of the gift giving spirits of the season (such as Woden and
Befana etc.). In the Netherlands, children put their wooden clogs (or
sometimes baskets) by the hearth on the Eve of St. Nicholas, hoping that St
Nicholas, riding through the air on his white horse, will pause, come down the
chimney and fill them with sweets. Carrots and hay are left out for his white
horse. This is plainly a Christianisation of the legend of Woden flying through
the air on his eight legged horse around the winter solstice. In some cases,
children spread a white sheet on the floor and sing special songs welcoming
St Nicholas. The door suddenly opens and a shower of treats falls upon the
sheet. Then St Nicholas (or rather, the man playing him) appears, dressed in
his bishop's robes, and questions the children about their behaviour. He is
accompanied by Zwarte Piet ('Black Peter'), who carries a thick rod and a
sack and threatens to carry the children off if they have been naughty. After
the children are sent to bed, adults exchange gifts and feast on hot punch,
chocolate and boiled chestnuts served hot with butter and sugar. [87]

In Czechoslovakia, children believe that St Nicholas comes down a
golden cord carrying a basket of apples, nuts and sweets. In Hungary, shoes
are left outside the window to be filled by the passing saint. In France, children

---

86   http://en.wikipedia.org/wiki/Saint_Nicholas

87   http://www.schooloftheseasons.com/decdays1.html

hang stockings near the fire saying:
Saint Nicholas, mon bon patron,
Envoyez-moi quelque chose de bon.[88]

Knecht Ruprecht

In Tyrol children prayed to the saint on his Eve and left out hay for his white horse and a glass of *schnaps* for his servant. He appeared dressed in bishop's robes, tested children on their catechism and rewarded the good children with sweets, while bad children were shown his servant, the hideous Klaubauf, a shaggy monster with horns, black face, fiery eyes, long red tongue, and chains that clanked as he moved. [89] In Lower Austria the saint is followed by a similar figure called Krampus or Grampus, in Styria by a horrible attendant called Bartel. Sometimes St. Nicholas himself appears in a non-churchly form like Pelzmärte, with a bell or with a sack of ashes which gains him the name of Aschenklas. Sometimes, however, he is accompanied by St Peter, an angel and even Jesus Christ. These are represented by children, who perform a kind of mumming play, during which the children in the audience are accused of various misdeeds and are defended by the *Heiliger Christ* who eventually rewards them with nuts.

The protestant reformer Martin Luther tried to get rid of Catholic elements of Christmas, and replaced Nicolas with *das Christkindl* (an angel-like Christ Child) who brought Christmas gifts. This figure later evolved into Kris Kringle in America.[90]

In Germany, St Nicholas' Eve is called *Nikolausta* and in the Catholic regions a man dressed as Nicholas goes from house to house taking gifts to children, carrying a book which is supposed to list all their naughty and good behaviour. He is accompanied by scary figures like Krampus, who jokily scares the children, threatening them with a switch. In other regions, Krampus is called Knecht Ruprecht, who sometimes brings the gifts in place of Nicholas. Sometimes they don't make a personal appearance, and in this case children leave their shoes by the window or door on December 5th in the hope

---

88   *Ibid*

89   Clement A. Miles, *Christmas in Ritual and Tradition*, Christian and Pagan, T. Fisher Unwin, 1912

90   http://german.about.com/library/blnikolaus.htm

that they will be filled with treats. In past times, naughty children would have had a switch left instead, though this aspect has faded away. In parts of France and Luxembourg, he is accompanied by Père Fouettard, a hairy Wildman figure with a red beard.

Amongst Albanians, Saint Nicholas or Shen'Kollë is widely venerated. His feast is celebrated on 5th December, and is known *Shen'Kolli i Dimnit* (Saint Nicholas of Winter). On the eve of the feast day, Albanians light a candle and abstain from meat, preparing a feast of roasted lamb and pork to be served to guests after midnight. Guests will greet each other, saying, *"Nata e Shen'Kollit ju nihmoftë!"* ("May the Night of Saint Nicholas help you").

The three purses he left for the three impoverished virgins are said to be the origin of the pawnbroker's sign, making him the patron saint of pawnbrokers. The Low Countries interpret the three gold balls as oranges or other fruits, which were imported seasonally from Spain, giving rise to the idea that the saint lived in Spain and visited each winter, bringing oranges and other winter delicacies. [91]

SANTA'S LITTLE HELPERS

In Europe, Saint Nicholas and other gift-giving spirits had (and in some places still have) a variety of helpers that bear no resemblance to the cute elves of the American Santa. These are ragged, sinister spirits, sometimes horned, often hairy with blackened or hideous faces, which carry rods to punish naughty children and evil doers, even dragging some away to hell. They go by a variety of names in various regions and include Knecht Rupprecht, Pelznickle, Zwarte Piets, Furry Nicholas, Rough Nicholas and Klapperbock. They are often identified with demons or the devil himself.

Santa's helpers often carry brooms and come down the chimney. Chimney sweeps often carry a broom, an attribute of St. Nicholas. Chimney sweeps are a lucky charm for the New Year in Germany and elsewhere. The chimney is the way to the otherworld. As the dwelling place of the living flame, the hearth was a holy place, a threshold between this world and the realm of the gods. Its rising smoke took prayers to the gods of the Upperworld, while the gods of the Worlds Below could be contacted through the hearthstone. In many tales, the hearth and chimney it is the entrance and egress of spirits. In lore, various fairies are said to live behind the hearth, or to come down the chimney. [92]

91   http://en.wikipedia.org/wiki/Saint_Nicholas

92   Anna Franklin, *Hearth Witch*, Lear Books, Earl Shilton, 2005

Schimmelreiter

In Germany and Austria Woden was transformed into the Schrimmerlreiter ('White Horse Rider'). In the Mittelmark the name of *de hêle* (holy) Christ was given to a skin or straw-clad man. In the Ruppin district a man dresses up in white with ribbons, carries a large pouch, and is called Christmann or Christpuppe. He is accompanied by a Schimmelreiter and by other men dressed as women with blackened faces called *Feien*. The procession goes from house to house. The Schimmelreiter as he enters has to jump over a chair; this done, the Christpuppe is admitted. The girls present begin to sing, and the Schimmelreiter dances with one of them. Meanwhile the Christpuppe makes the children repeat some verse of Scripture or a hymn; if they know it well, he rewards them with

Krampus

gingerbreads from his wallet; if not, he beats them with a bundle filled with ashes. Then both he and the Schimmelreiter dance and pass on. Only when they are gone are the *Feien* allowed to enter; they jump wildly about and frighten the children.[93]

Knecht Ruprecht

Knecht Ruprecht is a prominent figure in the German Christmas. His name means 'Farmhand Rupert' or 'Servant Rupert', though older mythologists interpreted it as meaning 'shining with glory' from *hruodperaht*, and identified its owner with the god Woden.

Tradition holds that he appeared in homes on Christmas Eve, and was a man with a long beard, wearing fur or covered in pea-straw. He sometimes

---

93   Clement A. Miles, *Christmas in Ritual and Tradition*, Christian and Pagan, T. Fisher Unwin, 1912

carried a long staff and a bag of ashes, and wore little bells on his clothes. According to some stories, Ruprecht began as a farmhand; in others, he is a wild foundling (an archetypal Wildman) whom St. Nicholas raised from childhood. Ruprecht sometimes walks with a limp, because of a childhood injury. Often, his black clothes and dirty face are attributed to the soot he collects as he goes down chimneys.

On Christmas Eve in the north he went about clad in skins or straw and examined children; if they could say their prayers perfectly he rewarded them with apples, nuts and gingerbread; if not, he punished them.

In the south-western part of Lower Austria, both St. Nicholas and Ruprecht appeared on Christmas Eve in an elaborate ceremony. The children welcomed the saint with a hymn; then he went to a table and made each child repeat a prayer and show his lesson-books. Meanwhile Ruprecht in a hide, with glowing eyes and a long red tongue, stood at the door to overawe them. Each child next knelt before the saint and kissed his ring, whereupon Nicholas bade him put his shoes out-of-doors and look in them when the clock struck ten. After this the saint laid on the table a rod dipped in lime, solemnly blessed the children, sprinkled them with holy water, and departed.

In some of the Ruprecht traditions, the children would be summoned to the door to perform tricks, such as a dance or singing a song to impress upon St Nicholas and Ruprecht that they were indeed good children. Those who performed badly would be beaten soundly by Servant Ruprecht, and those who performed well were given a gift or some treats. Those who performed badly enough or had committed other misdeeds throughout the year were put into Ruprecht's sack and taken away, variously to Ruprecht's home in the Black Forest to be consumed later, or to be tossed into a river. In other versions the children must be asleep, and would awake to find their shoes filled with either sweets, coal, or in some cases a stick.

Rough Nicholas

In Mecklenburg the servant was *rû Klas* ('Rough Nicholas'). Sometimes he wore bells and carried a long staff with a bag of ashes at the end, hence the name *Aschenklas* was occasionally given to him.

Krampus

Saint Nicholas's most frightening companion can be found in parts of Austria Slovenia and Croatia. Krampus is a terrifying figure, most probably originating in the Pre-Christian Alpine traditions. Local tradition typically portrays these figures as children of poor families, roaming the streets and sledding hills during the holiday festival. They wore black rags and masks, dragging chains behind them, occasionally hurling them towards children in their way.

These *Krampusumzüge* (Krampus Runs) still exist. In Schladming, a town in Styria, over twelve hundred Krampus gather from all over Austria wearing goat-hair costumes and carved masks, carrying bundles of sticks used as switches, and swinging cowbells. Proceedings can get very rowdy, as they are usually young men who often get very drunk. They hit passersby with their switches and young women often avoid the areas they roam in.

In many parts of Croatia, Krampus is described as a devil, wearing chains around his neck, ankles and wrists, and wearing a cloth sack around his waist. As a part of the tradition, good children receive a golden branch from St. Nicolas, while if the child has misbehaved, Krampus will take the gifts for himself and leave only a silver branch to represent the child's bad acts. Children are told they must be asleep when St Nicholas comes or the Krampus will think they are bad and steal their presents.

In Hungary, the Krampusz is often portrayed as mischievous devil, wearing a black suit, with a long red tongue, a tail and little red horns that are funny rather than frightening. The Krampusz wields a *Virgács*, a bunch of gold coloured twigs bound together. Hungarian parents often frighten children with getting a *Virgács* instead of presents if they do not behave. *Virgács* are sold on the streets.

Belsnickel or Pelsnickel
Belsnickel ('Fur Nicholas') is a companion of Saint Nicholas in north-western Germany. He is played by a man wearing fur which covers his entire body, and he sometimes wears a mask with a long tongue. If the children were not good, he would leave coal or switches in their stockings.

Pelznickel traditions were maintained among immigrants in America into the nineteenth century. *Brown's Miscellaneous Writings*, by Jacob Brown (1830) recorded that people had never heard of Santa Claus, but instead people were visited by Kriskinkle, Beltznickle or the Christmas Woman. A man, heavily disguised and often wearing female costume, would appear after dark. He carried a sack filled with cakes, nuts and fruits, and a long hazel switch.

Zwarte Piet (Black Peter)
To the medieval Dutch, Black Peter was another name for the devil. Somewhere along the way, he was subdued by St. Nicholas and forced to be his servant. Although portrayed as the slave helper of Saint Nicholas, the two

are, in many villages, blended into one character.

In Belgium and the Netherlands, children are told that Zwarte Piet leaves gifts in the children's shoes or punishes naughty children. He enters the house through the chimney, which explains his black face and hands. Black-faced, red-lipped Zwarte Piet dolls are displayed in shop windows.

In the Troppau district of Austrian Silesia, three figures go round on Christmas Eve - Christkindel, the archangel Gabriel, and St. Peter - and perform a little play before the presents they bring are given. Christkindel announces that he has gifts for the good children, but the bad shall feel the rod. St. Peter complains of the naughtiness of the youngsters: they play about in the streets instead of going straight to school; they tear up their lesson-books and do many other wicked things. However, the children's mother pleads for them, and St. Peter relents and gives out the presents.

In the Erzgebirge appear St. Peter and Ruprecht, who is clad in skin and straw, has a mask over his face, a rod, a chain round his body, and a sack with apples, nuts and other gifts.

THE EVOLUTION OF THE MODERN SANTA

Santa Claus is generally stated to have his origins in Saint Nicholas, but modern representations of him don't seem to bear much relation to a bishop. In 1809, Washington Irving published his satirical *A History of New York* poking fun at New York's Dutch past. He represented St Nicholas as a jolly pipe-smoking Dutchman with baggy trousers, who rode over the tops of trees in a horse-drawn wagon dropping presents on children's houses as he went. [94] However, rather than the austere bishop, he was drawing on the tradition of the saint's helpers, the *Zwarte Pieten* (Black Petes) who dressed in baggy trousers and wore pointed caps of the same colours.

St Nicholas was known as *Sinterklaas* in Holland. Children there would put their shoes in front of the fireplace with a present for his horse and sing songs such as:

Sinterklass, castrated cock
Throw something in my show
Throw something in my boot.

In 1821, a New York printer named William Gilley issued a poem about a *Santeclaus* who dressed all in fur and drove a sleigh pulled by one reindeer.

On Christmas Eve of 1822, another New Yorker, Clement Clarke Moore, wrote down and read to his children a series of verses; his poem was published a year later as *An Account of a Visit from St. Nicholas* (more

94   http://www.feedback.nildram.co.uk/richardebbs/essays/sceptic.htm

commonly known today by its opening line, "'Twas the night before Christmas . . ."). Moore gave St. Nick eight reindeer (and named them all), and devised the now-familiar entrance by chimney. Moore's Nicholas was still a tiny figure, a 'jolly old elf' with a miniature sleigh.

The image further developed in 1863 when an American political cartoonist called Thomas Nast was commissioned by *Harper's Weekly* magazine to produce a Christmas cartoon, and drew one of Santa. As time went on, his annual cartoon developed and incorporated a range of Christmas imagery drawn from around the world. In 1866 the cartoon was published in colour for the first time, giving us Santa's familiar red suit. Nast drew him walking on rooftops and going down chimneys, and gave us Santa's workshop at the North Pole and his association with Mother Goose characters.

It is speculated that Nast based his image of Santa Claus not on Saint Nicholas, but on Pelznickle, his helper. Unlike Saint Nicholas in his bishop's robes, the saint's companions were hairy, bearded and fur clad. Nicholas didn't come down the chimney, but his helpers did, and were subsequently covered in ashes and soot. The helper carried the bag and handed out the treats (or punishments) to children, not the saint.

By the early 1900's Santa Claus had become a favourite in Christmas cards and advertising and in 1927 the New York Times described him in detail - the sack full of toys, red costume, white whiskers and jolly, ruddy cheeks.

There is an urban legend that an advertising campaign by Coca Cola created our modern image of Santa Claus. It is true that Haddon Sundblom, in 1931, created a series of Santa Claus ads for Coca-Cola, but his Santa image was very close to Nast's, though it emphasised the red and *white* nature of the robes to echo Coca Cola's famous brand more closely.

Chapter 5
WILDMEN

Santa's hairy little helpers (and hence Santa himself) may be traced back to the wildman or woodwose characters that pop up in practically every mythology.[95] A huge number of nature spirits across the world are described as or partly or completely covered in hair and they are often horned with something of the animal about them, and are probably related to the classical Pan and Faunus.[96] They are sometimes mischievous and sometimes vicious, capable of bestowing enormous bounty or terrible punishment.

One of the wildman's guises was Robin Goodfellow or Puck, depicted with horns, furry legs and cloven hooves. In *The Mad Pranks and Merry Jests of Robin Goodfellow* (1628) Robin is described as a chimney-sweep whose practical jokes were followed by his traditional cry of "Ho, Ho, Ho!" (remind you of anyone?).

Hood, Hod, Wood and Woode are common names for the wildman, and this may be the real origin of the legends of Robin Hood. Consider his name, his green clothing, his forest home and his deadly arrows; perhaps he was the nature god of the ordinary people who could seek him in the forest. A depiction of Robin and his men at the fourteenth century chapter house at Southwell Minster in Nottinghamshire shows them as twelve green men merging with various sacred plants such as hawthorn and ivy. Furthermore, Robin Hood's death came the day before Christmas which may represent the annual death of vegetation before its renewal with the rebirth of the sun.

Wild men are often carved into church buildings, much like the foliate heads known as Green Men to which they are certainly related. The Green Man has foliage for hair and either a leafy beard or with leaves growing out of his mouth and nose; sometimes he has horns on his head. The French called

---

95   Phyllis Siefker, *Santa Claus: Last of the Wild Men*, McFarland & Company, 1996

96   Anna Franklin, *The Illustrated Encyclopaedia of Fairies*, Vega, London, 2002

him *tete de feuilles* (head of leaves) and the Germans called him *blattmaske* (leaf mask). No one really knows the purpose of the Green Man in churches, and theories have extended from people smuggling their old deities onto church premises (green men certainly appear in Classical Pagan iconography) to illustrations of the threatening character of the natural world which could only be redeemed by Christianity.

Green Man Winchester Cathedral

We find the wildman too in the Arthurian Yuletide tale of the Green Knight (see Appendix 3) a mixture of Pagan ritual and the confused teachings of medieval Christianity. The Green Knight has long green hair which covers his back, a green beard, and carries a holly club in one hand. He is beheaded and through his sacrifice demonstrates that life still goes on.

The wildman or woodwose was a common character at various festivities in mediaeval England from May Day to Yule. At midsummer pageants and parades the frightening and comical woodwoses were commonly dressed in ivy and carried oak clubs. At the Scottish court at Yuletide, the Abbot of Unreason was attended by men dressed in "branches of pine, yew, oak, fern, boxwood, or flowering heath". [97] Henry VIII held Yuletide festivities in 1515 with a play in which eight wild men, in green moss and with ugly weapons, fought eight knights.

An old folk play in Thuringia involved a wildman, covered in ivy and moss, who hid in the woods but was hunted and captured by men. He collapsed in a mock death before being revived by a doctor. [98] This was is a common theme of seasonal mumming plays in Britain. In some Plough

---

97   Thomas K. Hervey, *The Book of Christmas*, The Folklore Society, 1888

98   Robert Hillis Goldsmith, "The Wild Man on the English Stage", *The Modern Language Review*, 1958

Monday plays (the Monday after Twelfth Night), the fool mates with a woman, a fight breaks out over her between the fool and the hero, the fool is killed and then resurrected by a doctor.

In whatever country they appear, Father Christmas's companions invariably included a Bessy (a man dressed as a woman) and assorted merrymakers dressed in goat or bear skins or wearing goat or bear masks. Usually there is a comic doctor and often an archer. The company went door-to-door, demanding entry. One inside, they acted out a play. The leader, who dressed in goat or bear skins, argued with another character or with the woman figure. He was killed, the woman lamented, and the doctor comically resuscitated him, or he spontaneously revived, declaring he wasn't dead after all. Before the troupe left to visit the next house, they demanded gifts. The famous Abbots Bromley Horn Dance originally took place at Yule, though now it is enacted in September. Significantly there are twelve dancers, six of which carry the horns, and they are accompanied by a musician, Maid Marian (a man in a dress), the hobby-horse, the Fool, a boy with a bow and arrow and another youngster with a triangle.

In 1906 R. M. Dawkins recorded a ritual in the Balkans in which large, blackened, humpbacked goat-men shambled through the village with bells around their waists and ankles. The leader carried a huge phallus while another carried a crossbow. An old woman carried a doll in a basket. As they went from house to house, the phallic goat-man pounded the phallus on the door and demanded money. In the course of the parade, the baby grew to manhood quite suddenly and demanded a bride. When she was supplied, the pair copulated, the archer shot the newly satisfied groom, the bride grieved, and the goat man revived. After receiving a gift from the homes where they performed, the processors dragged a plough through the village. [99]

Similar rituals are found in the Arctic Circle among the Lapps, the Vogul, and the Gilyaks and among the Ainu, the aboriginal Japanese. Joseph Campell, in *Primitive Mythology*, described a ritual amongst the Ainu, to whom the bear was a god. A young black bear cub was caught in the mountains, taken to the village and suckled by one of the women. When it matured, it was put into a cage until it was judged that the time had come to

99   R.M.Dawkins, *The Modern Carnival in Thrace and the Cult of Dionysos*, 1906

release the spirit of the divine bear to return to the mountains by being shot
with an arrow through the heart, with the injunction:

> *"O Divine One, you were sent into this world for us to hunt. When
> you come to them, please speak well of us and tell them how kind we
> have been. Please come again and we shall do you the honour of a
> sacrifice."*[100]

The bear's head was put on a pole and taken to share in the feast, with food
being laid before it. Finally the man presiding cried out "The little god is
finished; come, let us worship!" The flesh and blood of the bear was then
consumed, and its skull laid with those of earlier sacrifices. [101] The scenario
is similar to that of the folk plays: the wild beast-god/wildman is taken from
its wild home and killed by an archer. The spirit is returned to the gods until it
returns next year in a new body.

Archaeological evidence suggests that similar (cave) bear sacrifices
were carried out more than 75,000 years ago. At Wildkirchi, Drachenloch and
Wildermannlisloch ('the Wild Man's Cave') in the High Alps, Emil Bächler
discovered altars with bear skulls and leg bones ritually treated exactly as in
the Arctic. [102] These rituals speak of the death and resurrection of the beast-
god.

The beast-man still survives in folk customs. The wildman is known
in various regions as Chläus, Div, Djadek, Jass, Kinderfresser ('child eater'),
Klapperbok, Old Scratch, Thomasniklo and Schrat. Over the ages, the brutal
wildman figure evolved into a character more like a clown or fool. [103] In
Switzerland there are hair covered revellers called *Chlaus,* the beast-masked
Narren leap through Black Forest villages; the blackened, goat-bearded *berika*
romp in Georgia and the *Perchta* runners re-enact a death and resurrection
ritual on the fields of Austria. The animal-man character may be seen in the
straw bear festival of Whittlesey, near Peterborough in East Anglia. Originally
a Plough Monday custom, a man was costumed as a 'bear' all in the best straw
from the local farms and went around from house to house demanding money
and drink. The costume was then burned. The custom was stamped out by the
authorities at the beginning of the twentieth century, but revived in the 1980s,

100   Joseph Campbell, *Primitive Mythology*, Arkana, New York, 1991 (1959)

101   *Ibid*

102   *Ibid*

103   Jeffrey Vallance, Lapp of the Gods
      www.forteantimes.com/features/articles/134/lapp_of_the_gods.html

and he is now accompanied by morris dancers, molly dancers and mummers.

Today, the Saami still await a Yuletide visit from a giant horned and hairy wildman called Stallo ('metal man'). He rides in a sleigh seeking mischief, and if drink is not left out for him, he might suck the brains and blood from a child's skull to quench his thirst. On Christmas Eve he searches for children to stuff into his sack and take away.

In Sweden, the Jultomten is akin to the forest wildman. He is stout, bearded and dressed in furs. He cares for animals and has powers over the elements. According to legend, Jultomten lived deep in the forest long before he showed himself to humans.

For Christians, the wildman was a dangerous and despised figure, a rebellious force that threatened the values of orderly society; he represented untamed Nature as opposed to Christian civilisation. He dwelt in the dark forests and wild woods which were still haunted by all the ancient forces of the Old Gods. He is raw nature, the shamanistic feral god of beasts and vegetation whose annual death and resurrection must be acknowledged.

Chapter 6
THE TWELVE DAYS OF YULE

TWELVE DAYS OUT OF TIME

Between Samhain and Yule, the nights darken and grow longer - the sun is dying. With the reduction of its protective power, the shades of the dead and the spirits of chaos are gradually released from the underworld and this intensifies as the shadows lengthen. As the winter solstice approaches they threaten to engulf the sun and bring about a return to primordial chaos.

The sun reborn at Yule is a weakling babe and for twelve days all is still uncertain. Only at their conclusion does the sun gain enough power to turn the tide and send the Winter Spirits back to the underworld. These first twelve days are the most dangerous and uncanny days of the year. They exist outside of normal time and do not belong to the year proper - time is in suspension. Finnish shamans call this period 'the Dreaming' or 'God's Trance Hour'.[104] The strangeness of these days is reflected in many of their other names: the Balkan 'unbaptised days'; the Slovenian 'wolf nights'; the Germanic 'raw nights' and the Bulgarian 'heathen days' or 'dirty days' when demons attack the World Tree.[105] In Scotland, no court had power during the Twelve Days. The Irish believed that anyone who died during these days escaped purgatory and went straight to Heaven.[106] In Finland and Sweden the Twelve days of Christmas were declared to be time of civil peace by law and anyone committing a crime during them could expect a stiffer sentence than normal.

The ancient Egyptians, Mesopotamians and Teutons (among others) all had a twelve day festival around the winter solstice. The idea was adopted by Christianity in the fourth century, because, the apologists said, it took

---

104   Nigel Jackson, *Compleat Vampire*, Capall Bann, Chieveley

105   The "Pagan Days" by Max Dashu, http://www.matrifocus.com/IMB07/scholar.htm

106   (For Pagans there are twelve days from the solstice to New Year's Day, and for Christians this is twelve days from Christmas to the Epiphany).

the Wise Men twelve days to find Jesus. They start on Boxing Day because 'Christmas Day was a holy day', or maybe because the old way of counting days was that they began at sunset, so Boxing Day starts on the eve of December 25th.

Others say that the Twelve Days do begin on Christmas day, which makes Epiphany the Thirteenth Day of Christmas. Epiphany, on January 6th, brings an end to the Christmas period. Epiphany means 'revelation' as in the manifestation of a god. In parts of Europe the festive period is still sometimes celebrated for thirteen days and is referred to as 'the Thirteen'. In Germany, Belgium, Sweden and Holland, Epiphany is called 'the Thirteenth'.

Many of the ancient beliefs and customs surrounding the Twelve Days remain to this day. They are a time of danger, the eerie and the supernatural, haunted by spirits which might punish or reward. The Wild Hunt rides out to collect souls, and in Iceland it goes by the name of the 'Yule Host'. In Guernsey the powers of darkness are supposed to be more than usually active on the twelve days between St. Thomas's Day (the solstice) and New Year's Eve. In Greece the Kallikantzaroi appear to wreak havoc. In Sweden the trolls are abroad, and elsewhere werewolves roam. According to Barnaby Gouge:

Wherein they are afraid of sprites,
And cankered witches spite,
And dreadful devils black and grim,
That then have chiefest might.

The dead return and traditions surrounding Yule include feasts left out for them.

The Twelve Days represent the twelve signs of the zodiac the sun must pass through and the twelve months of the coming year, and many omens were taken from them. In England it was said that the weather on the first day would reflect the weather in January, the weather on the second day the weather in February and so on. In Brittany it is supposed that the wind which prevails on the first twelve days of the year will blow during each of the twelve months, the first day corresponding to January, the second to February, etc.

Because a new era was beginning it was a prime time for divination of various kinds. In England, for example, girls would place onions in the chimney breast, named for their suitors, and the one that sprouted first would be their husband. Or they might go to the wood stack and draw out a stick. If it was straight and even, with no knots in it, their future husband would be gentle, but if it was crooked, he would be crabbed and churlish. In Poland, wax from the candles was dripped into glasses of water and then held to the light to interpret the patterns. Young girls would go out to the road and listen to the wind - if they could hear a voice or an animal, it would be from that direction that their future beckoned. If they heard nothing, they would yell and listen for the distance and direction of the echo. On the Isle of Man, *goggans* (small mugs) were filled with symbols of various trades such as water for a sailor, meal for a farmer and so on. These were laid in front of the hearth, and the unmarried girls were brought in and according to the *goggan* they laid their hands upon, such was the trade of their future husband.

THE FIRST DAY OF CHRISTMAS
26th December

The Twelve Days of Christmas begin - According to some they are the last six days of the old year and first six days of the new year.

Boxing Day – In Britain, the day after Christmas is called Boxing Day. It was a day of gift-giving, though the gifts only went one way – from the rich to the poor, from the master to the servant, or from the employer to the tradesman.

There are several possible explanations as to why the day is so called. In churches, it was traditional to open the church's donation box and to distribute the money to the poor. Then again, servants and children had earthenware or wooden boxes to collect money at this season:

When Boxing Day comes round again
O then I shall have money
I'll hoard it up and Box and all
I'll give it to my honey.[107]

Families kept lists of tradesmen and others who were considered to have a claim upon them for a Christmas-box, and such people were sure to call on Boxing Day to collect their dues. Pepys, in his diary (1668), records his having been " called up by drums and trumpets" and "these things and boxes," he adds, " have cost me much money, this Christmas, and will do more."

St Stephen's Day - St Stephen is called the first Christian martyr. He declared that Christian law must come before Mosaic Law and was stoned to death in 35 CE, becoming the patron saint of stonemasons with the usual Christian irony. He is said to have been a keeper of alms for the apostles, and this was why alms were doled out on St Stephen's Day, though in reality, the Romans gave gifts and money at the Saturnalia. Collecting alms was called 'Stephening'.

Blessed be St Stephen

---

107   Charles Kightly, *The Perpetual Almanack of Folklore*, Thames & Hudson 1987

There's no fast at his Even

Not much is known about the St Stephen of the New Testament, and inventive stories were used to overcome the deficit. An old English carol makes him a servant in King Herod's hall who saw the star which heralded the nativity, and pledged himself to the new-born king:

"Stephen out of kitchen came,
With boarës head on hand,
He saw a star was fair and bright
Over Bethlehem stand." [108]

An old Swedish folk song, *Staffansvisa* '(Saint Stephen was Riding'), relates that St Stephen caused a roasted cock to rise up out of its gravy and crow as proof to Herod that a greater king than him had been born. [109]

This song confuses two different personalities, the martyred St Stephen and the eleventh century missionary Staffan who travelled to Sweden and established a church there, from which he rode out to spread the Christian message, supposedly taking with him a string of five horses, two white, two red and one dappled. Whenever one horse got tired, he would switch to the next. One day he was attacked by a band of robbers who killed him and tied him to the back of a broken colt which took him to Norrala, where his grave became a place of pilgrimage where sick horses were brought for healing.[110] From this confusion of the two saints, Staffan shares many of the customs of December 26th including the 'Stephen-Cup,' drunk to good health.

St Stephen took over the horse associations of the season which formerly belonged to Pagan deities such as Poseidon and Epona. His feast day was a day for horse races and hunts, when in England the usual hunting laws were suspended and anyone could catch whatever they liked.

In England and elsewhere it was traditional to bleed horses on St Stephen's Day in the belief that it would benefit them. [111] In the Tyrol, in addition to bleeding horses, it was the custom to give them consecrated salt and bread or oats and barley. In some of the Carinthian valleys where horse-breeding was a speciality, the young men rode into the villages on unsaddled horses and raced four or five times around the church while the priest blessed

---

108 Clement A. Miles, *Christmas in Ritual and Tradition*, Christian and Pagan, T. Fisher Unwin, 1912

109 *True Christmas Spirit,* by Fr. Edward J. Sutfin, http://www.internetpadre.com/Christmas/advent.html

110 John Matthews, *The Winter Solstice*, Godsfield Press, Hampshire, 1998

111 Clement A. Miles, *Christmas in Ritual and Tradition*, Christian and Pagan, T. Fisher Unwin, 1912

the animals, and sprinkled them with holy water. In some German districts the festival was called 'the great horse-day' when consecrated food was given to the animals, they were driven round and round the fields until they sweated violently, and at last were ridden to the blacksmith's and bled, to keep them healthy through the year. The blood was preserved as a remedy for various illnesses.[112]

St. Stephen's Day is known as *Gŵyl San Steffan* in Wales. An old Welsh custom, discontinued in the nineteenth century, included the bleeding of livestock and the *holming* (beating or slashing with holly branches) of late risers and female servants.

Day of Poseidon (moveable) (Greek) - In ancient Greece the lunar month in honour of Poseidon began with the new moon nearest to the end of the year. However, when the lunar calendar was changed into a fixed solar calendar by the Romans, the new moon of December was set aside on honour of Poseidon (Latin Neptune), the sea god who created the horse. The month of *Poseideôn* (roughly late December and early January) was dedicated to Poseidon and the eighth day was especially sacred to him. Poseidon's name seems to mean 'Husband of Earth' and he is sometimes described as married to Demeter, just as Saturn was the husband of Rhea.

Wren Day (Ireland) - In Ireland the day is one of nine official public holidays. It is sometimes called *Lá an Dreoilín* or 'Wren's Day'. (See Chapter 10, Animals of Yule.) An effigy of a wren or an actual caged wren (live or dead), was carried from house to house with the 'Wren Boys' playing music, singing and dancing. The same custom existed in England. The official explanation given was that wrens are hunted on St Stephen's Day because their chattering in the bushes gave away the saint's hiding place, leading to his martyrdom. The usually sacred and protected bird was ceremonially hunted and its decorated corpse carried about to bring luck:

The Wren, the Wren, the King of all Birds
St. Stephen's Day was caught in the furze
Although he be little, his honour is great
Therefore, good people, give us a treat.

---

112   *Ibid*

27th December
THE SECOND DAY OF CHRISTMAS

Haloa (Ancient Greece) - Women carried first fruits and the new wine of Dionysus from Athens in procession to the open threshing floors. Lucius says it endedwith a great feast:

> *"Much wine was set out and the tables were full of all the fields that are yielded by land and sea, save only those prohibited in the mysteries, I mean pomegranate and apple and domestic fowls and eggs and red sea mullet and black tailed brayfish and shark."*

St John's Day – This day commemorates St John the apostle and Gospel writer, rather than John the Baptist. According to one legend Aristodemus, the high priest of Artemis at Ephesus, challenged John, saying that he would become a Christian if John survived a drink from a poisoned chalice. Naturally, he did. This seems to have given licence to many drinking customs on St John's Day (though in reality, they date back to the older Pagan new wine traditions). Germans drink a loving-cup in his honour. In many parts of Catholic Germany and Austria a quantity of wine was brought to church to be blessed by the priest after Mass, and was taken away by the people to be drunk at home. In Tyrol and Bavaria it was supposed to protect its drinker from being struck by lightning, in the Rhenish Palatinate it was drunk in order that the other wine a man possesses might be kept from injury, or that next year's harvest might be good. In Bavaria some was kept for use as medicine in sickness. In Syria St. John's wine was said to keep the body sound and healthy and even babes in the cradle were made to join in the family drinking.

28th December
THE THIRD DAY OF CHRISTMAS

Traditionally an unlucky day – Supposedly the unluckiest day of the year, and the day of the week on which it falls will be unlucky throughout the coming year.

Holy Innocents or Childermas Day – This commemorates the innocent children massacred by Herod in his search for Jesus. It was a day upon which no one, if he could possibly avoid it, would begin any piece of work. Louis XI of France would never do any business on that day, and our own Edward IV postponed his coronation as it would have fallen on Holy Innocents Day. In Cornwall no housewife would scour or scrub on Childermas, and in

Northamptonshire it was considered very unlucky to begin any undertaking or even to do washing throughout the year on the day of the week on which the feast fell. In Cornwall it was there called *Dyzemas* and a saying ran "What is begun on Dyzemas Day will never be finished". In Ireland it was called 'the cross day of the year' and it was said that anything then begun then must have an unlucky ending.

It was a day of ritual scourging, which seems to be the remnant of a purification rite. The seventeenth-century writer Gregorie mentioned a custom of whipping children on Innocents' Day in the morning. In central and southern Germany the custom was called *pfeffern* or 'peppering'. In the Orlagau the girls on St. Stephen's, and the boys on St. John's Day, beat their parents and godparents with green fir-branches, while the menservants beat their masters with rosemary sticks, saying:

Fresh green! Long life!
Give me a bright thaler (or nuts, etc.).[113]

In the Saxon Erzgebirge the young men whipped the women and girls on St. Stephen's Day, if possible while they were still in bed, with birch-rods, singing:

Fresh green, fair and fine,
Gingerbread and brandy-wine.

Then on St. John's Day the women paid the men back. At several places in the Thuringian Forest children on Innocents' Day beat passers-by with birch-boughs and in return got apples, nuts and other dainties. In France children who let themselves be caught in bed on the morning of Holy Innocents' got a whipping from their parents.

The Boy Bishop – The curious custom of the Boy Bishop can be traced back to the early tenth century. A choir-boy, chosen by his fellows, was vested in cope and mitre, held a pastoral staff and gave the benediction. Other boys were attired as dean, archdeacons and canons. The election of the Boy Bishop generally took place on December 5th, the Eve of St. Nicholas, patron of children, and he was often called the 'Nicholas bishop'. Sometimes, as at Eton and Mayence, he exercised episcopal functions at divine service on the eve and the feast itself.

Minute details have been preserved of the Boy Bishop customs at St. Paul's Cathedral in the thirteenth century. He made the cathedral dignitaries act as taper and incense-bearers, thus reversing matters so that the lofty performed the functions of the lowly. In 1263 this was forbidden, and only clerks of lower rank might be chosen for these offices. On Innocents' Day

---

113   Clement A. Miles, *Christmas in Ritual and Tradition*, Christian and Pagan, T. Fisher Unwin, 1912

the boy bishop was given a dinner, after which came a cavalcade through the city so that the 'bishop' might bless the people. He had also to preach a sermon. In some places it appears, though this is by no means certain, that the boy actually sang Mass. He had usually the right to levy contributions on the faithful, and the amounts collected were often very large. At York, for instance, in 1396 the 'bishop' pocketed about £77, all expenses paid.

In the late Middle Ages the Boy Bishop was found not merely in cathedral, monastic, and collegiate churches but in many parish churches throughout England and Scotland. With the beginnings of the Reformation came the suppression of the custom. In Catholic Mary's reign the Boy Bishop reappeared, but after Elizabeth's accession he fell again into oblivion. In France he seems to have gradually vanished too, though traces of him were to be found in the eighteenth century at Lyons and Rheims. At Sens, in the nineteenth century, choir-boys played at being bishops on Innocents' Day. In Denmark a vague trace of him was retained until the nineteenth century in a children's game when a boy, dressed up in a white shirt, was seated on a chair while the other children sang a verse beginning, "Here we consecrate a Yule-bishop," and offered him nuts and apples.[114]

29th December
THE FOURTH DAY OF CHRISTMAS

Hooden Horse – In 1735-6 the Rev. Samuel Pegge referred in his *Alphabet of Kenticisms* to "Houding: a country masquerade at Christmas time, which in Derbyshire they call guising and in other places mumming". [115] In Kent, particularly the Isle of Thanet, the Hooden Horse appeared over the Christmas period. His head was either wooden or made from a real horse skull with snapping jaws, carried on a stick by a draped man. He also had a ribbon decked mane and a horse-hair tail, and was accompanied by a rider and a Mollie (a man dressed as a woman) with a broom, hand bell ringers and carol singers. He roamed from house to house seeking hospitality. If admitted he would jump about and snap his jaws at the inhabitants. The custom died out and has been revived several times in different forms. In its current form, a small band of villagers spend around four days before Christmas touring local pubs and private parties, performing a humorous play along the theme of death and resurrection.

114   Clement A. Miles, *Christmas in Ritual and Tradition*, Christian and Pagan, T. Fisher Unwin, 1912

115   http://www.japanesetranslations.co.uk/hooden/hoodening-history1.htm

30th December
THE FIFTH DAY OF CHRISTMAS

31st December
THE SIXTH DAY OF CHRISTMAS

New Year's Eve

New Year's Eve is a day of omens and taboos when it is important to banish the old year and ensure good luck and prosperity for the new one. Debts had to be paid before the end of the year to avoid starting the new one in debt, and thus setting a pattern for the future; lending as much as a light was considered very unlucky. If you got up early on New Year's Day, you would be an early riser for the rest of the year and so on.

It was necessary to protect the home and its inhabitants from the supernatural. In many places, New Year's Eve was considered the most dangerous and magically charged night of the year. In Iceland, for example, cows gain human speech, seals take on human form, the dead rise from their graves and the elves move house.

In the Scottish Highlands houses were decorated with holly on order to keep out the fairies. It was the tradition to keep the fire, which was usually damped down at night, burning away merrily all through New Year's night, fuelled along with a special incantation. Candles were also kept blazing in the belief that evil would be kept from the door. If the fire went out that night, it was a very bad omen for the coming year.

Evil had to be warded off and the old year banished. In Silesia it was the custom on both Christmas Eve and New Year's Eve for people to fire shots into bushes and trees and over meadows to drive out evil spirits and witches, and to wrap the trunks of fruit trees in straw to protect them from harm. In Romania there was a custom known as the 'little plough'. After dark, boys and men went from house to house, with long greetings, the ringing of bells and the cracking of whips. In Germany, elder twigs were cut, fashioned into a wheel and put in the house to protect it against fire. Animals were given a mixed bowl of corn and clover to ward off witches and fruit trees were beaten with little sacks of peas in order to make them bear fruit. A broth made from wild pears was placed on the threshold to ward off death in the coming year. In some parts of Macedonia on New Year's Eve men or boys went about making a noise with bells to drive away evil and the old year.

Fireworks were traditional in Germany to drive away evil spirits and bad weather. In Switzerland, the people parade through the streets dressed in costumes and hats, representative of good and evil spirits. In Italy the day is celebrated by throwing broken pots out of the window, firing guns and setting off firecrackers. In Denmark the same thing is done with the aim of chasing away trolls and evil spirits. This seems to be an end of year custom designed to make enough noise to chase away the spirits of darkness. [116]

Ritual purification was common. On the last night of the year, Strathdown Highlanders would bring home great loads of juniper, which was kindled in the different rooms, with all the windows and doors closed, to fumigate all the household members and all the farm animals. [117] In Germany, juniper twigs collected during the year were brought in and burned to protect the house. Austrians considered this a *rauchnacht* or smoke-night when all rooms and animals must be purified with the smoke of burning wormwood and holy water. Another kind of purification existed in the Scottish Highlands where it was believed that if a boy were whipped with a branch of holly it was an assurance that he would live for as many years as the drops of blood drawn by the sharp leaves.

In several places, it was customary to 'burn out the old year' with bonfires, as at Biggar in Lanarkshire, while at Burghead in Morayshire a tar-barrel called the *Clavie* was set on fire and carried about the village and the fishing boats (the latter is carried out on New Year's Eve Old Style, 11th January). People collected the embers as charms against witchcraft. In Allendale, in the northern Pennines, a burning out the old year ceremony is held. Guisers begin their rounds of the local pubs in the evening, and shortly before midnight form up into three columns, each man carrying a blazing tar barrel on his head. Led by a band, they process to the market place and circle a large bonfire and the barrels are thrown on. After a communal singing of *Auld Lang Syne*, the guisers spend the rest of the night first footing. [118]

In Herefordshire and surrounding counties, one tradition was the weaving a of a globe of hawthorn twigs which was then set alight and carried around the fields where crops had yet to be planted or where the seeds lay awaiting the warmer weather, possibly symbolising the returning sun and lengthening days. The custom was widespread on farms and in villages in Herefordshire and Radnorshire during the nineteenth century. In parts of Worcestershire, on New Year's morning, a crown was made of blackthorn

---

116   Prof. Philippe Walter, *Christianity, the Origins of a Pagan Religion*, Inner Traditions, Vermont, 2006

117   W. Grant, *Popular Superstitions of the Highlands of Scotland*, Archibald Constable, London, 1823

118   Charles Kightly, *The Customs and Ceremonies of Britain*, Thames and Hudson, London, 1986

which was then baked in the oven before being burned to ashes in a cornfield, the ashes then being scattered over the ground. Sometimes simple libations of cider or beer were made to crops or pieces of cake buried as offerings.

It was important to 'let the New Year in' in the proper manner. First footing customs are found throughout Britain. In Aberdeenshire it is considered most important that the first-foot (i.e. the first person over the threshold after the chime of midnight) should not come empty-handed but must offer a *handsel*, a gift of spiced ale, whiskey, shortbread, oak cakes, sweets or *sowens* or fuel for the fire. Occasionally the sowens were sprinkled on the doors and windows of the houses visited. An offering of food or drink must be accepted by sharing it with everyone present, including the visitor. Fuel must be placed onto the fire by the visitor with the words "A Good New Year to one and all and many may you see". The first foot had to be a man or a boy, and preferably dark haired, as it was very unlucky for a red-headed man – or in some places, a fair-haired man - to 'let in' the New Year. In parts of Cardiganshire it was lucky for a woman to see a man first, but unlucky for a man to see a woman first. In Pen-Coed it was unlucky to see a red-headed man first. In some places the initial letter of the person's name was also significant, H for happiness, J for joy etc, while T was for trouble, W for worry and S for sorrow. [119]

First footing was a common practice in the northern counties of England where it was generally called 'seeing the New Year in'. In Shropshire the first footer must not be a woman, and people often engaged a friendly man or boy to pay them an early visit. In Montgomeryshire little boys were paraded through the house to 'break the witch' if a woman or girl had been thoughtless enough to call on New Year's morning. In some places a bachelor was considered best, and had to bring a shovelful of coals, something to eat or whisky. In the East Riding of Yorkshire a boy called the 'lucky bird' used to come at dawn on Christmas morning as well as on New Year's Day and bring a sprig of evergreens. In the Isle of Man and Northumberland it was decreed that the first-foot should not be flat-footed but should be a person with a high-arched instep, a foot that 'water runs under'.

A strange custom, which hints at older rites, was found in the Highlands on New Year's Eve. The hide of a mart or winter cow was wrapped round the head of one of the men and he went off, followed by the rest of the party who struck the hide with switches so that it made a booming sound, like

---

119   Trefor M. Owen, *Welsh Folk Customs*, Gomer Press, Llandysul, 1994

a drum. The part of the hide used was the loose flap of the beast's neck. [120] The procession went three times sunwise round every house in each town, beating on the walls of the house and chanting their rhymes at the door. A rhyme such as the following was chanted:

Great good luck to the house,
Good luck to the family,
Good luck to every rafter of it,
And to every worldly thing in it.
Good luck to horses and cattle,
Good luck to sheep,
Good luck to everything,
And good luck to all your means.
Luck to the good-wife,
Good luck to the children,
Good luck to every friend,
Great fortune and health to all.[121]

On entering each house each member of the party was offered refreshments of oatmeal, bread, cheese and meat, followed by whisky. The man of the house was then given the *caisean-uchd*, or breast-skin of a sheep, goat or deer which was wrapped round the point of a shinty stick; this was singed in the fire, and carried three times sunwise round the family, grasped in the right hand, and held to the nose of each person. [122] This 'breast-stripe' was meant to convey luck to each family. It was an oval strip, and no knife might be used in removing it from the flesh. The inhaling of its fumes is a talisman against fairies, witches and demons. In the island of South Uist, each person seized hold of it as it burned, making the sign of the cross (if he was a Catholic) in the name of the Trinity, and it was put three times sun-wise about the heads of those present. If it went out it was a bad omen for the New Year.

Some form of *Duan Challuinn* ('Hogmanay Poem') would always be chanted. There were two types of visitation; in one instance the rhyme was recited outside the house and the chant described the ritual of approaching and entering the house. Another rhyme was sung after the house had been entered, when the *caisean Calluig* ('Hogmanay Hide') was beaten. [123] Alexander

120   Ann Ross , *The Folklore of the Scottish Highlands*, Barnes and Noble, 1976

121   *Ibid*

122   J.G.Campbell, *Witchcraft and Second Sight in the Highlands and Islands of Scotland*, 1902

123   Ann Ross , *The Folklore of the Scottish Highlands*, Barnes and Noble, 1976

Carmichael (*The Silver Bough*) gave the following example of a seasonal rhyme:

Tonight is the hard night of Hogmanay
I am come with a lamb to sell--
The old fellow yonder sternly said
He would strike my ear against a rock.
The woman, better of speech, said
That I should be let in;
For my food and for my drink,
A morsel due and something with it.

Apparently lads with no better rhyme use to chant the following:

I have no dislike of cheese
I have no disgust of butter,
But a little sip of barley bree
I am right willing to put down!

The giving of gifts was observed at New Year. In Wales the custom of *calennig* ('New Year's gift') began early in the day and continued to noon. The children in West Glamorgan went from house to house with good wishes for the New Year. They carried apples stuck full of corn, variously coloured and decorated with a sprig of evergreen, three short skewers serving as supports to the apple when it was no being held, and a fourth stuck through it to hold it. [124] A later account states the apples were studded with oats and raisins and powdered with wheat flour, touched with gold leaf with sprigs of box and rosemary. Half cracked hazelnuts were attached to the ends of the leaves so the shells would clasp the foliage.[125] Verses were sung at the doors in return for food and small gifts of money:

I came today out of my house with bag and sticks,
My errand here is to fill my bag with bread and cheese.
Or to ask for money in North Cardiganshire:
I rose early and walked as fast as I could to ask for calennig,
If you feel it in your heart give a shilling or a sixpence;
A happy New Year for a halfpenny or a penny.

In England, children would dress in their best clothes and carrying apples or oranges stuck with cloves, would sally forth to crave a gift from their godfathers and godmothers.

In the Highlands of Scotland, it was customary for the poorer children to wrap themselves in a great sheet, doubled up in front so as to form a vast

---

124   *Gentleman's Magazine*, March 1819

125   Trefor M. Owen, *Welsh Folk Customs*, Gomer Press, Llandysul, 1994

pocket, and then go along the streets in little bands, calling out "Hogmanay" at the doors of the wealthier people hoping for a gift of oatcake, which was called the *Hogmanay*:

> *Get up, goodwife, and shake your feathers,*
> *And dinna think that we are beggars;*
> *For we are bairns come out to play,*
> *Get up and gie's our hogmanay!*

The first water drawn in the New Year was believed to have magical properties. In Pembrokeshire, early on New Year's morning, around four am, crowds of boys went round the neighbourhood with a vessel of cold spring water and using a twig of box, rosemary or myrtle they would sprinkle the hands and faces of anyone they met in return for a copper or two. [126] The rooms of every house they entered would be sprinkled. While sprinkling, the following verses were recited:

> *Here we bring new water from the well so clear,*
> *For to worship God with, this happy new year;*
> *Sing levy dew, sing levy dew, the water and the wine,*
> *With seven bright gold wires, and bugles that do shine;*

> *Sing reign of fair maid, with gold upon her toe;*
> *Open you the west door and turn the old year go;*
> *Sing levy dew, sing levy dew, the water and the wine,*
> *With seven bright gold wires, and bugles that do shine;*

> *Sing reign of fair maid, with gold upon her chin.*
> *Open you the east door and let the new year in!*
> *Sing levy dew, sing levy dew, the water and the wine,*
> *With seven bright gold wires, and bugles that do shine.*

A Highland practice was to send someone on the last night of the year to draw a pitcher of water in silence, and without the vessel touching the ground. The water was drunk on New Year's morning as a charm against witchcraft and the evil eye. At Bromyard in Herefordshire it was the custom, at midnight on New Year's Eve, to rush to the nearest spring to snatch the 'cream of the well' (the first pitcher of water) and with it the prospect of the best luck.

---

126   Trefor M. Owen, *Welsh Folk Customs*, Gomer Press, Llandysul, 1994

A belief about the luckiness of 'new water' existed at Canzano Peligno in the Abruzzi. On New Year's Eve, the fountain was decked with leaves and bits of coloured stuff, and fires were kindled round it. As soon as it was lit, the girls would come as usual with their copper pots on their head; but the youths were, on this morning, guardians of the well, and sold the 'new water' for nuts, fruits and sweets. A similar custom was practiced in Carpathia, but on Christmas morning. When the first morning star was up, the whole family hurried to wash in a cold brook. They believed that the bath had a magical purgative function and that it would help them to maintain good health throughout the year.

Divinations were also practiced. One involved placing a ring in the filled bowl, with young unmarried people dunking for the ring; the one who succeeded in retrieving it without the use of his or her hands was guaranteed to be married within the year. The coming weather was also considered. According to one rhyme:

If New Year's Eve night wind blows South,
It betokeneth warmth and growth;
If West, much milk and fish in the sea,
If North, much cold and storms there will be;
If East, the trees will bear much fruit;
If North-east, flee it, man and brute.

In Lithuania on New Year's Eve nine sorts of things (money, cradle, bread, ring, death's head, old man, old woman, ladder and key) were baked into dough, and laid beneath nine plates, and everyone had three grabs at them. Whatever he got would be his lot during the year.

In Germany it was also a time of divination – if you put a leaf of periwinkle on a plate filled with water and it remains green until the following night, you can expect health during the coming year. If it stains, you can expect illness, and if it turns black, death will follow. One popular custom is *Bleigiessen*, where a candle is lit and small chunks of lead are melted in a spoon held over the candle. The molten lead is then quickly dropped into cold water, whereupon it hardens almost immediately. A heart or ring means a wedding, a ship foretells a journey and so on.

In Macedonia St. Basil's Eve (New Year's Eve) is a common time for divination: a favourite method is to lay on the hot cinders a pair of wild-olive-leaves to represent a youth and a maid. If the leaves crumple up and draw near each other, it is concluded that the young people love one another dearly, but if they recoil apart the opposite is the case. If they flare up and burn, it is a sign of excessive passion. St. Basil's Cake was baked with a silver coin and a cross of green twigs in it. When all were seated round the table, the father and

82

mother took the cake, and broke it into two pieces, then into smaller portions. The first portion was destined for St. Basil or the Holy Virgin or the patron saint whose icon stood in the house. The second was for the house itself. The third was the cattle and domestic animals. The fourth was for the inanimate property and the rest for each member of the household according to age. Each portion was successively dipped in a cup of wine, and the person who found the cross or coin in his piece would prosper during the year. The coin was considered sacred and used to buy a votive candle.

On the Isle of Man it was a custom to fill a thimble with salt and upset it on a plate, one thimble for every one in the house. This was put aside for the night and examined the next morning. If any of the heaps of salt had fallen over that person would die in the coming year.

St Sylvester's Day – Sylvester means 'forest' or 'wood'. He was a pope from the fourth century, but was invoked when threatened by a wild animal. This and the date of his festival give us the clue to his real identity as a wildman. [127]

An Austrian custom involved a masked figure called the Sylvester (a sort of wildman) who hid in the corner at inns and leapt out when a young man or woman passed to give them a kiss. The Sylvester wore a wreath of mistletoe, perhaps an emblem of the fertility which he bestows with the kisses. When midnight came, he was driven out of the room as a representative of the old year.

1st January
THE SEVENTH DAY OF CHRISTMAS

New Year's Day

The order of months in the Roman calendar has been January to December since King Numa Pompilius in about 700 BCE, according to Plutarch and Macrobius. The first month was called *Januarius* by the Romans, after the god Janus (from *janua* meaning a door or gate), a son of Apollo the sun god. Romans prayed to Janus whenever they undertook a new work. During January, offerings to the Janus were made of new meal, frankincense and new wine. Janus was often portrayed as double headed, looking back to the past and forward to the future, or as the god of the year with the number three-hundred in one hand and the number sixty-five in the other.

127   Prof. Philippe Walter, *Christianity, the Origins of a Pagan Religion*, Inner Traditions, Vermont, 2006

The goddess Juno was also portrayed as two-faced at this time of year, looking backwards to the old year and forwards to the new. Juno's backward looking aspect is called Postvorta and her forward looking aspect is Antevorta.

Libanius, the famous Greek sophist of the fourth century wrote:

The festival of the Kalends is celebrated everywhere as far as the limits of the Roman Empire extend.... Everywhere may be seen carousals and well-laden tables; luxurious abundance is found in the houses of the rich, but also in the houses of the poor better food than usual is put upon the table. The impulse to spend seizes everyone. He who the whole year through has taken pleasure in saving and piling up his pence, becomes suddenly extravagant. He who erstwhile was accustomed and preferred to live poorly, now at this   feast enjoys himself as much as his means will allow.... People are not only generous towards themselves, but also towards their fellow-men. A stream of presents pours itself out on all sides.... It may justly be said that it is the fairest time of the year.... The Kalends festival banishes all that is connected with toil, and allows men to give themselves up to undisturbed enjoyment...Another great quality of the festival is that it teaches men not to hold too fast to their money, but to part with it and let it pass into other hands."

The old customs of New Year have persisted into the modern age. A firm break with the past, and the previous year, must be made, and all tasks must be finished before the new year begins. Everything done or seen on New Year's Day had a magical or symbolic significance, and it was important to begin the year as you meant to go on. This included feasting well to ensure food for the coming year, not starting the year as a debtor, not giving anything away, which would mean giving your luck away and so on, and the taking of taking omens.

In the eleventh century, Buchard of Worms wrote, in the *Penitential*, of the superstitious customs associated with January 1st:

"Have you celebrated the calends of January according to pagan customs? Have you undertaken an exceptional or uncommon task on the occasion of the New Year, a task that you work on neither before or after – to wit: arranging stones on your table or giving a feast, leading dancers or singers through the streets and squares, taking a seat upon your roof while wearing your sword in order to see and know what will happen in the new year, sitting atop of a bull's hide where the roads cross to read the future, on the night of January 1 cooking bread for yourself to know whether the new year will be prosperous according to whether the dough roses? If yes, because you have abandoned God your

creator, and have turned to vain idols and become apostate, you will
fast on all the official days for two years." [128]

In Britain, gifts were previously given at New Year, rather than
Christmas, and survived in the tokens (called *hogmanays* in Scotland) given to
children at New Year. [129] In Radnorshire, children sang:

We wish you a Merry Christmas and a Happy New Year
A pocket full of money and a cellar full of beer
A good fat pig to last you all year
Please give to us a New Year's gift.

Gifts at this time symbolise prosperity in the coming year. For the same
reason, on the Borders care was taken that no one entered a house empty-
handed on New Year's Day. In England, a visitor must bring something to
eat or drink. Everyone should have a new outfit, and if its pockets contained
money of every description they would never be empty throughout the year.
On New Year's morning Rumanians threw handfuls of corn at one another
with some appropriate greeting, such as:

May you live,
May you flourish
Like apple-trees,
Like pear-trees
In springtime,
Like wealthy autumn,
Of all things plentiful.

In Russia, corn sheaves were piled upon a table and in the midst of them was
set a large pie. The father of the family took his seat behind them, and asked
his children if they could see him. When they replied in the negative, he would
declare that he hoped that the corn would grow as high in his fields and that he
would be just as invisible when he walked there at harvest time. In some of
the Greek islands, when the family returned from church on New Year's Day,
the father would pick up a stone and leave it in the yard, with the wish that the
New Year may bring with it as much gold as the weight of the stone.

In Scotland, New Year's Day was also known as the Day of Little
Christmas. The word Hogmanay has never been satisfactorily explained. Some
think it derives from the Anglo-Sazon *Haleg Monath* ('Holy Month') others
from the Gaelic *oge maiden* ('good morning') or, more improbably, from the

128   Quoted in Prof. Philippe Walter, *Christianity, The Origins of a Pagan Region*, Inner
        Traditions, Vermont, 2006

129   Charles Kightly, *The Customs and Ceremonies of Britain*, Thames and Hudson,
        London, 1986

French *au gui mener* ('lead to the mistletoe').

After the family had got up in the morning, the head of the house gave a dram of whisky to each member of the household. In some breakfast consisted of half-boiled *sowens* (porridge from oak husks and siftings) which was supposed to bring luck to the household.

No substance of any kind was allowed to be removed from the house on New Year's Day - dirty water, sweepings from the floor, ashes and so on. One of the unluckiest things to do was give a neighbour fire from one's hearth. It would ensure a death within that family during the coming year; it also gave power to the black witches to take away the produce from the cattle.

On New Year's Day in the Orkneys it was believed that some of the local standing stones would walk away and dip their heads in the nearby loch, so they were avoided on this day. However, people would dance around the Stan Stane, a solitary standing stone on North Ronaldsay and feast around the standing stones of Steness for the five days of the New Year.

In Athens models of war-ships were carried round by men who collected money in them. They were called 'St. Basil's ships' since this is Saint Basil's Day and were supposed to represent the vessel on which St. Basil sailed from Caesarea. This is most likely a gloss on an old Pagan custom, the old Greek practice of bearing a ship in procession in honour of Dionysus.

Yemaya-Olokun, the Mother of the Sea, is honoured on New Year's Eve in Brazil. The natives of Rio de Janeiro go down to the beaches to celebrate. And at midnight, people either eat twelve grapes, one for each month of the year, while making twelve wishes, or jump seven waves. Flowers are thrown into the waves, little wooden boats are launched, and little altars are arranged in the sand in honour of Yemaya, who likes candles, fruit, fish, rice and items associated with personal adornment: mirrors, combs, perfumes and powder.

2nd January
THE EIGHTH DAY OF CHRISTMAS

January 3rd
THE NINTH DAY OF CHRISTMAS

January 4th
THE TENTH DAY OF CHRISTMAS

Mari Lwyd – In South Wales, the hobby horse called the Mari Lwyd ('Grey Mare') goes around from Christmas Eve until Twelfth Day. She has a head made either from a real horse skull or wood, with snapping jaws, mounted on a pole and carried by a man in a white sheet. She is accompanied by the Merry Dancers and goes from place to place. In Glamorgan her companions are the Mare Leader, the Sergeant, a fiddle-playing Merryman and a black faced Punch and Judy, the latter played by a man. Before entering any house, they must sing a verse battle of questions and answers against those within, which can continue for some time until one side runs out of steam. If the householders fail first, the Mari Lywrd can enter and rush about 'biting' the occupiers. The Punch tries to kiss the women, and the Judy chases him with a broom. There may be carols and dancing. Then, after food and drinks supplied by the home owner, there is a final verse wishing the host a happy New Year and the horse continues on its rounds.[130]

<h3 style="text-align:center">5th January
THE ELEVENTH DAY OF CHRISTMAS</h3>

Twelfth Night – Twelfth Night (5th January) and Twelfth Day (6th January) were considered to be the ending of the Christmas season. There is some cross-over with Christmas customs since the change over of calendars in 1752 caused twelve days to be 'lost' and rural people persisted in keeping the 'real Christmas' on 6th January.

Twelfth Night was surrounded by myths and customs. It was a time for one last fling with games, dressing up and plays, all managed by the Lord of Misrule. Shakespeare's play *Twelfth Night* was probably written for a Twelfth Night celebration at Elizabeth I's court in 1601.

It was both a propitious and a dangerous time, standing between the holiday period and the return to work, between winter and the coming spring, between the Old and New Year. Any such liminal time is surrounded by taboos and propitiations.

In many places bonfires were lit, sometimes thirteen fires, one for each of the Twelve Days of Christmas, and a thirteenth called the Judas Fire which was put out during the proceedings to extinguish any negativity that might attach to the coming year. At Brough in Cumbria the fire was a burning bush of holly and ash faggots which were carried about, and the occasion was known as Holly Night, and pieces of the charred wood were collected by the crowd for good luck.

Celebrations were held on Twelfth Night and special cakes were

---

130   Charles Kightly, *The Customs and Ceremonies of Britain,* Thames and Hudson, London, 1986

served. In Victorian England the shops were open late selling cakes decorated with stars, castles, lions, dragons, kings, knights and serpents etc, painted onto white icing. In the Vale of Glamorgan a large loaf or pile of cakes was prepared at farmhouses, and the cake was divided between the Virgin, the Magi and the company. The king and queen were chosen by a concealed ring on the cake, or a pea and bean hidden in the cake, as was the Lord of Misrule, who makes the master wait on the servants in a reversal of social mores, a direct descendant of the practices of the Roman Saturnalia winter solstice festival. The king of the Saturnalia was also elected by beans. Our old friend Herrick wrote in 1648:

Now, now the mirth comes
With the cake full of plums,
Where bean's the king of the sport here;
Besides we must know,
The pea also
Must revel as queen in the court here.

Begin then to choose
This night as ye use,
Who shall for the present delight here
Be a king by the lot,
And who shall not
* Be Twelfth-day queen for the night here*

Which known, let us make
Joy-sops with the cake;
And let not a man then be seen here,
Who unurg'd will not drink,
To the base from the brink,
A health to the king and the queen here.

Twelfth Night and Twelfth Day were traditional times for wassailing the apple trees, waking up the spirit of vegetation for the coming year (see Chapter 7, The Customs of Yule). A Twelfth Night ceremony described by Hugh Hughes in early nineteenth century Wales concerned the making of wassail with warm, spiced beer poured over baked apples and cakes, layered with sugar in a special twelve-handled wassail bowl. The bowl was passed around, each of the company drinking the ale, and afterwards sharing out the cakes and apples. On Twelfth Night the wassail was taken to the home of a recently married couple or a family that had moved into a new home. Young men and women from the locality would take it to the door and sing a wassail song outside the closed door, answered in song by those indoors. Eventually the wassailers were admitted and were sung to by the householders, and sung to again when they left.

In Kidwelly in Wales the custom was called *perllan* after the small rectangular board with a circle marked at its centre and ribs running from the centre to the four sides. In each of the corners an apple was fixed, and within the circle, a miniature tree with a bird on it. It was taken round on New Year's Day by young men, accompanied by a large wassail cup of beer. The song included the words:

And with us we have a perllan
With a little wren flying in it
He is the king of all birds

This custom ran alongside the Mari Lwyd, also popular in the district. In Wales, the Yuletide wassailing was often accompanied by a horse figure such as the Mari Lwyd ('Grey Mary'), Y March ('The Horse') or Y Gynfasfarch ('The Canvas Horse') among others.

Occasionally the seasonal wassailers were accompanied by a man dressed as a bull. At Kingsgate in Gloucestershire he was called The Broad, and in Coventry Old Bronzen Face. At Tetbury a wooden bull's head wrapped in sacking was carried round, and at each door the sacking was pulled away to reveal the face. The bull is a symbol of virility and plenty, and the custom may date back to Pagan times, and may even be a representation of the Horned God.

Twelfth Night and Twelfth Day was the time to expel the spirits of chaos and send them back to the underworld. At Brunnen in Switzerland boys went about in procession with torches and lanterns and made a great noise with horns, bells and whips to drive away the wood spirits. In Labruguière in southern France the inhabitants rushed through the streets, making a great uproar to scare away ghosts and devils. In parts of the eastern Alps the *Berchtenlaufen* Lads ran about with masks, cowbells, whips and all sorts of weapons, shouting wildly. In Nuremberg up to the year 1616 on *Bergnacht* or Epiphany Eve boys and girls used to run about the streets and knock loudly at the doors. At Eschenloh near Partenkirchen in Upper Bavaria three women used to *berchten* with linen bags over their heads, with holes for the mouth and eyes. One carried a chain, another a rake, and the third a broom. Going round to the houses, they knocked on the door with the chain, scraped the ground with the rake, and made a noise of sweeping with the broom.[131]

This night is sacred to the hag goddess Percht or Bercht, guardian of the souls of unborn children. She is honoured with *Perchtenlauf* ceremonies, and Percht's night is a magical time when animals are said to be able to speak, and wishes can come true.

January 6th
THE TWELFTH DAY OF CHRISTMAS

Birth of Dionysus – Dionysus (Roman Bacchus) is a god of vegetation, especially the grape vine. His epithets reflect this – *Bakchos* ('shoot'), *Anthios* ('Holy Flower'), *Dendrites* ('Tree God') and *Kissos* ('Ivy'). Pliny the Elder reported that the people of the island of Andros believed that wine flowed from a spring in his temple every *nonen* of January, and the day was called 'God's gift'. Later Jesus was said to have similarly changed water into wine on the same day. Church father Clement of Alexandria commented "The birth of God happened with a lot of Dionysian wonders, such as the changing of water into wine".

Birth of Aion - St. Epiphanius (fourth century CE) stated that in Alexandria the birth of Aion was celebrated on the night before 6th January with a festival before the image of Kore. Aion was the head of the divine hierarchy in Mithraism, the Alexandrian god of Eternity or deified time (like Chronos) and he regulated the revolutions of the stars. [132] According to Epiphanius the feast took place at the Koreion in Alexandria, a temple in the sacred to Kore, the daughter of

Aion

---

131   Clement A. Miles, *Christmas in Ritual and Tradition*, Christian and Pagan, T. Fisher Unwin, 1912

132   http://hermeticmagick.com/content/deities/aion.html

Demeter. Throughout the whole night the people keep themselves awake by singing hymns and by flute-playing before the image of the god. At cock-crow they descended, carrying torches, into an underground chapel and thence they carried up a wooden image of Aion lying naked upon a bier. This image had a golden cross on its forehead and a cross on each hand. This was carried seven times around the inner sanctuary of Kore's temple. At the height of the ceremony the announcement was made "*Today at this hour the virgin Kore has given birth to Aion.*" Epiphanius added that such ceremonies also occurred in Petra, with the hymns sung in Arabic tongue and in praise of a virgin called Chaamu and her son Dusares, whose name means 'Only Son of the Ruler of All'.

EPIPHANY - This Christian festival took its name from the ancient Greek mysteries of Kore and Demeter. *Epiphania* meant 'divine appearance', in the sense of the appearance of a god. Christianity also incorporated other customs of the Pagan Epiphany. In Christian lore it marks the visit of the Wise Men to the infant Jesus. The earliest reference to Epiphany as a Christian feast was in 361 CE. St. Epiphanius wrote that that January 6th was Christ's Birthday, his Epiphany, and added that the miracle of Cana and the turning of water into wine happened on the same day (both previously attributed to Dionysus).

In Greece and Cyprus customs revolve around the Great Blessing of the Waters. It marks the end of the traditional ban on sailing, and banishes the havoc-causing *kalikántzaroi*. The purifying power of the Epiphany waters was combined with the fructifying powers of the Yule-log at Mount Olympus, where ashes were taken from the hearth where a cedar log had been burning since Christmas, baptised and blessed in the blessed waters of a river, then taken to the vineyards and orchards and thrown to the four corners and at the foot of apple and fig trees. In Romania, where a similar sprinkling is performed, the priest was invited to sit on the bed, which had grains under the mattress, in a piece of sympathetic magic to make hens lay.

In Poland, water was consecrated and dispensed to each corner of the home with an evergreen branch, to purify and protect it. Symbols and runes were marked in chalk over the doors and windows to guard against adversity.

On the Isle of Man Bishop Phillips, in the *Manx Prayer Book* written early in the seventeenth century, calls Twelfth Day *Shen lail chibbert ushtey*, 'old feast-day of the water-well' suggesting new water customs similar to those of Wales.

Chapter 7
THE CUSTOMS OF YULE

BRINGING HOME CHRISTMAS

One of the most widespread features of the season, up until recent decades, was collecting greenery from hedgerows, woodlands and gardens to decorate hearths, make wreaths and bedeck churches. Hervey reported:

> "...in the neighbourhood of every town and village, the traveller may meet with some sylvan procession, or some group of boys, returning from the woods, laden with their winter greenery, and engaged in what we have heard technically called 'bringing home Christmas'." [133]

Stow, in his *Survey of London* (1603), recorded that not only were houses and churches decorated with evergreens, but also the conduits, standards, and crosses in the streets. The plants most commonly used were holly, ivy, laurel, rosemary and mistletoe, but also cypress, yew, pine and fir (see Chapter 9, Herb Craft).

These decorations were either taken down on Twelfth Night or as late as Candlemas, according to Herrick:

> *Down with the rosemary, and so*
> *Down with the baies and misletoe,*
> *Down with the holly, ivie, all*
> *Wherewith you drest the Christmas hall;*
> *That so the superstitious find*
> *Not one least branch there left behind*

For the old Pagans, the evergreen was a symbol of immortality as it had the power to survive the winter death that struck down all other forms of vegetation. Particularly precious were plants like the holly, the ivy and the mistletoe which actually bore fruit in the winter-time. The Romans decorated their houses with evergreens during the Saturnalia and Kalends, and in spite of church condemnations they survived. In the sixth century the Bishop Martin of

133   Thomas K. Hervey, *The Book of Christmas*, The Folklore Society, 1888

Braga forbade the adorning of houses with laurels and green trees.

The Christmas evergreens had a sacred nature, as evidenced by their careful hanging and disposal. In Shropshire people never threw them away for fear of misfortune, but either burnt them or gave them to the cows; it was very unlucky to let a piece fall to the ground. The Shropshire custom was to leave the holly and ivy up until Candlemas, while the mistletoe-bough was carefully preserved until the time came for a new one next Yule.

CHRISTMAS CORN

The magic of the season was used to solicit blessings on the coming year's harvest. In Malta, grains and canary-seeds are sown on cotton balls in flat trays on the first day of Advent to represent the future crops. In Sweden green boughs were not used for decoration, but instead the floor was strewn with the fragrant needles of pine or juniper, or even with rye-straw. This straw probably came from the last sheaf at harvest (which embodied the corn spirit) and when scattered on a barren field afterwards was said to make it productive.

This bringing of the corn-spirit into the house at Christmas was important in several places. In Poland, before the tablecloth was laid on Christmas Eve, the table was covered with a layer of hay or straw, and a sheaf stood in the corner. This straw was then given to the cattle as a charm to keep them healthy in the coming year or used to bind up fruit trees to make them productive. Farmers sat on a log and threw Yule straws one by one up to the roof, and as many as lodged in the rafters, so many would be the sheaves of rye at harvest time.

In Carpathia, farmers covered the floor with straw. An unthreshed

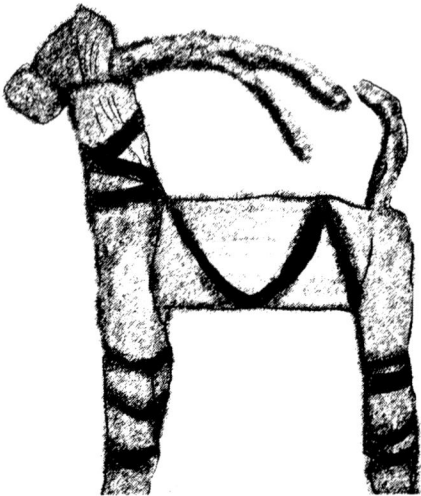

grain sheaf, the *Didko* or *Diduch*, was placed on the honourable seat at the table, under the icons (the corner formerly reserved for the Old Gods). Oats or straw were also used for decorating the festive table on which there had to be seeds from all crops. In the spring these very seeds were used in the first sowing. The festive bread was put in the place of honour too, and decorated with wintergreen or periwinkle and various small figures. Prosperity was symbolized by a 'mountain' of bread at the end of the table. At the beginning of the evening meal the farmer hid behind this mountain, asking "Can you see me from behind the bread mountain?" The children replied "We can't," after which the farmer concluded "Let us wish you'll not see me either in the spring from within the hay or in the summer from within the wheat!"

In Norway, the *julbukk* ("Yule buck") and *jolegeiti* ("Yule goat") are represented by straw figures or by youths disguised with straw or skins in their role. The Yule Goat is one of the oldest Scandinavian and northern European Yule traditions. As such it is now a customary decoration or gift in Scandinavian homes. The straw effigy is handmade out of braided straw and a few wheat ears. In Sweden it is known as the *Julbock*, in Norway it is the *Julebukk*, (both names translating as Yule Buck) and in Finland it is the *Olkipukki* - meaning Straw Buck. Scandinavian families would gather the harvest and save some of the wheat sheaves to create a goat effigy out of them (in remembrance of the goats which pulled Thor's chariot), gently tying the wheat together with red ribbons. It would be left to dry completely for Yule time celebrations, at which time it would be burned as a sacrifice to Thor.

KISSING BOUGH

One of the most enduring customs in England is the kissing bough, which has evolved into the bunch of mistletoe we still know today.

In Britain, recorded from the fifteenth century onwards, there was a tradition of creating a hoop or sphere woven from ash, willow or hazel. In the middle of this was placed an image of the Christ Child or Holy Family. These were blessed by the local priest, and anyone visiting over the festive season was embraced under these hoops to show that they brought only good will with them. Eventually, this 'bough' was treated as a status symbol with families vying with each other to produce a more opulent one with ribbons, gilded nuts and apples hanging from them. After the Reformation, the holy figures were removed to avoid accusations of popery. The Victorians continued the custom of hanging up an evergreen bough or bunch under the name of Holly ('holy') Bough. Then it became a kissing bough or bunch. Here is an account from Derbyshire:

"The 'kissing bunch' is always an elaborate affair. The size depends upon the couple of hoops--one thrust through the other--which form its skeleton. Each of the ribs is garlanded with holly, ivy, and sprigs of other greens, with bits of coloured ribbons and paper roses, rosy-cheeked apples, specially reserved for this occasion, and oranges. Three small dolls are also prepared, often with much taste, and these represent our Saviour, the mother of Jesus, and Joseph. These dolls generally hang within the kissing bunch by strings from the top, and are surrounded by apples, oranges tied to strings, and various brightly coloured ornaments. Occasionally, however, the dolls are arranged in the kissing bunch to represent a manger-scene....Mistletoe is not very plentiful in Derbyshire; but, generally, a bit is obtainable, and this is carefully tied to the bottom of the kissing bunch, which is then hung in the middle of the house-place, the centre of attention during Christmastide." [134]

Echoing the mediaeval tradition, in parts of Germany and Sicily a large bough was set up in the principal room, hung with little presents for each member of the household. [135]

The Welsh had the *Calennig,* an apple on three twig legs, stuck with almonds or cloves or thorns. It was offered to householders by carolling children in return for a small gift of cakes, money or sweets.

WREATHS
It is not known where the idea of a Christmas wreath originated. The circle shape may represent eternity or the sun, especially as they are fashioned from evergreens.

CHRISTMAS WAITS
In Britain and elsewhere, it was the custom to greet Christmas day at midnight with the singing of carols: "the night which ushers in the great day itself is filled, throughout all its watches, with the continued sounds of sacred harmony".[136] Groups of singers and musicians who played and sang carols at Christmas

134   Clement A. Miles, *Christmas in Ritual and Tradition*, Christian and Pagan, T. Fisher Unwin, 1912

135   Thomas K. Hervey, *The Book of Christmas*, The Folklore Society, 1888

136   *Ibid*

for money were called 'Christmas Waits'. The name wait or wayte appears to relate to the German *wachen*, 'to be awake'. In mediaeval time, watchmen in British towns and cities sounded the watch three or four times a night on trumpets, shawms or pipes, a practice mentioned as early as the reign of Edward III. The term seems to have been transferred to musicians at the end of the thirteenth century, and the waits became a group of wind musicians kept at public expense by a town or city to play on ceremonial or festive occasions. From the latter part of the eighteenth century, the practice of waits being employed by a municipality have slowly died out, and the name was transferred to self-appointed musicians and singers who perambulated the streets playing and singing carols and other appropriate music at Christmas in hope of reward.

They were considered a nuisance by many. According to Bernard Shaw's Diary for 1889:

"The only music I have heard this week is waits; to sit up working until two or three in the morning, and then - just as I am losing myself in my first sleep - to hear 'Venite Adoremus' welling forth from a cornet English pitch, a saxhorn Society of Arts pitch (or thereabouts), and a trombone French pitch, is the sort of thing that breaks my peace and destroys my goodwill towards men!"

GHOST STORIES

Throughout Northern Europe there were traditions that the family ghosts returned at Christmas time to share the festival with their living relatives, along with other less welcome spirits. [137] Anne Boleyn, for example, was seen haunting her old homes during the Twelve Days of Christmas, her headless ghost reported at Rochford Hall in Essex and Hever Castle in Kent. For this reason, it was a tradition to tell ghost stories at Christmas time. Charles Dickens penned several such tales for his readers, and until recently, the BBC televised a dramatised supernatural tale every Christmas Eve.

PANTOMIMES

The pantomime is a time-honoured British entertainment over the festive season. Many of its elements can be traced back to the Roman Saturnalia and Kalends and the later Twelfth Night customs, such as role reversals and general buffoonery: the principle boy is always played by a girl; the

---

137   In Brittany there was the custom of leaving food for the ghosts while the family attended
church.

pantomime dame is always a man in drag and there is an animal (e.g. the pantomime horse) played by humans, harking back to the guisers in animal skins.

MUMMERS AND GUISERS

The mummers who still go about in some parts of Britain and Europe carry on the traditions of the ancient seasonal revellers. Christmas masking was recorded during the reign of Edward III and by the sixteenth and seventeenth century, the court masques involved elaborate trappings and splendid costumes. In *Henry VIII* Shakespeare mentions the king and his party dressed as shepherds breaking in on a banquet held by Cardinal Wolsey.

Amongst the ordinary people bands of mummers, calling themselves guisers or 'geese dancers' (Cornwall), tipteerers (Sussex) or morris/ merry dancers (Shropshire), would go about with men dressed as women and women dressed as men, from house to house, claiming the right to enter and partake of food and drink, and sometimes performing a rude play.

In Northern England there was a ceremony called the 'Fool Plough' in which a number of sword-dancers dragged a plough, accompanied by music and a Bessy (a man dressed as an old woman) and a Fool (or 'Tommy') who was almost covered with skins, wearing a hairy cap and the tail of a fox or some other animal hanging from his back. In England the sword-dance is found chiefly in the north but, like the morris dance, it was characterised by the wearing of jingling bells. Sword dances have a long history, and were described by Tacitus amongst the Germanic tribes (*Germania*, first century CE) as being performed at public gatherings. Naked youths would dance among swords and levelled lances and at certain times the swords would be brought together on the heads of the performers. Sometimes they were accompanied by sets of verses containing the story of a quarrel and the violent death of one of the performers. In one of the dances, too, there was even a doctor who revived the victim.

A commonly performed mumming play at Yule is St. George and the Dragon or St. George and the Turkish Knight. The central figure is always St. George and the main drama, after a prologue and the introduction of the characters, is a fight and the arrival of a doctor to bring back the slain man back to life. The central motif of death and revival may refer to the resurrection of the spirit of the year or of vegetation, reminiscent of the Thuringian custom of executing a wild man covered with leaves, which a doctor brings to life again by bleeding (see Chapter 5, Wildmen).[138]

---

138   Clement A. Miles, *Christmas in Ritual and Tradition*, Christian and Pagan, T. Fisher Unwin, 1912

Similar customs were found in Eastern Europe. Mr. J. C. Lawson described a performance in Greece:

> *"At Pharsala there is a sort of play at the Epiphany, in which the mummers represent bride, bridegroom, and 'Arab'; the Arab tries to carry off the bride, and the bridegroom defends her."* [139]

In various parts of Greece, boys carrying bells would go round houses singing songs during the Twelve Days, with one or more of their company dressed up with masks and bells and foxes' brushes. [140] In Russia, too, mummers used to go about at Christmastide, visiting houses, dancing and performing. Prominent parts were always played by human representatives of a goat and a bear. Such maskings are described in Tolstoy's *War and Peace* in the year 1810.

In Poland, the festival was marked with processions of guisers in animal masks or men dressed as women. They were accompanied by a goat head on a stick and someone carrying a spinning solar symbol. [141] A child on horseback represented the sun reborn. The Turon would follow along at the rear. The Turon was costumed in sheep's wool, adorned with goat's horns, cow's ears and a horse's tail. His companions drummed, banged pots and rang bells as he approached each home, laughing and dancing. The head of the household answered the door, and the Turon ran in, swirling and leaping, and generally destroying everything he came in contact with. After a gift of a drink

---

139   Quoted in Miles

140   Clement A. Miles, *Christmas in Ritual and Tradition, Christian and Pagan*, (1912)

141   http://www.slavpaganism.com/beliefs

of mead and honey vodka or some silver, the Turon and his party moved to the next house.

THE STAR WATCH

In Eastern Europe, it is the convention to set someone to watch for the first star rising on Christmas Eve, which signals the end of the day's fast and the time to feast. In Poland this was called the *czuwaœ* ('star watch') and the honour went to the youngest member of the household. When the star was spotted, a great cheer went up. In Lithuania the feast must only commence once the first star can be seen in the sky, as it represents the star of Bethlehem and announces the arrival of the Saviour. In Russia, there is a fast until the first star appears on Christmas Eve, when *kutya* is eaten, a symbolic dish of various grains for fertility and honey and poppy seed for happiness and peace.

CHRISTMAS GIFTS

The custom of exchanging Christmas gifts comes directly from the Roman Saturnalia, despite the fact the church tried to explain it in light of the gifts given by the Wise Men to the infant Jesus. *Strenae* were offered to the Emperor or exchanged between private citizens at the January Kalends. They were originally merely branches plucked from the grove of the goddess Strenia, but by the time of the Empire they had become more elaborate and costly, and included honeyed things, that the year of the recipient might be full of sweetness, lamps that life might be full of light, copper and silver and gold that wealth might flow. With the adoption of the Roman New Year's Day its present-giving customs appear to have spread far and wide.

THE TREE

Many people instinctively feel that a tree has a spirit or consciousness. We still honour this spirit of the tree when we decorate the evergreen Christmas tree and place the fairy, which represents its living spirit, at the top. The decorating of a tree is a common folk custom, and widespread in tribal and shamanic cultures. Pliny noted how 'barbarian people', unlike the Romans, could not understand how the gods could be locked up in temples and portrayed with human faces, but instead dedicated clearings and groves to the gods.

Trees were objects of veneration in ancient times. While the life span of humankind is short, trees can live for many centuries. When all else fades in winter evergreens remain changeless in a changing world, strong enough to resist the death time. Thus the tree became identified with the power of the deity or was seen as a deity itself. As symbols of the god, or a god in actuality, trees were associated with fertility. There was a desire to stimulate the fertility of trees in the dead time of winter by placing pieces of cake and bread in their branches. At the festival of Dionysus anyone with a tree in the garden would dress it up to represent the god. Romans hung evergreens around their houses during the Saturnalia. Ancient Egyptians brought in palm branches on the shortest day of the year to symbolize Ra's victory over death. In the fourth century CE, the Empower Theodosius forbade Pagan rituals, particularly decorating trees:

> *"If someone burns incense in front of man-made idols, they are damned; or if such a person worships idolatrous images by decorating a tree with ribbons, or if he sets up an altar outside – he is guilty of blasphemy and sacrilege."* [142]

In the shamanic world-view, the cosmic axis bisects the realms at the centre of the world, connecting to the worlds of above and below. The cosmic axis and sacred centre is the still point around which creation turns. It is often visualised as the World Tree, with its roots in the netherworld, trunk in middle earth, and branches in the heavens. The most famous example is the Norse Yggdrasil, an evergreen ash. It is likely that the reverence for sacred trees amongst the Germanic tribes was related to the concept of the World Tree. Thor's Oak was an ancient tree sacred to the Germanic tribe of the Chatti. It stood near the village of Geismar, and was the main focus of the veneration of the god. In 723 CE, the Anglo-Saxon missionary Winfrid (St. Boniface) had the oak felled to demonstrate the superiority of the Christian god over the native Pagan religion.

In Judaic and Christian myth, the tree of knowledge grew in Paradise ('Orchard'), but the first man and woman, Adam and Eve, were forbidden to pluck its fruits. Tempted by the serpent at its roots, Eve plucked the fruit of knowledge and gave it to Adam. [143] God grew angry at this trespass, and flung them from Paradise. The biblical Tree of Knowledge was unlikely to have been an apple, but a fig or date palm. Miracle plays depicting biblical stories performed during medieval times and one of the most popular plays featured

---

142   Quoted in Christian Ratsch et al, *Pagan Christmas,* Inner Traditions, Vermont, 2006

143   Eve's original Hebrew name was Hawwah from the Akkadian word *Hayah* meaning 'to live'. She is thus called Hawwah because she was 'Mother of All Living' according to Genesis. This was a title of the Sumerian goddess Ninhursag, from whom the myth was appropriated by the Hebrews. In the Sumerian version the god Enki (possibly cognate with Yahweh or Jehovah) was cursed by Ninhursag because he stole forbidden plants from paradise. His health began to fail and the other gods prevailed on the Mother Goddess to help him. She created a goddess called Ninti (literally *nin*= lady, *ti*= rib i.e. 'lady of the rib', a play on words since the phrase also means "to make live"). Enki claimed his rib hurt him and she healed him. Eve is in fact the Great Goddess, who initiates Adam into her mysteries via the World Tree.

Adam and Eve in the Garden of Eden. The only prop would be an evergreen tree (the Paradise Tree) to which was affixed a red apple. Most commonly the Paradise Play was performed on December 24th because this was the feast day of Adam and Eve on the old Christian calendar. It was forbidden by the Church in the fifteenth century.

Christian convention credits Saint Boniface with the invention of the Christmas tree when he chopped down the sacred oak of Thor at Geismar. Another story is that Martin Luther (1483 - 1546) was so impressed by a forest scene that he allegedly cut down a small fir tree, took it home, and decorated it with lighted candles.

The first known references to a fir tree decorated specifically for Christmas was in Latvia around 1510. Evergreen trees decorated with artificial roses were burned in the squares of Riga and Reval by local guilds as an entertainment on Christmas Eve. By 1531 there was a thriving market for Christmas trees in Strasbourg. The red apples of the Adam and Eve tree were retained, along with figures of Adam, Eve and the serpent. In some areas, the trees were hung upside down from the ceiling. A description of Christmas trees in Strasbourg in 1604 tells us:

> *"On Christmas they put fir trees in the rooms at Strasbourg, they hang red roses cut from many-coloured paper, apples, offerings, gold tinsel, sugar. It is the custom to make a four corned frame around it".* [144]

In Britain, the Christmas tree was popularised by Prince Albert who brought the tradition over from Germany. Newspaper illustrations in 1848 showed the royal family with a Christmas tree decorated with glass-blown ornaments, candles and ribbons in Windsor Castle.

Modern American fundamentalist Christians condemn the use of Christmas trees citing *Jeremiah 10: 2-4* :

> *"Thus says the Lord, Do not learn the way of the nations, And do not be terrified by the signs of the heavens Although the nations are terrified by them; For the customs of the peoples are delusion; Because it is wood cut from the forest, The work of the hands of a craftsman with a cutting tool. They decorate it with silver and with gold; they fasten it with nails and with hammers so that it will not totter."*

Decorate your tree with:

Apples – these are a symbol of fertility for the coming year. Dried apple rings can be hung on the tree.

---

144   E.M.Kronfield, *Der Weihnachtsbaum*, quoted in *Pagan Christmas* by Christian Ratsch and Claudia Muller-Ebeling, Inner Traditions, Vermont, 2006

Bread – shaped folk breads, including gingerbread and biscuits, were (and still are in some countries) used to bring blessing and healing. The Romans used shaped breads as gifts at the New Year. Suitable shapes include stars, suns, trees etc.

Candles – the Romans gave each other gifts of candles during the Saturnalia to represent the continuation and regeneration of light during the dark days of winter.

Dried Fruits – dry out the first fruits at Lughnasa to represent the continuation of the harvest spirit for the coming year.

Fly Agaric Mushrooms (either dried out or pottery representations) – these represent good luck at Yule and are a reminder of shamanic flight.

Globes – coloured glass balls represent the sun.

Nuts – symbolise fertility, especially as they are easily stored to provide nutrition during the winter. Hazelnuts are a Celtic symbol of concentrated knowledge, while walnuts symbolise immortality.

Pinecones– represents eternal life an resurrection, these can be used jn their natural state or painted gold.

Poppy Seed Heads – represent fertility because of the many seeds they produce and because they are connected with the harvest goddess.

CHRISTMAS DIVINATIONS

Christmas Eve divination was a common practice. In England, a Dumb Cake was made by single girls from salt, wheat and barley, and baked in complete silence. It was placed in the oven and the front door opened at midnight. The spectre of the girl's future husband was supposed to enter the house and march into the kitchen to turn the cake. In some areas the cook would prick her initials on the cake and in due course her future husband would materialise to add his initials to hers. Children would cut an apple and counts the pips. The one whose apple had the most pips could look forward to the most happiness in the twelve months ahead. In Scotland, the ashes of the fire were checked on Christmas morning. A foot shape facing the door foretold a death in the family, while a foot facing into the room meant a new arrival. Anyone born at Christmas had the power of seeing and commanding spirits. According to Walter Scott,

Philip II of Spain always looked haggard and downcast because his birthday subjected him to this dubious privilege.

THE YULE LOG OR CLOG

According to Frazer, the old custom of the Yule log, clog or block was widespread in Europe, but seems to have flourished especially in England, France and among the Southern Slavs. It was the winter counterpart of the midsummer bonfire, kindled indoors instead of in the open air.

The Yule clog was a huge block, frequently the root of a large tree, brought into the house with great ceremony, and accompanied by music. Herrick wrote:

Come, bring with a noise,
My merrie, merrie boys,
The Christmas log to the firing;
While my good dame she Bids you all be free,
And drink to your heart's desiring.

The Yule clog lay on the floor till all had sung their Yule songs, standing around it, and then it was placed on the hearth. It was lit with the brand of the last year's log, carefully saved for the purpose, and music was to be played during the ceremony of lighting, as Herrick wrote:

With the last yeere's brand
Light the new block, and
For good successe in his spending,
On your psaltries play,
That sweet luck may
Come while the log is a teending.

It was an evil omen if the log went out during the night. The remains of the log were also supposed to guard the house against fire and lightning. The Yule log must never be bought but should be received as a gift, found or taken from you own property. Often the log to be burned at midwinter was chosen early in the year and set aside.

Tradition varies about the type of wood to be used. Oak logs were popular in the north of England, birch in Scotland and ash in Cornwall and Devon. It was important that the Yule log be the biggest log available since the Christmas festivities would last only as long as the Yule log burned.

In some parts of the Scottish highlands, the head of the household would find a withered stump and carve it into the likeness of an old woman, the Cailleach Nollaich or Christmas Old Wife, a sinister being representing the evils of winter and death. Burning her drove away the winter and protected the occupants of the household from death.

Until the middle of the nineteenth century the old rite of the Yule log was kept up in some parts of Central Germany. A heavy block of oak was fitted into the floor of the hearth. The remains of the old log were ground to powder and strewed over the fields during the Twelve Nights, which was supposed to promote the growth of the crops. In some villages of Westphalia, the practice was to withdraw the Yule log from the fire as soon as it was slightly charred and it was then kept carefully to be placed on the fire whenever a thunderstorm broke, because the people believed that lightning would not strike a house in which the Yule log was smouldering. In other villages of Westphalia the old custom was to tie up the Yule log in the last sheaf cut at harvest. [145]

In several provinces of France, the custom of the Yule log or *tréfoir*, was observed. A superstition had it that a piece of it kept under the bed protected the house for a whole year from fire and thunder. It also guarded against chilblains on their heels in winter and cured cattle of many maladies. If a piece of it was steeped in the water from which cows drank it helped them to calve. The ashes of the log were strewn on the fields to save the wheat from mildew. [146]

In Serbia the log was usually a block of oak, but sometimes of olive or beech. People believed that they would have as many calves, lambs, pigs, and kids as they struck sparks out of the burning log. People carried a piece of the log out to the fields to protect them against hail. In Albania the ashes of the fire were scattered on the fields to make them fertile. In Yugoslavia, the Yule Log was cut just before dawn on Christmas Eve and carried into the house at twilight. The log was decorated with flowers, coloured silks and gold, and then doused with wine and an offering of grain.

In Italy, the Yule log is called the *Ceppo*. Boccaccio, in the fourteenth century, described a Florentine family gathering about the hearth and pouring a libation of wine upon the glowing wood, then sharing the remaining wine.

THE FEAST
Feasting at the winter solstice and New Year was a common practice, exploiting the power of the season to ensure plenty in the coming year with sympathetic magic. The more that was provided and eaten, the more that would come with the harvest. Portions of the last sheaf or corn were often included, or the food was symbolic and contained mixtures of each grain, seeds, nuts, fruit and so on. Different seasonal dishes evolved in each locality.

---

145   James Frazer, *The Golden Bough*, Macmillan Press, London, 1976

146   *Ibid*

In the Orkneys it was considered to be lucky to feast and drink at Yule, and penalties were imposed on those who refused – even the youngest child was required to take a sip of whisky. Each of the children received a 'Yule Cake', a round oatcake decorated around the outside with pinch marks, and with a hole cut into the centre, which undoubtedly symbolised the sun and celebrated its rebirth. [147] Pork and mutton were eaten, and the spirits of the ancestors welcomed in to share in the feast.

Mince Pies

Mince pies originally contained minced meat, hence the name of the filling 'mincemeat' which today consists of dried fruit and spices instead. There was a superstition that you should eat a mince pie every day of the Twelve Days, and each one eaten would give you a month of good health in the coming year.

The Christmas Pudding

The Christmas pudding began its career as the plum pudding, a concoction of plums, spices, wines, meat broth and breadcrumbs. The plums and meat have disappeared from the modern pudding and have been replaced by dried fruits and nuts. Traditionally, it should be made with thirteen ingredients. Lucky charms and silver coins were incorporated in the mix to bring good fortune, such as a silver coin meaning wealth, a ring meaning a marriage and so on. The round pudding is covered with brandy and flamed and we can choose to see a resemblance to the fires of the sun if we really want to.

The Christmas Cake

Most countries have their own version of the Christmas cake, which is supposed to have originated with the cake presented by the people of ancient Rome to their senators.

A custom among Scots demanded that the cook should rise in the early hours of Christmas Day and bake *sowen* (oatmeal) cakes. These were distributed to the family at Hogmanay. If a cake happened to break, bad luck followed, but if it remained unbroken the eater could look forward to a happy New Year.

In France various sorts of cakes and loaves were made, including Christmas morning loaves called *cornaboeux*, made in the shape of horns or a crescent, which were distributed to the poor. In Lorraine people gave one another *cognés* or *cogneux*, a kind of pastry in the shape of two crescents back to back. In some parts of France the *cornaboeux* are known as *hôlais*, and

---

ploughmen gave to the poor as many of these loaves as they possessed oxen and horses. [148] Sometimes French Christmas cakes had the form of complete oxen or horses.

In Sweden and Denmark, the 'Yule Boar' was a loaf in the form of a boar, which stood on the table throughout the festive season. It was often made from the corn of the last sheaf of the harvest. Often it was kept till sowing-time in spring, when part of it was mixed with the seed corn and part given to the ploughman and plough-horses or plough-oxen to eat, in the expectation of a good harvest. [149]

Among German peasants there was a belief in the magical powers possessed by bread baked at Christmas, particularly when moistened by Christmas dew. In Franconia such bread, thrown into a dangerous fire, stilled the flames; in the north of Germany, if put during the Twelve Days into the fodder of the cattle, it made them prolific and healthy throughout the year.

In Eastern Europe, Christmas loaves or cakes were made to resemble the sun, baked flat with a hole in the middle with lines radiating out from it. They were broken by the man of the house on Christmas Day, and a small piece was eaten by each member of the family. In some places one was fixed on the horn of the eldest ox.

The Yuletide Goose
Before the introduction of the turkey, the traditional Christmas bird was the goose in Britain. Between Samhain and St. Martin's Day)11th November) the birds migrate, and their departure signifies the coming of winter. Even in China the bird was a sun animal, and signified the seasonal change to autumn and was depicted with the autumn moon. Amongst the Celts the goose was a sacred solar bird, and eating its flesh was taboo, except at the midwinter feast when a ritual meal of goose flesh was eaten. Goose remained a traditional food at Michaelmas and Yuletide until quite recently.

ANIMALS AT CHRISTMAS
Animals were often especially cared for at Christmas, no doubt initially as a magical invocation of fertility. Up till the early nineteenth century the cattle in Shropshire were always better fed at Christmas than at other times, in Cheshire poultry were double portions of grain. In Silesia on Christmas night all the beasts were given wheat to make them thrive and it was believed that if wheat

148   Clement A. Miles, *Christmas in Ritual and Tradition*, Christian and Pagan, T. Fisher Unwin, 1912

149   James Frazer, *The Golden Bough*, Macmillan Press, London, 1976

be kept in the pocket during the Christmas service and then given to fowls, it would make them grow fat and lay many eggs. In Sweden on Christmas Eve the cattle were given the best forage the house could afford, and afterwards the remains of the Christmas feast; the horses were given the choicest hay and ale. In Poland, flat bread wafers were then taken out to the barn and shared with the animals, for it was believed that this was the one night that animals were given the gift of speech. On the way back into the house, the trees in the yard were awakened - three knocks on the trunk, to let the spirits know that the year had turned, and then a garland made of sheaves of wheat was wrapped around the branches to protect them from frost.

Wild animals were not forgotten. In Hungary the last sheaf of the harvest was given on New Year's morning to the wild birds. In southern Germany corn was put on the roof for them on Christmas Eve, and in Sweden, an unthreshed sheaf was set on a pole.

There was a widespread belief in Europe that animals can speak on Christmas Eve or that animals would be found kneeling in reverence in their stalls at midnight. Howison, in his *Sketches of Upper Canada,* related that an Indian told him that "on Christmas night all deer kneel and look up to Great Spirit."

WASSAILING

Today, most people think of wassailing only in connection with toasting the apple orchards in the south of England on Twelfth Night. However, in the past, wassailing was a wide-spread custom, associated with wishing health to people, crops and animals; apple trees were wassailed to make them bear fruit, and even bees were wassailed to make them produce more honey. It was carried out at various times of the year, notably at Yule, Candlemas, May Day and Halloween. In Ireland, for example, after apple gathering in autumn, it was the custom to mix a bowl of *la mas nbhal*, a drink of spiced ale, wine, or cider with small apples and pieces of toasted bread. Each person present had to take an apple and wish good luck to the other members of the party.

The word 'wassail' comes from the Anglo-Saxon phrase *Wæs hal*, which was used as a greeting. *Wæs* means 'to be' and *hal* means 'hale' or 'whole'. The greeting often accompanied the welcoming of a guest with a cup of ale or mead, and so became a toast (the correct response to which is *Drinc Hale* meaning "I drink to your good health") and eventually wassailing, the act of toasting someone or something on special occasions with spiced ale or wine.

It was also a good opportunity for the poorer members of the community to collect money, going from door to door, singing wassailing songs for a penny or two. The practice of singing songs to accompany drinking from the wassail bowl was probably the origin of Christmas carolling and has lead to the more modern equation of the terms wassailing and carolling during the Christmas and New Year period.

Wassail bowls were often very ornate, decorated with birds, berries, oak leaves and other figures. The Welsh folk museum houses one made of lignum vitae. The actual drink was usually combination of ale, sherry, wine or cider and spices, topped with bread or apples, occasionally fluffed up with beaten egg.

A variation of wassailing was vesselling or besselling (a corruption of 'wassailing') where people carried boxes containing dolls to represent Jesus and Mary, and the dolls were revealed to those who gave alms. This custom is also known at other times of the year, for example as in Leicestershire when May Dolls, mounted on broomsticks, were revealed for a small payment.

A wassail bowl was often carried from house to house, offering drink to each householder for luck. A wassailing song went thus:

A wassail, a wassail, throughout all the town,
Our cup it is white and our ale it is brown,
Our wassail is made of the good ale and true,
Some nutmeg and ginger, the best we could brew.

A similar wassail rhyme which has been recorded over quite a wide area is:

Wassail, oh wassail all over the town
The cup it is white, the ale it is brown
The cup it is made of the good ashen tree
And so is the beer of the best barley

The wassailers often wore disguises and costumes to remove them from the everyday to something 'other', as is often the case with ritual actors at special times of year. In the Gower Peninsula, the wassailers went around with blackened faces or masks, or wore disguises such as the Bessy (a man dressed as a woman) who carried a besom, while others whacked each other with stave. In the 1660s and 1670s a Sussex clergyman gave money to boys who came to 'howl' his orchard, the custom being performed by the 'Howlers' or the 'Howling Boys'. In *Stations of the Sun*, Ronald Hutton describes a photograph from the 1890s showing the captain of the Dunction Howlers, Richard ('Spratty') Knight, dressed in a suit of floral material, with a string of apples around his neck and a large hat decorated with apples.

In some cases, the wassailers engaged in a series of challenging verses or riddles with the householder or sought to gain entry to the house by wit or persuasion. One such verse, which was popular in Staffordshire and Warwickshire, was recorded by a Mr Rann of Dudley in 1819 and was published in *The Every-Day Book* as *The Carroll for a Wassell Bowl*:

A jolly Wassel-Bowl
A Wassel of good ale,
Well fare the butler's sole
That setteth this to sale - Our jolly Wassel
Good Dame, here at your door
Our Wassel we begin
We are all maidens pure
We pray now let us in - With our good Wassel
Our Wassel we do fill
With apples and with spice
They kindly will agree
To take a good carouse - Of our Wassel
But here they let us stand
All freezing in the cold
Good Master give command
To enter and be bold - With our Wassel

Some farms would only let the men take part in the wassailing and when they returned to the farmhouse they would find that the women had locked them out. They were made to stay outside until they had guessed what type of meat was cooking on the spit or titbit held on the end of a stick. Whoever correctly guessed would then be rewarded with the titbit or a small gift. There was a belief, especially amongst the women, that if this custom was omitted then the following harvest would be doomed to failure.

It seems to have been the tradition to wassail the orchards and farm animals on Twelfth Night. Cattle were toasted to keep them healthy. The prize cow was given a special cake with a hole in the middle (a symbol of the sun) and regaled with the words:

Fill your cups my merry men all!
For here's the best ox in the stall!

Oh he is the best ox, of that there's no mistake,
And so let us crown him with the Twelfth cake!

The cake was hooked over one of its horns. In Herefordshire and Monmouthshire a plum pudding might be stuck on a cow's horn and the beast frightened into running until it tossed the pudding - if the pudding fell forward, a good harvest was predicted, but if it fell backwards, the harvest would be poor.

In parts of Scotland, the sea was similarly honoured, with ale poured into the waves in hope this would encourage good fishing in the coming year.

The first recorded example of wassailing the orchards was at Fordwich, Kent, in 1585, when groups of young men who went between orchards performing the rite for a reward. The Devonshire poet Robert Herrick's *Hesperides* was written in the year 1647 and states:

Wassail the trees that they may bear
You, many a plum, and many a pear;
For more or less fruits they will bring,
As you do give them wassailing.

Wassailing the orchards usually involved either the land owner or specially selected bands of wassailers, like the Howlers, visiting the orchard at night, selecting the oldest or most fruitful tree (known in Somerset as the Apple Tree Man) to represent the whole orchard. The tree might be beaten with sticks in order to wake it up after its winter sleep. Bread or cakes soaked in cider would be placed in the tree's branches and the wassail song sung, then loud noises made to frighten evil spirits away from the orchard. One ceremony in Devon involved hoisting a young boy, who represented the spirit of the tree, into the branches, and he would be given offerings of bread, cheese and cider.

Wassailing had all but died out at the beginning of the twentieth century, but has been revived in many cider areas, usually on Twelfth Night. Since the 1970s wassailing has often been associated with morris dancing, as it was usually morris sides who initiated the revival of old traditions generally.

LIGHTS

A prominent feature of Yule is the prevalence of lights of various forms to drive away the powers of darkness; Christmas was formerly called the 'Feast of Lights'.

Crofton Croker reported that huge dip candles, called Christmas candles, were sold in the chandlers' shops in Ireland. It was the custom to burn the three branches down to the point in which they united, and the remainder was reserved to 'see in' the New Year. Considerable ceremony was observed in lighting the candles on Christmas Eve. It was thought unlucky to snuff one and auguries were drawn from the manner and duration of their burning.

All of the Celtic countries have a similar custom of lighting a candle at Christmas to light the way of a stranger. In Scotland was the *Oidche Choinnle,* or Night of Candles when candles were placed in every window to light the way for the Holy Family on Christmas Eve and for first footers on New Years Eve. Shopkeepers gave their customers Yule Candles as a symbol of goodwill wishing them a "Fire to warm you by, and a light to guide you".

In the Orkneys on Yule morning, islanders were awoken by travelling fiddlers who wandered the neighbourhood for the purpose. The sun didn't rise till 9 am, so children brought out the candle stumps they had hoarded especially during the year, to make the house a blaze of lights. The overnight candle or lamp was taken to the byre and used to singe the tail of each animal to make them thrive in the coming year. They were given extra food to mark the season.

THE BATTLE OF LIGHT AND DARK

The winter solstice marks the triumph of darkness over light, with the longest night and shortest day. However, its triumph is brief, from the dawn of the following day, the days begin to lengthen and the sun's power waxes. On the darkest night, the light is reborn. Stories surrounding the winter solstice often tell of the battle between light and dark during which the light triumphs. The battle of the summer and winter king at Augsburg, where summer wears ivy and evergreens and winter is masked, is marked by a fight between the two in which summer wins. In Steiermark winter and summer are teams of young men. The winter men wear fur jackets and have baker's shovels, flails and reels of twine. The summer men have sickles, scythes and pitchforks.

Carlo Ginzburg in *Ecstasies* quotes a description of Croatian lore by seventeenth century author Tommasini in which that some men are born under certain constellations or with a caul go to crossroads at night in spirit, and at the four ember weeks go to crossroads to fight against each other for the abundance or scarcity of all sorts of products. The night battles represent the ritualised battles between white and black shamans, representatives of polarised forces of life and death, creation and destruction. [150]

---

150   Carlo Ginzburg, *Ecstasies, Deciphering the Witches Sabbath,* Hutchinson Radius, London, 1990

Chapter 8
CHRISTMAS

Modern Christians claim that 25th December is the birthday of Jesus Christ, but this is a date that was not fixed until the fourth century and which is still not accepted by some Eastern Churches. Various sects have celebrated Christmas on one hundred and thirty-six separate dates and every month of the year as been mentioned as the possible one in which Christ was born. The first evidence of the birth of Jesus being celebrated was in Egypt in around 200 CE, when it was celebrated on 25th May. Others placed it in April. The *De paschæ computus*, written in 243 CE, stated that Christ was born on 28th March because on that day the material sun was created. When examined, Christmas seems to be nothing more than an amalgam of earlier traditions, dates and myths. In fact the early Gnostics did not believe in Christ as an historical personage, but rather as an ideal.

The Nativity of Christ was not considered an important festival by early Christians, unlike Easter (which celebrated the resurrection). The celebration of a birthday was rejected as a Pagan tradition by most Christians during the first three hundred years of Christianity. However, partly in reaction to the claims by Gnostics that Jesus had not been mortal, Christians began to emphasize the Nativity, though a date could not be agreed.

There is *no* contemporary account of Christ's birth and life; even the historians and scholars living in Jerusalem at the time did not mention him. For information we have to turn to the Gospels which were written at least seventy years later than the events they purport to describe. The first three Gospels of Mark, Luke and Matthew disagree with each other on salient points, and only Matthew and Luke say anything about Christ's birth and origins. The last Gospel is assigned to John, composed about 100 CE in Turkey and very different to the other three.[151]

---

151   In fact, the New Testament itself is only a choice selection of extant texts chosen in CE 367 by Bishop Athanasius of Alexandria and ratified by the Church Council of Hippo in 393 and the Council of Carthage four years later. The works or 'Gospels' that most agreed were cho-

Though the Gospels of Matthew and Luke give no date for Christ's birth, they do suggest that it could not have been December. The shepherds are supposed to have paid a visit to the new born babe after watching their flocks by night - shepherds would not have been out watching their flocks during the exposed nights of the winter season, and would only have watched them all night during the lambing season. Then again, Mary and Joseph are said to have returned to Bethlehem because a census was being conducted that required them to do so – a census would not have been conducted during the winter months which would have made travelling difficult.[152]

FOLLOWING THE STAR

The early church flourished in Egypt, with the result that many elements of ancient Egyptian mythology were incorporated into the Jesus story. The most prominent Egyptian deities of the time were Osiris and his consort Isis who had been worshipped for thousands of years, and who had gradually assumed the powers of various other gods. Osiris was a god who chose to become a man to guide his people; as such he was called 'the Good Shepherd' and depicted with a shepherd's crook. As a corn god he died, was buried, and was brought back to life. As corn he fed his people and was called the 'Resurrection and the Life'. His flesh was eaten in the form of wheaten cakes. Like Mary, Isis was called 'The Star of the Sea' and 'Queen of Heaven', a virgin who brought forth a son titled 'the Saviour of the World', the hero who brings order back into the universe. Isis and her son were forced to hide from an evil king until Horus became a man.

Isis gave birth to Horus each year at the winter solstice. When he was born a voice proclaimed "the ruler of the earth is born". His birth was heralded by the evening rising of the three stars of Orion's (Osiris's) belt just before the rising of the birth star Sirius (Isis) shortly afterwards in the east, marking the place where the new born sun would rise. Thus the coming of the Light of the World was heralded by a star as that of Jesus was later said to be.

A much more important association of Sirius and the rebirth of a god was at the summer solstice (because of the precession of the equinoxes in later ages it was July to August) which heralded the rebirth of Osiris at

---

sen and others ignored and even deliberately suppressed. During the next few centuries the New Testament was subject to heavy editing and revision. The earliest version of Mark, for example, ended with the crucifixion and contained no resurrection scene, until one was forged in the late second century and appended.

152   You might think the weather in Israel would not have been as cold in winter as it is in Britain, but the Gospels report Christ as saying "Pray that your flight be not in the winter" and in the Old Testament, Jacob complained of frosts at night.

the inundation of the Nile which began the Egyptian year in the month *Wep-renpet* or 'Opener of the Year'. Of all the stars only the heliacal rising of Sirius coincides with the length of our solar year of 365.25 days. Each year it started time - and therefore order, the seasons and creation. The Egyptians noted that every ten days one of the thirty six decans (the stars that kept the calendar, chosen because they followed the same pattern as Sirius) disappeared into the west and remained unseen for a period of time before reappearing with the dawn in the east. As one 'died' another was 'reborn' every ten days, according to *Papyrus Carlsburg 1*. During the period the star was missing, it was said to have entered the *Duat* ('Embalming House') or netherworld, where its impurities were shed, preparing it for rebirth. [153] The Egyptian mummification process took seventy days, the period of time the decans spent in the *Duat*.

The Egyptians called the star Septit [154] (or Sothis in the Greek form), titled 'the Water Bringer' and identified it with Isis. Isis appears in the Pyramid Texts as the chief mourner for her husband, the vegetation god Osiris (identified with the constellation Orion), whom she brought back to life with magic. In Upper Egypt, on Orion's first heliacal appearance over the eastern horizon he seems to appear feet first, as if he is lying on his back as a corpse. By the time Canis Major is fully visible (originally the summer solstice but now late July-August), Orion has become upright, as Isis breathes new life into him and he is resurrected.[155] Remembering that the early Christians did not fix the date of Christ's birth for several centuries, this may well be the origin of our 'star in the east'.

Christian scholars have made many attempts to account for the star that is said to have heralded Christ's birth, looking for evidence of a comet or some other celestial phenomena during the period. However, many gods, such as Krishna, Mithras, Horus and Osiris are also said to have had their births heralded by a star.

THE WISE MEN
Jesus was said to have been visited by wise men following a star in the east. The Bible does not say that they were kings, or even mention how many of them there were. The Syrian church claimed there were twelve Magi. The idea that there were three Magi came from the third century theologian Origen, possibly to account for the three recorded gifts of gold, frankincense

153   Dr. E.C. Krupp, *Beyond the Blue Horizon*, Oxford University Press, Oxford, 1991

154   A Greek form of her Egyptian name Aset or Eset, meaning 'throne'.

155   http://www.astrolodge.co.uk/astro/diary/astronomy/2007Q1/january2007.html

and myrrh. This was probably included in the story to fulfil the prophecy in *Isaiah 60:6* of Gentiles coming with camels to bring "gold and incense in praise of the Lord". Our concept of the three kings comes from mediaeval times, and in Christian tradition they are known as Melchior, Balthasar and Caspar. In the fourth century CE the mother of Constantine brought bones purportedly belonging to the three wise men to Constantinople.

There is an old, but not ancient, tradition of calling the three stars of Orion's belt 'The Three Kings', which seems to be a later Christian interpolation that indicated a knowledge of an original star myth. Much more widely spread was the tradition of calling the seven stars of the Plough 'wise men' or 'sages' and these play a bigger role in the myths of the winter solstice.

THE VIRGIN BIRTH

The various myths of the sun god share common themes – he is born at the winter solstice in a cave, he is the saviour of mankind and he is born of a virgin. This might mean he is born of the virgin dawn, the maiden moon or purified earth, or perhaps the constellation Virgo. And of course, the rising of the sun is preceded each morning by the rising of Venus, the morning star, as Herrick says:

Hark! the cock crows, and yon bright star
Tells us the day himself's not far :
And see ! where, breaking from the night,
He gilds the eastern hills with light!

The 'virgin mother' was a common Pagan theme. In ancient times, virgin did not mean a woman who had never had intercourse, but a woman who had never been married and was antonymous. Many goddesses were called 'virgin' despite being married or having lovers.

Any children of gods who mated with mortal women were considered virgin-born. Such immaculate conceptions might take place through dreams and visions, by 'eating the god', bathing in the sea or river, by the action of the wind and so on. In ancient Greece, children born out of wedlock were called *parthenioi* meaning 'virgin-born', and were regarded as the sons of Zeus, the universal Father.

Isis was called 'the Immaculate Virgin' (the inviolable goddess of the dawn), despite conceiving from the dead form of her husband. According to Eratosthenes (276-194 BCE), the celestial Virgin was Isis, the symbol of the returning year who gave birth to Horus, the divine child. The Egyptians represented the new-born sun Horus by the image of an infant which they brought forth and exhibited to his worshippers. [156] The celebrants retired into certain inner shrines, from which at midnight they issued with a loud cry, "The Virgin has brought forth! The light is waxing!" Macrobius (395–423 CE) reported that a figure of the baby Horus was laid in a manger and a statue of Isis was placed beside it:

> *"...at the winter solstice the sun would seem to be a little child, like that which the Egyptians bring forth from a shrine on an appointed day, since the day is then at its shortest and the god is accordingly shown as a tiny infant."* [157]

The festival lasted twelve days (the origin of the twelve days of Christmas) to reflect the twelve months of the year. The inscription over the temple of Isis at Sais reads "The fruit I have begotten is the sun". Like other sun gods, Horus was a saviour god who defeated the powers of darkness and chaos. Like the Holy Family of the New Testament, Isis and Horus were forced to flee from persecution and hide in the wilderness. This is a common theme in the myths of sun gods, and may refer to the season of darkness and want that corresponds to winter until the sun comes to full strength at the spring equinox.

Isis was often portrayed as the Madonna holding her child, and her statues were even used by later Christians to represent the Virgin Mary and the baby Jesus.

The virgin mother and her child was a widespread Pagan icon with the Teutonic goddess Hertha - the virgin earth impregnated by the divine sky - shown with a child in her arms, and Quetzalcoatl, the (crucified) saviour of the Aztecs, was the son of the Virgin Queen of Heaven.

St. Epiphanius (fourth century CE) stated that in Alexandria the birth of Aion was celebrated on the night before 6th January before the image of the goddess Kore ('Virgin'). Aion was the Alexandrian god of Eternity or deified time (like Chronos) and he regulated the revolutions of the stars. [158] The ritual ended with bringing forth from beneath the earth the image of Aion, which was carried seven times around the inner sanctuary of Kore's temple. At the height of the ceremony the announcement was made "Today at this hour the virgin Kore has given birth to Aion". Gregory Nazianzen (329-389 CE) described the Greek form of this celebration in which the cry was heard: "the virgin has brought forth, the light grows". John Cassian in *Collations* (written

---

156   James Frazer, *The Golden Bough*, Macmillan Press, London, 1976

157   Macrobius, *Saturnalia*

158   http://hermeticmagick.com/content/deities/aion.html

418-427 CE) reported that the Egyptian monasteries still observed the 'ancient custom' of this Epiphany but on 25th December. The Epiphany was celebrated as early as the second century CE by an obscure sect called the Basilidans as a festival of both the birth and baptism of Jesus, undoubtedly an update and usurpation of the earlier Pagan festival.

The birth of the Greek god Dionysus had also been celebrated on January 6th, another god born of a virgin who wandered the earth teaching humankind, and who underwent a death and resurrection. Similarly, the Indian god Krishna was born of a virgin in a cave at the winter solstice, and his birth was announced by a star. In order to destroy him, innocents were massacred, but he escaped and went on to perform miracles, healing the suck, curing lepers and raising the dead. He was killed by being shot by an arrow (or some say crucified) and rose from the dead to ascend into heaven. He will return on the last day to be the judge of the living and the dead.

The Roman poet Virgil wrote (in *Eclogues* 37 BCE) that the 'return of the virgin' would bring about the birth of a boy "in whom the golden race (shall) arise". The boy was the sun and the virgin was the constellation of Virgo, which rises on the horizon at midnight on December 25th. Albertus Magnus (1193?-1280), the teacher of Thomas Aquinas, wrote:

"We know that the sign of the celestial Virgin did come to the horizon at the moment where we have fixed the birth of our Lord Jesus Christ. All the mysteries of the incarnation of our Saviour Christ; and all the circumstances of his marvellous life, from his conception to his ascension, are to be traced out in the constellations, and are figured in the stars."

The constellation of Virgo is usually represented by a virgin with a sheaf of corn in her hand (the bright star Spica). However, it is also represented by a woman and child, as at the Temple of Denderah in Egypt and on the Arabian and Persian globes. Many goddesses were portrayed as Madonnas, with their sons on their knees: Devaki was shown with the Krishna in her arms; Istar, with a crown of stars, was depicted with her son/lover Tammuz on her knee. Virgo has been associated with nearly every prominent goddess, including Ishtar, Isis, Cybele, Mary the Mother of Jesus, Athena and Persephone.

In ancient times, while Sirius was at midnight on the Meridian at the winter solstice, the constellation of Virgo would have been rising on the horizon in the east, signifying the Virgin in the East who will give birth (at sunrise) to a renewed and reborn sun.

THE HOUSE OF BREAD

Bethlehem – the town of Jesus' birth - means 'house of bread' [159] as, according to the early church father St Jerome (who lived in Bethlehem from 386 to 420 CE), there was a site sacred to Tammuz/Adonis in Bethlehem. Tammuz was a corn-god of death and resurrection born on December 25th, a festival spoken of by Tertullian, Jerome and other Church Fathers, who wrote that the ceremonies took place in a cave, and that the cave in which they celebrated his mysteries in Bethlehem was the same one in which Christ Jesus was born. Tammuz was killed, placed in a tree and was resurrected at the spring equinox (when the sun undergoes his final 'resurrection' from darkness):

Trust, ye saints, your Lord restored,
Trust ye in your risen Lord;
For the pains which Tammuz endured
Our salvation have procured. [160]

His mother was the virgin Myrrha who was identified with Mary by early Christians who called Jesus' mother 'Myrrh of the Sea'.

HAPPY MITHRASMAS

When Constantine replaced the Pagan Diocletian as Emperor of the Western Roman Empire in 305 CE, he ended all persecutions of the Christians. Constantine was said to have accepted Christianity in 312 CE on the eve of a battle when he had a vision of a cross of light superimposed upon the sun. He sought to unify sun-worship and Christianity into a single monotheistic state religion and summoned the Council of Nicea in 325 CE to settle disputed points of doctrine and orthodoxy. This was a political, not a spiritual decision, as Constantine was hardly a godly man. He drowned his wife in boiling water, murdered his own son and the husbands of his two sisters, his father in law and his twelve year old nephew.

The council opted to mark Christmas on December 25th to coincide with the Roman festival celebrating *Natalis Invicti*, the Birth of the Unconquered Sun (god). [161] In 386 CE St Chrysostom, Archbishop of Constantinople, preached

"But Our Lord, too, is born in the month of December . . . the eight
before the calends of January . . ., But they call it the 'Birthday of the
Unconquered'. Who indeed is so unconquered as Our Lord . . .? Or, if

---

159   James Frazer, *The Golden Bough*, Macmillan Press, London, 1976

160   Ctesias (400 BCE), *Persika*

161   The Eastern Church refused to accept 25th December for another three hundred years.

they say that it is the birthday of the Sun, He is the Sun of Justice."
With refreshing honesty he stated this was so that

"*…while the heathen were busied with their profane rites, the
Christians might perform their holy ones without disturbance".*

Paulinus of Nola wrote in fourth century Italy

"*For it is after the solstice, when Christ born in flesh with the new sun
transformed the season of cold winter, and, vouchsafing to mortal man
a healing dawn, commanded the night to decrease at his coming with
advancing day."*

In 274 CE the Pagan Emperor Aurelian had attempted to unite the
religions of the empire, fusing the cults of various sun gods under the state cult
of *Sol Invictus*, the whose birthday was December 25th or the winter solstice in
the Roman calendar.

Many of the myths of Christmas seem to have come from the cult of
the god Mithras, which was more popular than Christianity (only about 10%
of the Empire was Christian), and which almost became the state religion of
the Roman Empire. Mithras was born of a human virgin on December 25th, his
birth attended by shepherds. When he reached adulthood, Mithras healed the
sick, made the lame walk, gave sight to the blind and raised the dead. Before
returning to heaven at the spring equinox, Mithras had a last supper with
twelve disciples, representing the twelve signs of the zodiac.

This identification of Jesus with the Pagan sun god was a doubled
edged sword for the Christians however, and Tertullian had to assert that
Sol was *not* the Christians' god, while Augustine denounced the heretical
identification of Christ with Sol. Pagan customs and observances persisted.
Tertullian condemned Saturnalia customs such as exchanging of gifts and
decorating homes with evergreens:

"*By us who are strangers to Sabbaths, and new moons, and festivals,
once acceptable to God, the Saturnalia, the feasts of January, the
Brumalia, and Matronalia, are now frequented; gifts are carried to and
fro, new year's day presents are made with din, and sports and banquets
are celebrated with uproar; oh, how much more faithful are the heathen
to their religion, who take special care to adopt no solemnity from the
Christians."*

The friend and biographer of Saint Eligius recorded that the bishop would
caution his flock

"(*Do not*) *make* vetulas (little figures of the Hag), *little deer or* iotticos
*or set tables at night or exchange New Year gifts or supply superfluous
drinks".*

The celebration of Christmas arrived in Britain around the early fifth century. A letter addressed in 601 by Pope Gregory the Great to Abbot Mellitus, giving him instructions to be handed on to Augustine of Canterbury, is illuminating with regard to how the Church appropriated Pagan festivals as Christian ones:

"Because (the Anglo-Saxons) are wont to slay many oxen in sacrifices to demons, some solemnity should be put in the place of this, so that on the day of the dedication of the churches, or the nativities of the holy martyrs whose relics are placed there, they may make for themselves tabernacles of branches of trees around those churches which have been changed from heathen temples, and may celebrate the solemnity with religious feasting. Nor let them now sacrifice animals to the Devil, but to the praise of God kill animals for their own eating, and render thanks to the Giver of all for their abundance; so that while some outward joys are retained for them, they may more readily respond to inward joys. For from obdurate minds it is undoubtedly impossible to cut off everything at once, because he who strives to ascend to the highest place rises by degrees or steps and not by leaps." [162]

By 529 CE Christmas had became a civic holiday, and all work or public business (except that of cooks, bakers etc.) was prohibited by the Emperor Justinian. In 563, the Council of Braga forbade fasting on Christmas Day, and four years later the Council of Tours proclaimed the twelve days from December 25 to Epiphany as a sacred, festive season.

By 1100 Christmas was celebrated all over Europe. The word 'Christmas' comes from the late Old English *Cristes Maesse* ('Christ Mass') and was first recorded in 1038.

THE PURITANS BAN CHRISTMAS

The Protestant Reformation in sixteenth century Europe saw a rejection of the Roman Church, citing the need to return to scripture as the ultimate source of spiritual authority, rather than the Pope. Turning to the Bible, they found no evidence of a date for Christ's birthday, and no commandment to celebrate it. The *Anatomie of Abuses* by the Calvinist Philip Stubbes, first published in 1583, complained:

"Especially in Christmas tyme there is nothing els vsed but cardes,

162   Quoted in Clement A. Miles, *Christmas in Ritual and Tradition*, Christian and Pagan, T. Fisher Unwin, 1912

*dice, tables, maskyng, mumming, bowling, and suche like fooleries; and
the reason is, that they think they haue a commission and prerogatiue
that tyme to doe what they list, and to followe what vanitie they will.
But(alas!) doe they thinke that they are preuiledged at that time to doe
euill? The holier the time is (if one time were holier than an other, as it
is not), the holier ought their exercises to bee. Can any tyme dispence
with them, or giue them libertie to sinne? No, no; the soule which
sinneth shall dye, at what tyme soeuer it offendeth.... Notwithstandyng,
who knoweth not that more mischeef is that tyme committed than in all
the yere besides?"*

In 1583 the Presbyterian Church suppressed the observation of Christmas in
Scotland and the Church of Scotland continued to discourage the celebration
of Christmas, which remained a normal working day in Scotland until 1958.

By 1613, German Calvinists preached against feasts honouring Saint
Nicholas, condemning them as heathen idol worship.

The most extreme reaction, however, came from the English Puritans
during the years of Cromwell's Commonwealth. Oliver Cromwell campaigned
against the Pagan practices of feasting, decorating and singing. Puritans called
Christmas by such pejorative names as 'the Papist's Massing Day' and 'Old
Heathen Feasting Day' and abolished the Christmas celebration by an act
of Parliament in 1647, a ban not lifted until the Restoration. The *Ordinance
for the better observation of the Feast of the Nativity of Christ* stated that
Christmas should be marked with humility and fasting rather than feasting.
Parish officers were subject to penalties for allowing the decking of churches
and allowing services to be conducted on Christmas Day. However, the
much loved feast was not so easily suppressed and many people protested;
there were riots in several places. When it was ordered that Christmas Day
should be a market day like any other, folk refused to take their provisions to
town, and those few shopkeepers who opened their premises were attacked
by the populace and their wares thrown down the street. In 1647 evergreen
decorations were defiantly hung up in London, and the Lord Mayor and City
Marshal had to ride about setting fire to them.

In 1645 a pamphlet was published called *An Hue and Cry After
Christmas,* printed by 'Simon Minc'd Pye for Cisseley Plum-Porridge',
which described the arraignment, conviction and imprisoning of Christmas
on St Thomas' Day, and how he broke out of prison leaving his hoary hair and
grey beard sticking between the prison bars.

The Massachusetts Pilgrims in America passed a similar law in 1659
and condemned wassailing as a source of public disorder. Modern Jehovah's

Witnesses and some Christian fundamentalists do not celebrate Christmas, regarding it as an unchristian holiday and condemning the trappings of the modern Christmas such as Santa Claus, elves and flying reindeer as Pagan or even satanic. The more extreme groups regard the word 'Christmas' as blasphemous.

The Puritans had a point – every element of the Christmas story, and every Christmas custom is Pagan in origin.

Chapter 9
HERB CRAFT

Nor shield for shoving, nor sharp spear for lunging;
But he held a holly cluster in one hand, holly
That is greenest when groves are gaunt and bare
Sir Gawain and the Green Knight

APPLE *Malus sp.*

There are many associations of the apple with Yule. Apples appear in Santa's sack, as decorations on Christmas trees and as pomanders, as well as being a vital ingredient in the wassail "when roasted crabs hiss in the bowl". Apple gifts, mounted on tripods, were trimmed with nuts and yew, representing sweetness, fertility and immortality ,were offered in the Forest of Dean, Gloucestershire on New Year's Day.

The apple is a symbol of, and sacred to, the sun. In Baltic lore the sun stops and washes her horses in the sea, then drives to her apple orchard in the west. The setting sun is a red apple that falls from the orchard. The sun goddess is sometimes also described as a rosy apple. This tree, or iron post stands beyond the hill of the sky next to a grey stone. In Balkan lore, the World Tree is an apple. The sun goddess, Saule rests in it, hanging her belt up and sleeping in the crown. At dawn, when she rises, the belt turns red.

In Greek myth, the Hesperides were three maidens who lived in the western paradise where the golden apples of immortality grew. Originally there were seven, but they were later reduced to three, Aegle which means 'brightness'; Erythraea meaning 'the red one' and Hespera meaning 'evening light.' They seemed to have been nymphs of the setting sun or possibly a trio representing Dawn, Noon and Evening. When the Argonauts approached them for the apples, Hespera turned herself into a poplar, the tree of sun maidens. Apples, like the sun, are associated with immortality. In the Edda, the old Scandinavian saga, Iduna kept in a box, apples that she gave to the gods to eat, thereby to renew their youth.

Great honour has been paid to apple trees down the centuries, and in some places still is. In parts of Britain apple trees are wassailed at Yuletide. The trees are visited and cakes or bread soaked in cider are placed in the branches, and cider poured over the roots as a libation. Occasionally roasted apples floating in cider are offered. Sometimes shots are fired to scare away evil spirits from the orchards. The health of the trees is toasted with cider and they are asked to continue to produce abundantly.

Here's to thee, old apple tree,
Whence thou may'st bud, and whence thou may'st blow!
And whence thou may'st bear apples enow!
Hatsfull! Capsfull!
Bushel-bushel-sacksfull,
And my pockets full too! Huzza!

Trees that are poor bearers of fruit are not honoured. Wassailing was also observed in parts of America, notably the apple growing regions around Yakima, Washington, introduced by those who had visited the English apple wassailing rites.

The dried peel and tree bark may be used in incense. Apples, as sun and fertility symbols, can be used to decorate the Yule tree, in wreaths and Twelfth Night ornaments. I change over my Yule decorations for Twelfth Night ones which are quite different, and consist of apples, corn, fruits and nuts etc. to reflect the waking up of the land after the Yule season has finished. Fruit trees in your garden should certainly be wassailed on Twelfth Night, and cider and apple pieces are traditional ingredients of the wassail cup.

BAY LAUREL

For the ancient Romans, the bay laurel was a symbol of celebration and victory. The name laurel said to be connected with the Latin word *laus* meaning 'praise' In Victorian England it was used in Christmas divinations, looking for omens in the crackling and curling of leaves, according to Herrick:

When laurell spirts i' th' fire, and when the hearth
Smiles to itselt'e and guilds the roofe with mirth;
When up the Thyrse is rais'd, and when the sound
Of sacred orgies flyes around, around, "

At Oxford and Cambridge universities, the windows of the college chapels were carefully decked with laurel.

In Greek myth laurel was sacred to the sun god Apollo who, having slain the Python (representing darkness and chaos), fled for purification to the laurel-groves of the Vale of Tempe. There he fell in love with the nymph

Daphne, the daughter of the river Peneus. She fled from him and to save her from being ravished her father turned her into a laurel. Apollo, returning to Delphi, instituted the Pythian Games to commemorate his victory over Python, and the prizes there awarded were crowns of laurel leaves and berries. Daphne (*Daphoene* 'the Bloody One') was the dawn (Sanskrit *Dahana* or *Ahana*) pursued by the rising sun, but Daphne came to mean the laurel, a wood which burns easily.

For the Norse, bay laurel and rosemary crowned the boar's head at the winter feast.

Bay is infused with the power and energy of the sun, and may be powerfully used to invoke the Sun Lord and his gifts of divination, healing and protection. It can be used in the ritual bath, to attune with the sun's energies, and thrown onto the ritual bonfire or used in the incense, as well as being used in decorations and cooking.

BEAN *Leguminosae*

The bean is an obvious fertility symbol, shaped like a testicle, and in the vernacular 'bean soup' referred to semen.[163] Beans have several connections with the season. A bean was baked into the Twelfth Night cake in order to choose the king of the revels, and in Germany, the Christmas period was called a 'bean feast'.

The taboo against eating beans was widespread in early cultures. Egyptians made it an object of sacred worship and were forbidden to eat it. Jewish high priests were forbidden to eat beans on the Day of Atonement. The Mystœ of Eleusis practised chastity abstaining from certain food and above all from beans before the great sacrament. The Greek philosopher Pythagoras strongly believed that beans contained the souls of the departed. Legend has it that this caused his death; pursued by enemies he mistakenly ran into a bean field. Rather than trample on the souls of the dead, he stood stock still, thus allowing his enemies to catch him. The Pythagoreans continued to abstain from beans on the grounds that their ancestors' souls could be resident in them. If a man as opposed to a woman ate a bean he might be robbing an ancestor of his chance of reincarnation.

In ancient Rome the head of the household would go out three days of the year, spitting beans from his mouth to rid the home of evil spirits.

Beans should be incorporated into the Yuletide feasts, both as symbols of fertility and in honour of the ancestors. A bean is incorporated into the Twelfth Night cake to choose the king of the revels.

---

163   Christian Ratsch, *Pagan Christmas*, Inner Traditions, Vermont, 2006

CHERRY

There is an old custom of cutting cherry branches on December 4th and putting them in water and encouraging them to blossom. They are commonly called St Barbara's boughs. If they bloom in time for Christmas, it indicates a good harvest for the coming year, if not, it portends bad luck. In lower Austria it was customary to put up a branch for each family member, and the branch that developed best would have the best luck in the following year. If a person's branch failed to flower at all, they would die in the coming year. In Silesia, girls would put aside a branch for each of their suitors, and the one that opened first would be the one they would marry.

An old English carol relates how Joseph and the pregnant Mary were walking in a cherry orchard when Mary asked Joseph to pick her some cherries. Joseph remarked unkindly that she should get whoever 'brought thee with child' to pick the cherries for her. The unborn Christ child then communicated with the cherry trees, asking them to lower their branches so that Mary could pick her own cherries, and Joseph was suitably repentant.

Try bringing in a cherry branch before Yule and encourage it to blossom by putting it in water in a warm place. The flowering is a blessing for the coming year.

FIR *Pincaceae Sp.* – *Abies Alba* (Silver Fir), *Abies siberica* (Siberian Fir)

Fir trees and spruce trees look very similar, apart from the fact that fir cones point up and spruce cones point down. Fir needles are softer than the pointed spruce leaves, and spruce needles grow in a circle around the branches. Fir trees can grow up to 200 feet tall. The German word *tanna* means both 'fir' and 'forest' and we find it in the German word for the Christmas tree, the *tannenbaum*. The Black Forest in Germany got its name from the dense growth of fir trees in the area.

Tacitus described a Germanic midwinter feast where people carried fir branches. In the Alps, firs were often considered to be holy, and the dwelling place of gods. In Phrygia, the fir was sacred to the goddess Cybele, while the Romans dedicated it to the goddess Diana, seeing in the closed cone a symbol of virginity. The Siberian Jakuten said that the souls of their shamans were born in a fir tree on the mountain Dzokua. [164]

In Germany, fir branches were hung outside doors and animal stalls at Christmas to prevent disease and ward off evil. According to the abbess Hildegard Von Bingen:

---

164   Christian Ratsch & Claudia Muller-Ebeling, *A Pagan Christmas*, Inner Traditions, Rochester, 2003

"The fir is more warm than cold, and holds many powers within itself, and it is associated with bravery. Wherever the fir wood stands the spirits of air hate it, and shun it. Enchantments and magic spells have less power to effect things there, than they do in other places." [165]

The first modern record of a fir as a Christmas tree comes from Strasbourg in 1604, where it was recorded that people put fir trees in the rooms, hung with red roses cut from coloured paper, apples, offerings, gold tinsel and sugar.

As well as affording the Yule tree and decorations, fir resin and dried needles can be added to incense.

FLY AGARIC *Amanita muscaria*

Found commonly throughout much of the world, the white-gilled, white-spotted red poisonous mushroom is of the most recognizable and widely encountered plants in popular culture.

Fly agaric is psychotropic and has a long history of use among European mystics and shamans. In Finno-Ugric languages words denoting ecstasy and intoxication are traceable to root expressions meaning 'fly agaric'. The effects of the mushroom include auditory and visual hallucinations and spatial distortions. Subjects commonly report sensations of flying, or seeing little people or red-hatted mushrooms dancing. Fly agaric grows under pine and birch trees and the Siberian shaman's seven-stepped pole was made of birch. In other words, the shaman ingested the mushroom and flew up the cosmic axis tree to the spirit realms, seeing the spirit of the agaric as a red-capped fairy. [166]

To some commentators, the Father Christmas costume of white and red also suggests the mushroom. He wears a red cap or hood, like dozens of European fairies, which may be a code for the mushroom itself. Many writers have speculated that Santa may originate in the figure of the shaman. Siberian winter dwellings were excavated holes with a birch log roofs; the only entrance was through a smoke hole in the roof. Even the summer dwellings had smoke-hole exits for the spirit of the shaman to fly out of when he was in a trance. This might explain why Santa enters and exits through the chimney. The shaman is the middleman between humans and spirits and brings back knowledge from the spirit world. Ordinary individuals would write requests

165   Hildegard Von Bingen, *Physica*, III

166   Anna Franklin, *The Illustrated Encyclopaedia of Fairies*, Vega, London, 2002

on pieces of paper and burn them, so their messages would be carried to the spirits on the smoke.

As we have already seen, Father Christmas may originate with Odin, the shamanic god of knowledge and wisdom. When Odin rode out with the Wild Hunt at Yule, wherever the red blood and white froth from his horse's mouth touched the ground, the earth would give birth nine months later to fly agaric mushrooms. In Germany, fly agaric mushrooms were also called 'raven's bread' associating them with Odin's (Woden's) ravens. Huginn (from Old Norse *hugr* 'thought') and Muninn (from Old Norse *munr* 'memory' or 'mind') fly all over the world, and bring Odin information. Odin's ability to send his 'thought' and 'mind' relates to the trance-state journey of shamans. In Skaldic poetry the mushrooms are called *munins tugga* ('food of the ravens') indicating they bring about the shamanic trance and journey.

Thor drove his cart through the air, causing thunder and lightning when he threw his hammer through the air. Where the lightning struck, or where the thunder stones fell, they were thought to inseminate the ground and make mushrooms grow. The same was said of the Greek sky god Zeus's thunderbolts.

The *Rig-Veda* speaks of the mysterious soma; a plant that was considered a god, an aspect of Agni, the god of fire. The plant had no roots, leaves, blossoms or seeds but possessed of a single eye like the sun - the red cap of the fly agaric.[167] Spoken of as an eye, the cap of the fly agaric represents the opening of inner vision, as well as the sun.

In Siberia it was believed that the creator spat on the earth, and that spittle became the fly agaric mushroom. Great raven, the first helper of the people, ate one of the mushrooms and began to dance and became clairvoyant, declaring "Let the fly agaric mushroom live forever on the earth, and let my children see what it has to show them." [168] Siberian shamans regularly use fly agaric mushrooms.

Mushrooms appear in Greek mythology in connection with the sun god Apollo. Carl Ruck speculated that the votive offerings sent to Apollo's shrine at Delos from Hyperborea (sometimes identified with Siberia and sometimes with Britain) were actually fly agaric mushrooms.[169] Along the

167 Gordon Wasson, *Soma: The Divine Mushroom of Immortality*, Harcourt Brace Jovanovick Inc, 1968

168 Christian Ratsch and Claudia Muller-Eberling, *Pagan Christmas*, Inner Traditions, Vermont, 2003

169 Carl Ruck, *The Offerings from the Hyperboreans, Persephone's Quest*, Yale, New Haven, 1986

route the offerings travelled lived a race called the Arimaspeans ('One-eyed'). The murder of the Cyclops ('Round-eye') occasioned Apollo's sojourn amongst the peoples of his northern homeland, Hyperborea. There was also a race of one-footed creatures called Shade-foots who, according to Aristophanes, were implicated in a profane celebration of the lesser Eleusinian mysteries. The Shade foots were also known as Monocoli ('One-legs'). In Vedic Sanskrit, soma is described as 'Not-born Single-foot'.

Fairy food, which is generally described as being red in colour, is prohibited for humans. Should they eat it, they can never return to the realm of men. This is comparable with the taboos placed on shamanic substances, forbidding them to ordinary men and women. Among the Selkup, fly agaric was believed to be fatal to non-shamans. Among the Vogul consumption was limited to sacred occasions and it was abused on peril of death. The Indo-Europeans strictly limited the important ritual of soma to certain classes and the profane user risked death at the hands of the angry god. Amongst the Celts, red foods and mushrooms were taboo, designated as the food of the Otherworld or the dead. As the mushroom aids the shaman to visit other realms in spirit flight, see spirits and contact the spirit or god within, Robert Graves argued that ambrosia, the food of the gods, was in reality hallucinogenic mushrooms. [170]

Descriptions of visits to fairyland might easily describe a drug induced visionary experience - enhanced colours, unearthly music, spatial distortions, the loss of any sense of the passage of time, and food and drink tasting wonderful. However, when the traveller returns (or the vision ends) fairy gold turns to withered leaves or common rubbish.

The active ingredient is excreted in the urine of those consuming the mushrooms, and it has sometimes been the practice for a shaman to consume the mushrooms, and the rest of the tribe to drink his urine: the shaman, in effect, partially detoxifying the drug. This 'second round' for the substance is easier on the body than direct consumption. (See also 'Reindeer' in Chapter 10, Animals of Yule.)

Decorate your tree with fly agaric mushrooms, either dried real ones or decorations. These represent good luck at Yule and are a reminder of shamanic flight.

FRANKINCENSE *Boswellia thurifera*
Frankincense is a gum resin obtained from the *Boswellia thurifera* tree, native to the Middle East and Somalia. To obtain the gum a narrow strip is peeled off

---

170   Robert Graves, *The White Goddess*, Faber and Faber, London, 1961

the bark, and the tree bleeds a milk-like substance which hardens with expose to air. The tears are scraped off and collected. These are then burned to provide fragrant incense.

Frankincense has been used as a religious and magical herb for thousands of years. The earliest record comes from Egypt 5000 years ago where it was used to honour the sun god Ra. In Babylon it was used to honour the sun god Bel. It is said to have been taken as one of the gifts of the wise men to the Christ child.

Frankincense may be used in all rituals of the sun, especially the winter solstice. It cleanses, purifies, consecrates and raises vibrations. The fragrance concentrates the mind and drives away negativity.

GERMANDER SPEEDWELL *Veronica chamaedrys*
In Germany, this is given the name of *niklasl*, and is associated with St Nicholas.

HAWTHORN
Joseph of Arimathea supposedly brought a hawthorn staff with him when he came to Britain from Palestine, or some say the thorn from the crown of thorns that Christ wore. It is claimed he visited Britain during the first century CE in his capacity as a tin trader, accompanied by the Christ Child. After the crucifixion he returned, sometime after 37 CE and made contact with the druids. When he landed at Glastonbury, in despair he thrust his staff into the ground at the foot of Wearyall Hill and knelt down with his followers to pray, whereupon it miraculously rooted and thereafter flowered on Old Christmas Day (January 5th). In 1752, two thousand people watched to see if the Quainton thorn would flower on Christmas New Style; and as it did not, they refused to keep the New Style festival.

Actually this species of hawthorn is the *Crataegus monogyna biflora* which flowers twice a year. When the famous Glastonbury Abbey was built the hawthorn was moved to its precincts. The stump of the thorn was venerated until 1750 when it was replaced by a stone marker. Grafts have been sent all over the world, including one to Central Park in New York. Every Christmas the blossoms are cut by the mayor of Glastonbury and sent to the Queen's breakfast table, a custom said to have begun during the reign of Queen Anne. A fanatical puritan is said to have tried to cut down the thorn during Cromwell's Commonwealth, but only splintered the trunk. A splinter struck him in the eye and blinded him. Death or injury is said to overtake those who try to cut down holy thorns.

HAZEL

The rod carried by St Nicholas's helpers may relate to Donar (Thor). He carries a hazel wand to punish bad children. The hazel was sacred to Donar, and the hazel rod was a symbol of life and fertility and a protector against evil spirits and lightning, as lightning never strikes a hazel tree. Mary and the baby Jesus are supposed to have found protection under a hazel during a thunder storm.

In Poland, Koljada (Yule) songs were sung from house to house and the singers were rewarded with pastries shaped like goats or cows. If the singers were not rewarded they would play tricks on the misers. One of the company would gently tap the woman of the house with small stick and wish her happiness and health in the coming year, a leave a hazel twig from a bunch he carried, which would later be nailed above the door for good luck. [171]

Bunches of hazel twigs may be used in the Yule decorations, and may also be used as aspergers. The nuts can be used in the decorations, on the tree and in the food for fertility (of all kinds) in the coming year.

HELLEBORE (CHRISTMAS ROSE) *Helleborus sp.*

The Christmas rose is supposed to blossom on Christmas Eve, and in mild winters, it does. In Germany several cities had a 'Christ's Rose Day' during Advent, during which artificial hellebore flowers were sold in the streets to help the poor. [172]

In Christian myth, there is a story of a little shepherd girl who stood weeping outside the stable where Jesus was born because she had no gift for him. A watching angel caused the snow at the little girl's feet to disappear, revealing the Christmas roses which were formed by the angels from each tear of the little shepherdess.

Hellebore is known as the 'oracle flower' as it was used to predict the weather. People would cut twelve flowers of the Christmas rose and place them into a vase. Each flower symbolized one month of the following year. The weather was forecast by the way the flowers opened. Closed flowers represented bad weather and open flowers good weather for that month.

The plant was formerly known by the name of *melampode* after Melampus, a physician of around 1,400 CE. He used hellebore to treat nervous disorders and hysteria. According to the Greek tradition Melampus was originally a herdsman who first realised the properties of hellebore after observing the effects of the herb on his goats. He is said to have later used the

---

171   http://www.slavpaganism.com/beliefs

172   Christian Ratsch and Claudia Muller-Eberling, *Pagan Christmas*, Inner Traditions, Vermont, 2003

milk of the goats that had eaten hellebore to cure mental derangement in the daughters of Proetus, King of Argus.

Once, people blessed their cattle with this plant to keep them from evil spells, and for this purpose, it was dug up with certain mystic rites. In an old French romance, the sorcerer, to make himself invisible when passing through the enemy's camp, scatters powdered hellebore in the air, as he goes.

Hellebore is ruled by the planet Saturn which is called 'the great teacher' and 'the planet of karma'. Saturn rules responsibilities, restrictions and limitations as well as the lessons you must learn in life. Saturn plants have been used for breaking patterns, Hag Goddess rituals, banishing and necromancy. Hellebore can be used in incense and talismans for breaking the patterns and limitations of the past, especially at this time of endings and new beginnings.

NB. *Hellebore is a poisonous herb, so should be used with caution. Taken internally it can cause convulsions and heart failure.*

HOLLY *Ilex aquifolium*
So sacred was the holly tree to our ancestors that in many areas it was given the alternative name 'holy tree'. It is also known as the hulver bush, hulm, holme chase, and the Christ thorn.

The holly's place in the Ogham alphabet is *Tinne*, meaning 'fire'. From it we get the word 'tinder'. It is a dense, stable wood which contains little water and hence will burn when freshly felled. It is associated with thunder gods including Tannus (Gaul), Taran (Pictish) Donar (Germanic) and Thor (Scandinavian). It may be associated with *dann* or *tan* the Celtic word which denotes any sacred tree.

Holly was a decoration at the Roman Saturnalia. The club Saturn carried was made of holly. The Romans would send fresh holly boughs as a greeting to friends at the Saturnalia. In the Roman cult of Bacchus, the holly was paired with the ivy, and houses were decorated with both plants during the Saturnalia. Quintus Tertullian, in the second century CE, forbade the practice as a Pagan custom. However, the practice continued and the church were forced to re-interpret it by saying that the palms that greeted Christ on his entry into Jerusalem sprouted thorns heralding the ordeal he was to be put through, making the holly a Christian symbol of the crown of thorns.

The evergreen leaves and red berries contrast with the bare branches of other trees in winter. Shakespeare wrote:
Heigh-ho! the green holly!
This life is most jolly.

Any plant which bears fruit in winter is especially magical. The flourishing of the holly in the winter death-time led to it being identified with Christ, the white flower emblematic of his purity, the prickles his crown of thorns, and the red berries the drops of his shed blood: *"...of all the trees that are in the woods, the holly bears the crown"* in the words of the old carol. [173]

In the Middle Ages, Christian mythographers decided that St John the Baptist was born at the summer solstice at the time of the weakening sun, announcing his own power would wane with the birth of Christ at the winter solstice, the time of the strengthening sun. [174] John the Baptist is reported to have said of Jesus "He must increase, but I must decrease." [175] John is the only saint whose feast day is celebrated on the day of his birth, rather than his death. Christian scholars incorporated Pagan symbolism into their iconography to associate Christ with the waxing year and John with the waning, represented by the holly and oak respectively, though neither tree had any connection with Christianity or Judaism. It is this Christian myth that gave rise to the modern Pagan ritual of the battle of the Oak King and Holly King at the solstices. This bi-annual fight is reflected in the Arthurian tale of Gawain and the Green Knight, which may well draw on earlier Pagan traditions (see Appendix 3 for the story).

A curious carol, dating from the year 1456, shows that holly was pre-eminent amongst the evergreen decorations of the season:

"Nay, Ivy! nay, it shall not be I wys;
Let Holy hafe the maystry, as the maner ys.
Holy stond in the halle, fayre to behold;
Ivy stond without the dore; she ys full sore a cold.

Holy and hys mery men they dawnsyn and they syng,
Ivy and hur maydenys they wepyn and they wryng.
Ivy hath a kybe (Kybe, chilblain.); she laghtit with the cold,
So mot they all hafe that wyth Ivy hold.

Holy hath berys as red as any rose,
The foster and the hunters kepe hem from the does.

173   John Williamson, *The Oak King, the Holly King and the Unicorn*, Harper and Row, New York, 1986

174   Phillipe Walter, *Christianity, the Origins of a Pagan Religion*, Inner Traditions, Rochester, 2003

175   John, 3:30

Ivy hath berys as black as any slo;
Ther com the oule and ete hem as she go.

Holy hath byrdys, a ful fayre flok,
The Nyghtyngale, the Poppyngy, the gayntyl Lavyrok.
Good Ivy! what byrdys ast thou?
Non but the Howlet, that cryes 'How! how!'"

Many popular superstitions still linger round the use of holly at Christmas. Tradition says that no branch should be cut from a holly tree, but rather that it should be pulled free in a method considered fit for a sacred tree. In Rutland it is deemed unlucky to bring it into a house before Christmas Eve or to allow it to remain after Twelfth Night. To burn Christmas holly on the fire courts disaster before the year is out. In some western counties of England the boughs removed from churches were treasured for luck throughout the year following; and in Germany, they were looked upon as a sure protection against thunder. Folk custom has it that cattle will thrive and sheep produce twins if some holly is hung where they can see it on Christmas Eve. In Scandinavia, people put up holly to celebrate *Jul*, believing it will bring luck to the house.

Sterile holly (holly without berries) was unlucky in decorations and during poor berry year this would be countered by a sprig of ivy, sometimes reddened, in the wreath. In the north of Britain prickly holly leaves are called 'he-holly' and the smooth ones 'she-holly'. An old country saying states that if smooth leafed holly is brought into the house first at Yule-time the wife will rule the household in the coming year, if the prickly holly enters first the husband will rule.

In Somerset 'Holly Riders' with berry-wreathed hats rode around the hill farms singing carols in exchange for cider and pennies on Christmas morning. On Boxing Day there was a peculiar custom called 'holly-beating' when men and boys chased female servants to thrash them on their bare arms with prickly holly. In some places, St Stephen's day (Boxing Day) was actually known as 'Holming (holly) Day'. On New Year's Day, boys visited houses carrying a vessel of freshly drawn spring water and sprinkled the people and houses with a sprig of holly for luck.

Holly was also used for divination at Yule. In the north of Britain a future spouse could be determined by putting three holly leaves, named for the suitors and blessed in the name of the Trinity, under the pillow with the left hand. The first leaf to have turned over in the morning would be the future bridegroom.

Twelfth Night was Holly Night in Brough, Westmoreland. Hone, in his *Table Book* of 1838 gave a description of the festivities. The townspeople prepared a tree, fastening a torch to every branch. About eight o'clock it was taken to a convenient part of the town, where the torches were lit, the town band playing till all was completed. The tree was carried up and down the town in a stately procession which stopped every time they reached the town bridge and the cross, where the 'holly' was greeted with shouts of applause. Many of the inhabitants carried lighted branches and flambeaus. After the tree was thus carried, and the torches sufficiently burnt, it was placed in the middle of the town where it was again cheered by the populace. Then people would seize each end of the tree and endeavour to drag it to one of two inns they were contending for, and once this was accomplished, they would spend a merry night there.

In Germanic myth, the holly probably relates to Frau Holle (also Holde or Holda) the hag associated with winter and the Wild Hunt. In Scotland it was associated with another winter hag, the Cailleach Bheur ('Blue Hag') who brought winter to the highlands. Legends say her face was blue with cold, her hair white as frost and the plaid she wore the colour of winter stubble. Each year after Samhain she strode the moors and mountains smiting the earth with her heavy staff to beat down the grasses and harden the earth with frost. In winter she unleashed tempests and blizzards, but in the spring her power waned as the sap rose, weakening day by day until on the eve of Beltane, she gave up the struggle and flung her staff under a holly tree, where to this day no grass can grow. She stiffened and shrank to a solitary grey stone to wait out the summer.

For magical purposes, gather your holly on the solstice eve at midnight, in the forest and without a light. An offering of your blood or some red wine should be left in return.

It is particularly a tree of the winter solstice, the bright red berries representing the blood and sacrifice of the God, his life and spirit continuing with the evergreens throughout the dark time. Bring some holly indoors as the druids did as a home for the nature spirits during the winter.

The Sun Lord is reborn at the winter solstice after which the days lengthen. The berries also symbolise the sun, light, fire and warmth. It is no accident that the holly's totem bird, the red breasted robin, is depicted on Christmas cards. In Celtic lore the robin is one of the birds which gave the gift of fire to humankind, bringing a flaming branch from the sun. In doing so the robin was burned and its Welsh name *bronrhuddyn* means 'singed breast'. Offerings were placed out for the robin at Yuletide to ensure luck for the coming year.

The holly is a masculine tree and a tree of warrior magic and spiritual strength, protecting the new-born sun child until he grows to manhood. Holly was used in the making of spear shafts, imparting its masculine vigour and potent life force.

IVY *Hedera helix*

Ivy is an evergreen plant which begins to grow on the ground but which then climbs the nearest tree in a spiral fashion (*helix* is Greek for 'spiral'). This associates the plant with the sun, since the path of the sun during the year is a spiral one, depicted as such on monuments such as Newgrange. Any plant with a spiral growth pattern was thus considered a plant of immortality sacred to death and resurrection gods such as Dionysus and Osiris. As a symbol of rebirth, ivy it was carried in a basket representing Bacchus. In Christian allegory it symbolised the eternal life and the resurrection of Christ.

Church ivy saved from Christmas was fed to ewes to induce the conception of spring lambs. In Shropshire, children with whooping cough drank from ivy wood cups cut at the correct hour and phase of the moon. Wreaths of ivy with rowan and woodbine were placed near milk containers to protect the contents from invading sprits. An ivy leaf placed in water on New Year's Eve that was still be fresh on Twelfth Night meant that the year ahead would be favourable.

While the holly was considered a male plant, the clinging ivy was female ('holly be a man and ivy a girl' according to an old saying). A carol dating to the reign of Henry VI suggests that while holly was used as an indoor decoration, ivy was only used outside. In some old English Christmas carols holly and ivy are put into a curious antagonism, apparently connected with a battle of the sexes as in this fifteenth century example:

Holly and Ivy made a great party,
Who should have the mastery,
In landës where they go.

Then spoke Holly, 'I am free and jolly,
I will have the mastery,
In landës where we go.'

Then spake Ivy, 'I am lov'd and prov'd,
And I will have the mastery,
In landës where we go.'

Then spake Holly, and set him down on his knee,
'I pray thee, gentle Ivy,
Say me no villainy,
In landës where we go.'"

The red-berried holly, symbolizing light, warmth and light, was meant to prevail over the black-fruited ivy which signified the dark and cold of winter. One of the best known carols is the *Holly and the Ivy*, which has long been a traditional song for Christmas. In some traditions the Holly-boy and Ivy-girl take part in competitive games, playing forfeits with the singing of songs.

The ivy and the grape vine are often intermingled in myth, both having the power to change the consciousness. The chewing of ivy leaves can induce a temporary altered state. The ivy and vine are sometimes seen as partners and sometimes as enemies; whereas the vine releases mental and physical inhibitions the ivy facilitates an inward journey. During the Bacchanalian revels of Thrace and Thessaly, which took place in October, the drunken Bassarids, wreathed in ivy and carrying fir branches would rampage in the mountains in honour of Bacchus/ Dionysus, the ivy-wreathed vine god, (who was also called *Kisso* or 'ivy god') tearing animals and sometimes people apart in their intoxication, which was probably induced by spruce ale and magic mushrooms (fly agaric) which grow under fir trees. In folk belief, ivy could bring on madness or intoxication without drinking. Plutarch thought that when mixed with wine, ivy could bring about the kind of delirium usually only seen with the hallucinogenic henbane. Orpheus too was supposedly torn to pieces by the Bassairds, who had drunk a concoction of ivy and toadstool. In England the ivy bush was the sign of a tavern and ivy ale is a potent drink, stilled brewed at Trinity College.

The ivy is a symbol of life and rebirth as it remains green throughout the winter, and for its spiral growth. The spiral growth is symbolic of the path of the sun which is represented by the labyrinth or life-maze, spiralling inwards towards death and rebirth at the centre and outwards into new life. It teaches the lesson of sacrifice: the old self must be left behind or 'die' before a spiritual rebirth can take place.

The holly and ivy are both associated with the Roman Saturnalia which took place at the winter solstice. The holly was Saturn's club and ivy made the nest of his totem bird, the wren. On midwinter morning the first person over the threshold had to be Saturn's representative, a dark man, known as the Holly Boy. Women had to be kept out of the way.

Use ivy in your Yule decorations and wreaths. It can be twined with holly to symbolise the balance of God and Goddess, male and female, light and dark, summer and winter. A wand twined with ivy can be used to tap the trunks of wassailed fruit trees.

JUNIPER

The juniper bush is very widely distributed in the northern hemisphere from North America to south-west Asia, and from Siberia to the Mediterranean. It is a small tree or shrub which grows best on poor soil. The bark is reddish-brown in colour and the leaves are sharp pointed needles, usually about a third of an inch long, which grow in whorls of three. The male and female cones grow in the axils of the needles and usually on separate trees. The male cones are solitary, yellow, cylindrical and very small. The slightly larger female cones are greenish and globular. They take between two to three years to ripen into the blue-black berry-like fruits. Juniper 'berries' need to be crushed and ground for use; they are added to sauces, especially for game dishes, and are used to flavour bread and cakes. They are well known as the flavour in gin, and in mediaeval times they were used to flavour whisky in Scotland.

In European countries the juniper is associated with purification and healing. In Scotland, young men after sunset on Hogmanay (New Year) would go over the hills and return with juniper and dry it by the fire overnight. A member of the household was sent to collect water from the 'dead and living ford'. Next morning everyone would drink some water and the rest would be sprinkled around the house to purify it. All the windows and doors were then blocked and the house was then fumigated with the burning juniper. In Transylvania, Germany and the Alps, juniper was used at the Epiphany to drive out disease and evil things, and the initials of the three kings were written on the doors as an extra protection. Juniper was used in a purification ceremony in the Vogtland and Saxon Erzgebirge when young men 'beat' women and virgins with juniper rods.

Juniper was a symbol of the Canaanites' fertility goddess Ashera or Astarte in Syria. In the Old Testament, a juniper bush sheltered the prophet Elijah from Queen Jezebel's pursuit. Similarly a later apocryphal tale tells of how the holy family were hidden from King Herod's soldiers by a juniper during their flight into Egypt.

Juniper berries have a variety of medicinal properties, principally as an aid digestion and for various stomach ailments. In an Egyptian papyrus dating back to 1500 BCE there is a recipe utilising juniper to cure tapeworm infestations. The Romans used the berries for purification and stomach ailments, while the mediaeval English herbalist Culpepper recommended them the treatment of flatulence amongst other conditions.

Juniper was burned for its aromatic smoke, rather than its heat. In ancient times it was used for the ritual purification of temples. In central Europe juniper smoke was used in the spring-time cleansing and casting out of witchcraft, and during plague outbreaks. In Switzerland, hospital wards were fumigated with juniper smoke. In Germany, the smoke was believed to help asthma, rheumatism, depression and lunacy. Also in Switzerland, farmers put milk through juniper sieves to preserve its freshness.

The principle uses of juniper are in healing and purification rituals. It is an important incense plant, and the blossom pollen of juniper flowers was called 'blossom smoke'. Juniper banishes negativity and attracts healthy energies. It was believed to protect people from evil spirits, witches and demons. In England, the berries were used at burials to keep away devils. It is used particularly at the pivotal points in the wheel, at the New Year to drive out the old year, and at Yule the time of new life and rebirth. At Yule, all the participants in the ritual are smudged with juniper smoke, and your home should be cleansed with it and blessed to prepare it for the coming year.

MISTLETOE *Viscum album*

Mistletoe is an evergreen, woody parasite growing on the branches of trees, mainly apple and pear, but occasionally on ash, hawthorn and oak trees. It is native to Europe, North Africa and central and western Asia. It may form a bush of up to 5 ft. It has numerous branching stems. The leaves are leathery and lance-shaped. It forms its greenish flowers in threes between February and April; they appear both at the tip of the year's growth at its joints with the growth of the previous year. As soon as the flowering is over the buds form for the next year. These are followed in October by the greenish-white berries which do not become fully ripe until December.

In Cornish, its name is *ughelvarr*; in Breton *uhelvarr*; in Welsh, *uchelwydd*, all meaning 'high branch' signifying its growing habit or perhaps even its high status. In Irish, it is *uil-ioc,* meaning 'all heal'. In Anglo-Saxon it was *mistiltan*, from *tan* meaning 'twig' and *mistl* meaning 'different' from its habit of growing on other trees. The missel thrush is said to be so called from feeding on its berries.

The mistletoe was considered a potent magical plant because it did not grow on the earth, but on the branches of a tree in a 'place between places'. It grows into a ball, imitating the sun, and the leaves are fresh and green all year long, making it a plant of immortality and life surviving in the dead time. The berries ripen in December as though it is not affected by the seasons and the winter cold.

Pliny said that the mistletoe was one of the most important magical plants of the Celts and served as a symbol for the winter solstice. He recorded that the druids called mistletoe by a name which meant 'all healing'. They made preparation for sacrifice and a banquet beneath the trees and brought forth two white bulls whose horns were bound for the first time. Robed in white the druid ascended the tree and cut the mistletoe with a golden sickle (probably gilded bronze in actuality) and it was caught by others in a white cloak. The bulls were then killed with prayers. The berries are white and sticky and were associated with semen from the cosmic bull which impregnated the earth.

In Germanic myth, the mistletoe was sacred to Donar, the thunder and lightning god. In German, the plant was called *Donnerbesen* or 'thunder broom'. The Christians demonised it as a plant of the witches, calling it *hexennest* ('witch nest') or *teufelbesen* ('devil's broom').[176]

In Norse mythology the mistletoe was used to slay the sun god Balder. One day, Odin discovered Hel was preparing for Balder's arrival in the Underworld and the Vala prophesied that he would have a child with Rinda the earth goddess who would be called Vali and would avenge Balder's death. The gods persuaded everything on earth to swear not to harm Balder, except the mistletoe growing on the oak at the gate of Valhalla as it was thought that such a puny plant could not harm him. The gods amused themselves by casting harmless darts at Balder. Loki, god of fire, was jealous of Balder and made a shaft from the mistletoe and tricked Hodur, the blind and dark brother of Balder, into throwing it and killing him.

Odin sent Hermod to ask Hel for Balder's return and she agreed, on condition that all things should weep. All did, except Thok, a giantess, who may have been Loki in disguise, so Balder had to stay in the Underworld. In due course, Vali was born and on the same day, slew Hodur.

This is obviously a seasonal myth relating to the winter solstice. The sun (Balder) is killed by the darkness (Hodur). Vali's revenge is the breaking forth of new life after the winter darkness. The tears symbolise the spring thaw, when everything drips with moisture. Thok ('Coal') alone refuses to weep as she is buried deep in the earth and does not need the light of the sun. After Balder had been resurrected, owing to the pleadings of the other gods and goddesses, the mistletoe was given into the keeping of Frigga, the goddess of love, and it was ordained that anyone who passed beneath the mistletoe should receive a kiss to show that it had become a symbol of peace and love.

176   Christian Ratsch et al, *Pagan Christmas,* Inner Traditions, Vermont, 2006

In Greek myth, Ixion murdered his prospective father in law, but Zeus purified him and invited him to eat. Ixion planned to seduce Zeus's wife Hera but got drunk and Zeus was able to deceive him with a cloud shaped like the goddess. Zeus walked in on their lovemaking and ordered Hermes to whip him and then bind him to a fiery wheel which rolled without cease through the sky. According to Robert Graves (*The Greek Myths*) Ixion's name from *ischys* ('strength') and *io* (moon) suggests *ixias* ('mistletoe') speculating that he was an oak king with mistletoe genitals representing a thunder god virtually married to the rain making goddess of the moon then scourged so his blood and sperm fructified the earth. On an Etruscan mirror, Ixion is shown spread-eagled to a fire wheel, recalling the solar cross which represents the four stations of the sun in the year, the solstices and equinoxes.

The name of the Roman god of healing Aesculapius means 'that which hangs from the esculent oak' associating the mistletoe with healing. Though the berries of the mistletoe are toxic, the leaves and stems of the mistletoe have been used in herbal medicine. European mistletoe contains eleven proteins and substances called lectins which are currently being investigated for anti-cancer effects.

The Roman writer Virgil (in the *Aeneid*) compared the Golden Bough in the underworld to the mistletoe, saying the plant was not unknown in the religious ceremonies of the ancients, particularly the Greeks. The Golden Bough was a tree branch with golden leaves that enabled the Trojan hero Aeneas to travel through the underworld safely. It was sacred to Proserpina (Persephone), the queen of the dead. Two doves lead him to an oak tree that sheltered the bough of shimmering golden leaves.

Ancient Babylonian legend regarded mistletoe as a divine branch from heaven which was grafted to earthly trees.

Though other evergreens were included in the decorations of churches, mistletoe was the one omission, being considered a Pagan plant. The exception was at York, where on the eve of Christmas Day mistletoe was carried to the high altar of the cathedral and a general pardon and season of peace was proclaimed.

Because the evergreen mistletoe bears its fruit in winter, it is an emblem of fertility. In Swabia, people bound mistletoe to fruit trees during winter in the hope that it would ensure a good fruit harvest. In Austria people put mistletoe in the bedroom to ensure the conception of a child. In Switzerland, it was included in the bridal bouquets to ensure a good marriage.

The mistletoe formed the 'kissing bough' and often still does. There was a tradition that that the maid who was not kissed under it, at Christmas, would not be married in that coming year. [177] With each kiss, a berry had to be plucked off for luck. This seems to have been a purely English custom, though in Lower Austria a pine wreath was hung from the ceiling, while a masked figure hid in a dark corner. Known as 'Sylvester', he had a flaxen beard and a wreath of mistletoe. If a youth or maiden happened to pass under the pine wreath, Sylvester sprang out and imprinted a rough kiss. When midnight came he was driven out as the representative of the old year.[178]

Many traditions associate the mistletoe with the New Year, rather than Christmas. In West Shropshire tradition, the bough was not to be put up until New Year's Eve. Worcestershire farmers gave their Christmas mistletoe to the first cow to calve in the new year to bring luck to the dairy. At New Year, the first person to enter a house should carry a sprig of mistletoe in one hand and a sprig of evergreen in the other. Until quite recently in some rural areas farmers would burn a globe made of mistletoe and hawthorn or blackthorn in the New Year. The ashes would then be thrown onto the field that was to be ploughed first.

At midwinter the berries are ripe and should be cut. Mistletoe berries are used at the midwinter solstice in rituals to give strength to the weakened sun. Mistletoe is seen as a herb of fertility, as the berries represent the semen of the Bull of Heaven. It is a symbol of rebirth.

Mistletoe can be used as a sacrifice to the Underworld aspect of Cerridwen in return for her giving birth to the midwinter solstice sun. Hang over the doorway at Yule, tied with red ribbon for harmony and to represent a welcome to all who visit, all year round. Replace at the next Yule, burning the old piece in the Yule fire to burn away the old and welcome the new.

MUGWORT *Artemisia vulgaris*

Mugwort is an aromatic, perennial herb that grows to a height of between 2 - 4 ft. It is native to Europe and most of temperate regions of the northern hemisphere. It can be found growing along roadsides in hedgerows and on waste ground. The stems are erect, angular and branching. The leaves are lance-shaped, smooth above, whitish and downy, From July to September the small pinkish flowers bloom in flat, oval groups on long spikes at the end of the stems.

In Germany, mugwort was used to season roasts on the first day of Christmas. It is a herb with an ancient history and was found in large

---

177   Thomas K. Hervey, *The Book of Christmas*, The Folklore Society, 1888

178   Clement A. Miles, *Christmas in Ritual and Tradition*, Christian and Pagan, T. Fisher Unwin, 1912

142

quantities in the Ice Age caves of Lascaux, probably left by reindeer hunters 17,000 years ago. [179]

Mugwort gets it generic name *artemisia* from the fact that it is supposedly good for female complaints. It was sacred to Artemis the Greek goddess of the moon and childbirth. The herb is first mentioned by Pliny who recommended it for 'women's troubles'. Hippocrates and Discorides also recommended it for the same purpose. It was sacred to the northern love goddess Freya, and German women held a price of mugwort in their hands while giving birth.

It was also sacred to the German birth goddess Holla (Frau Holle) who helped the child make the transition into this world. For the same reason, mugwort was also used on graves and bonfires to help the soul pass from this world into the next.

At the Yuletide season it can be used in incense to mark the birth of the Child of Light.

MYRRH *Commiphora myrrha*
Myrrh is obtained from stout bushes which grow to a maximum height of around 9 ft. They are native to North Africa and Asia. The branches are knotted in appearance with smaller angular branchlets which end in a sharp spine. The oval leaves cover the bushes sparsely. The bark contains ducts, and due to the breakdown as tissue between them, large cavities are formed. These become filled with a granular secretion which released freely when the bark is wounded or from natural fissures. This is a pale yellow liquid at first which hardens into a reddish brown gum resin. The name 'myrrh' is derived from the old Arabic word *mur* which means 'bitter'.

Myrrh has been known and used since ancient times and is referred to in an Egyptian papyrus dated 2000 BCE. It was a funeral herb for the Egyptians, used in the embalming process and burnt it as incense during the funeral rites. It is mentioned in the Bible. In the Song of Solomon myrrh is compared to the joys of sexual love. In the gospel of Matthew it features as one of the gifts of the Wise Men to the infant Jesus.

Myrrh is associated with death and mourning. The tree itself seems to weep and the secretion is bitter. It is widely used in incenses, including those of the Catholic Church. Myrrh incense is used at funeral rites and may be employed at to mark the death of the God. Myrrh raises the vibrations and increases spiritual awareness.

179   Christian Ratsch et al, *Pagan Christmas,* Inner Traditions, Vermont, 2006

PEA

A pea is placed in the Twelfth Night cake to choose the queen of the revels, just as a bean is used to choose the king.

In German myth, peas belonged to the fairies during the Twelve Nights, and if a person ate one, it would bring bad luck. Pea fields were haunted by wild women (fairies) with long hair who would try to enchant young men who wandered there.

Peas were used in German love magic – if you put a pod containing nine peas behind a door, the next person who comes in will be compelled to utter the name of your future bridegroom. The pea was sacred to Donar (Thor) the god of marriage and was associated with fertility. Peas were thrown to animals on Christmas night to make them fertile. [180]

PENNYROYAL

According to Pliny the Elder: "On the day of the winter solstice, pennyroyal blossoms are hanging underneath the roof to dry, and the bubbles they produce – that are filled with air – burst".

PINE *Pinus sp. Pinus sylvestris,*

Pine trees occur in the mountains of Southern Europe, the Scottish Highlands and form a vast belt of forest land from across Siberia and Russia into Sweden and Norway and in former ages it spread over the lowlands of Denmark, England and Ireland. There are around one hundred and fifty species of pine but the Scots pine (*Pinus sylvestris*) is Britain's only native conifer. It can grow to a height of up to 120 ft. It acquires its characteristic flat top with age. The leaves are blue-grey or blue-green needles, which often grow in pairs. The male cones are small, yellow and rounded, clustered near the tips of the shoots in early summer. The female cones are globular and pink when fertilised. It is often used in reforestation, and also in erosion control. Scots pine is very resistant to urban pollution but prone to parasitic diseases.

Poets have often noted how the rising sun lights up the distant pines with silver. Wordsworth (*Stanzas composed in the Simplon Pass*) commented:
"My thoughts become bright like yon edging of Pines
On the steep's lofty verge: how it blacken'd the air!
But, touched from behind by the sun, it now shines,
With threads that seem part of his own silver hair."

The pine is associated with the slain and risen god. The vegetation god Attis castrated himself beneath the sacred tree of the goddess Cybele and bled

180   Christian Ratsch, *Pagan Christmas*, Inner Traditions, Vermont, 2006

to death; his body became a pine tree. The Romans honoured him on the Day of Blood (at the spring equinox) which was preceded by a pine tree carried into the temple of Cybele. This was carried by the Guild of Tree Bearers who hung a model of Attis, swathed it in woollen bands, from its boughs, and decorated it with violets. A wine was brewed from the seeds of the stone pine and used in the orgiastic rites of Cybele. The ancient Egyptians buried an image of the god Osiris in the hollowed-out centre of a pine tree.

Pine was often the World Tree, or tree of immortality. For the Phrygians the pine was the most sacred tree and representative of eternal life from its evergreen nature. An ancient Chaldean epic of 2000 BCE tells the story of Izdubar, a mighty hunter who visited the land of the pine trees, the seat of the gods and the sanctuary of the angels. "In front of the seed of the pine tree carried its fruit, good was its shadow, full of pleasure an excellent tree, the choice of the forest." [181] This was the black pine of Eridhu, the Tree of Life.

The pine tree was also sacred to Dionysus, another god who died and was resurrected. He is usually depicted as carrying a pine wand. His worshippers at Corinth were commanded to worship a particular pine tree 'equally with the god'. Masks of Dionysus were hung from a pine tree in the middle of the vineyard and turned in the wind, fructifying wherever they looked.

The pine's association with death and immortality is reflected in its use at funerals. An old custom was to place pine boughs on the coffin. At Orthodox Jewish funerals pine is the only wood allowed to be used for the coffin. The Chinese plant pine on graves to strengthen the spirit of the departed and keep the remains from decay. In the Highlands they were used to mark burial places of warriors, heroes and chieftains.

Dionysus carried a pinecone-tipped wand as a fertility symbol and the image of the pine cone has also been found on ancient amulets as a symbol of fertility. The pine cone is formed in a spiral growth pattern, and because of this and its phallic shape it is a symbol of rebirth and fertility of the Vegetation God. The cone is sometimes called the 'tree egg' (representing the egg from which the world hatched) and tops the fertility wand. Because of its power of rebirth and its phallic cones the pine is a tree of fertility. Pine cones were cast into the vaults of Demeter, along with pigs and other fertility symbols, to quicken the earth and the wombs of women. In Russia brides are traditionally given a decorated pine bough at spring marriages.

---

181   George Smith, *The Chaldean Account of Genesis*, 1876 at www.sacred-texts.com

Pan, the god of wild nature, had a sacred grove of pines on Mænalus, a mountain in Arcadia. Virgil wrote *'always has a vocal grove and shaking pines; he ever hears, the loves of shepherds, and Pan, the first who suffered not the reeds to be neglected.'*

Pine is a popular Christmas tree species because it grows to 6 feet in only eight years. It honours the death and resurrection god, and our own hopes of healing, fertility and immortality. The resin, needles and wood from the pine are used to invoke the god and to cleanse the sacred space. A reddish-yellow dye is obtained from the pine cones and used to dye robes. Pine may be used as an incense or bathing herb when working on becoming at one with the cycles of life, the ebb and flow of energy and accepting your self within it. Pine teaches how to let go of guilt and restrictive ideas.

Pine has many healing uses and was first investigated by Hippocrates, the father of Western medicine, for its benefits to the respiratory system. During the 1800s, tar from the pine was used in many medicines, especially for skin diseases like eczema and psoriasis. The needles were made into a stuffing called 'pine wool' that was thought to repel lice, fleas, and other pests.

ROSEMARY *Rosmarinus officinalis*

Rosemary is a hardy, evergreen perennial that grows to a height of 3 to 6 ft. It is native to the Mediterranean region but cultivated throughout the world. The stalkless leaves are leathery, needle-like and bright green, glossy above and silvery below. The pink, mauve, blue or white flowers (depending on the variety) grow on spikes at the top of the small branches in June and July. The flowers are followed by small, brown and oily seeds. It is said to grow better and smell sweeter in Britain than anywhere else in the world.

In Greek lore, rosemary was the daughter of the sun, Leukothoe who was changed into a plant after she incestuously seduced her father.

Rosemary is a revered ceremonial herb symbolizing remembrance, friendship and fidelity. It was thrown into, or placed on graves.

Pliny wrote that "its leaves smell like incense" and the French called it *incensier*, using it to purify the air, even in hospitals. At the winter solstice, the Berber tribes of Morocco used rosemary incense. Romans burned it on graves and dedicated it to the household gods.

In Germany it was dedicated to Faru Holle, and there was a legend that on Christmas Eve, at midnight, all water was changed to wine and all trees to rosemary.[182]

---

182   Christian Ratsch et al, *Pagan Christmas,* Inner Traditions, Vermont, 2006

A legend claims the flowers were originally white, only changing to blue when Mary, on the flight from Egypt, threw her blue cloak over a bush, changing its colour at the same time as giving it its distinctive fragrance. A variation of this legend says when the Holy Family fled to Egypt, they stopped to rest on a hillside, by a little stream where Mary washed the baby's clothes and spread them over a rosemary bush to dry. For its humble service, the plant was named rosemary, and God rewarded it with delicate blossoms of the same heavenly blue as Mary's robe.

Rosemary is a cleansing herb and repels negativity. According to medieval legends, rosemary decorating the altar at Christmas time brings special blessings to the recipients and protection against evil spirits. The wassail bowl has a sprig of rosemary in token of remembrance and it garnished the boar's head at the Christmas feast. Use it in the Yule incense and decorations and in the ritual bath, and to stir the wassail bowl or ritual cup.

ROWAN *Sorbus aucuparia*

The rowan is a member of the *Rosacea* – or rose – family, which is characterised by its pomme fruits. The rowan, white beam and service trees form a sub-genus known as *Sorbus*, all having small white flowers arranged in clusters. Rowans are native to Europe, including Britain, and the western portions of Asia, and grow across the northern hemisphere. The rowan is usually seen as a solitary specimen throughout woodlands or scattered in rocky and mountainous regions. For this reason, and because of a similarity of the leaves, it is sometimes called the mountain ash, though is not related to the true ashes (*Fraxinus* sp.).

In Scotland the rowan seems to have been the Tree of Life. Such trees stood at the sacred centre (often also the geographical centre) of a place, connecting it to the realms of above and below, as well as the four directions. Kings were crowned there, and all important decisions made under the auspices of the tree, giving them the authority of the Otherworld as well as this one. There were strong taboos in the Highlands against the use of any parts of the tree save the berries, except for ritual purposes.

In Germany country people would place burning candles in the branches of all the rowan trees on Christmas Eve at midnight. Rowan was associated with Thor (one of the important Yuletide gods), the red berries a sign of thunder. Rowan is said to protect against lightning as it is never struck by it, which may account for its connection with the thunder god in Northern Traditions. In Scandinavian mythology, Thor was trying to get to the land of the Frost Giants when an evil sorcerer caused the River Vimur to overflow just as he was trying to ford it. A rowan tree bent down so that he could grasp it and scramble to safety; consequently the rowan became known as 'Thor's helper' or 'Thor's tree'. Sometimes, the rowan is said to have sprung from a lightening strike, and to embody the lightening. [183]

In the ogham system, rowan is *Luis*, a peasant tree associated with birth and protection. By different authorities, its gender given as male or female. Its planetary ruler is the Sun and its associated element is fire.

SPRUCE *Picea sp.- Picea abies* (Norway spruce), *Picea mariana* (Black spruce)

Spruce is a member of the pine family but spruces differ from the pines, larches and cedars in that their leaves are arranged singly in a spiral along elongated shoots, and not tufted or grouped on lateral dwarf shoots. Their seeds ripen in a single year. The cones hang downwards after fertilization, from five to seven inches long and from an inch and a half to two inches broad. Spruces are found in Europe, North America and as far east as Asia.

Spruce resin is a valuable substance. The bark, when cut, oozes as a fine yellow turpentine, known as spruce rosin or even 'frankincense'. The genus name of spruce is *Picea* from the Latin name for the pitch pine; from *pix* or *picis* referring to the black sticky pitch that the Romans made by boiling down pine resin. This may come from the Proto-Indo-European root *pi* or *pa* meaning fat, resin, or sticky material. This is useful for making torches and for use in incense.

The spruce is cultivated for timber and Christmas trees. It has been the most popular Yule tree since the nineteenth century.

YEW *Taxus baccata*

The yew is found from Ireland to the Caucasus in north Iran, North Africa and the Himalayas. It is native to Britain, re-establishing itself after the Ice Age. The earliest yew fossil is 200 million years old. Unlike most conifers, the yew is deciduous and there are male and female trees. The male yew has tiny cones that bear pollen in the spring, disturbed by the slightest breeze. The flower is small, fleshy disc with a single ovule in the centre from which the red berry-like aril grows that bears the seed which is eaten and spread by birds.

The yew's success is due to its ability to regenerate itself, and for this reason it was called 'the tree of immortality'. The branches root in the earth forming widening circles of new trees. Many yews are thousands of years old. It is said that there is no natural reason why the yew should die - the decaying tree puts forth new life. When the yew is over 30 ft in girth, the heart wood

183   T.F. Thistleton Dyer, *The Folklore of Plants*, Chatto and Windus, 1889

148

is exposed to the elements and starts to rot away. Being hollow makes it more flexible and wind resistant. An aerial root may appear inside the trunk. Yews can also encase its dead wood in a sheath of new growth - new wood grows over the old, giving a gnarled appearance. Thus it appears immortal, regenerating from decay. The tree can even survive a fire. Even when slabs are cut off to make items, the tree can close all such wounds. The Hittite word for yew was *eya* which may relate to the Sanskrit *ayu* meaning 'energy' or 'life force'. [184]

In ancient times, yews were planted around burial mounds barrows. Trees to the east and west of a church were often planted in the Celtic period and aligned with the rising and setting sun.

The Norse god Ullr ('Glorious One'), stepson of Thor, is associated with the yew. He lived in a yew vale and was an archer making his bows from the yew tree. He seems to have been a god of winter and ruled Asgard while Odin was absent for the winter months, which may associate him with Sagittarius the Archer. Odin would return and drive him away and be greeted with rejoicing as he bestowed gifts on mankind. Ullr took refuge in the far north, or some say, the Underworld. He was also a god of death and rode in the Wild Hunt.

The yew was used at Christmas. The church did not celebrate Christ' birth till 353 CE and the winter solstice was not chosen till mid fourth century when it was deliberately conflated with the births of Osiris, Dionysus, Mithras, Balder etc., all gods of light. The yew sometimes furnished the Yule log, of which a piece was saved to be burned at Candlemas, and some saved for the next Yule. The Yule log represents the vegetation god who is reborn. Possibly there was an ancient Yule cult of the yew with its flame-like berries.

The Northern Tradition world tree Yggdrasil is often described as an evergreen ash. The alternative name for yew in Norse is *barraskr* meaning 'needle ash', leading some to conclude that Yggdrasil was a yew, rather than an ash.[185] The name is translated as 'horse of Odin, Yggr being one of Odin's names. The Old Norse for yew is *yr* so it may mean 'yew column'.[186] Yggdrasil binds together the three realms. It suffers from continual decay, but renews itself, like the yew. Odin the secret of the runes while hanging on Yggdrasil. The yew contains an alkaloid which is a powerful hallucinogen. On

184   Ananad Chetan and Diana Brueton, *The Sacred Yew,* Penguin Arkana, London, 1994

185   Gabriel Turville-Petrie, *Myth and Religion of the North,* Holt, Rinehart and Winston, New York, 1964

186   Quoted in Ananad Chetan and Diana Brueton, *The Sacred Yew,* Penguin Arkana, London, 1994

warm days, it emits a gas that lingers in the shade of the tree which has been known to cause people to hallucinate. Nigel Pennick reports that yew potions may have been prepared for shamanic use.[187] Yew is lethal, so a great deal of skill would have been required. Yggdrasil's roots extend into the underworld, the world of spirits.

The yew was one of the five magical trees of Ireland descried as 'the renown of Banbha' (the Crone or Death aspect of the Goddess), 'the spell of knowledge' and 'the king's wheel'. Every ancient Irish king wore a yew brooch in the shape of a wheel to remind him of the turning of the life's wheel and the inevitability of death.

The yew is a tree of death, but one which promises regeneration from that death. The yew may also be counted as a tree of the Nameless Day before the rebirth of the sun at Yule. The Celts regarded the sun that rose on the day before the solstice as a 'shadow sun', the real sun being imprisoned by Arawn, King of the Underworld. In a year of thirteen lunar months of twenty eight days there is a day left over, a Nameless Day, a time of chaos, a crack between the worlds.

---

187   Nigel Pennick, *Rune Magic*, Aquarian Press, London, 1992

Chapter 10
ANIMALS OF YULE

BEAR

The bear hibernates in the winter, entering a cave or some quiet, secluded place. It emerges in the spring, with the female often having given birth in the meantime, and appearing with cubs in tow. This led to the bear being associated with regeneration and rebirth, adopted as a solar symbol. The ancients believed that the sun sickened as the winter progressed, getting weaker and weaker as the hours of daylight diminished. Finally, at the winter solstice (the shortest day) it died and went into the underworld. At dawn it was reborn, emerging from the womb of the Mother Earth via a cave mouth, then growing stronger with each passing day. Many sun gods are said to have been born in a cave at this time. It seems likely that Arthur was originally a sun/bear god, with the solstice being called *Alban Arthur* or 'Arthur's Time' by modern Druids.

The Celts certainly venerated the bear, and had several bear gods and goddesses. The words *art* and *artos* or *math* and *matus* mean 'bear' in the various Celtic languages. Thus we find the goddess Andarta ('Powerful Bear'), the Gaulish bear god was Artaios, worshipped at Beaucroissant and Arduinna, who gave her name to the Ardennes. She was a deity of hunting in the manner of the Greek Artemis. The goddess Artio ('Bear') was venerated in Switzerland, worshipped by the Helvetian tribe near Bern (which also means 'bear') and a bear still appears on the city's coat of arms. He protected wayfarers.

Bears are rarely represented in Celtic art, and when they are, they are usually connected with burial goods. Jet amulets in the form of bears were found in northern Britain from the Romano-Celtic period, one was buried with a child at Malton in Yorkshire, and another at Bootle in Lancashire.[188] The bear

---

188   Miranda Green, *Animals in Celtic Life and Myth,* Routledge, London, 1992

seems to have been considered a protective spirit in the Otherworld realms of dreams and death.

The bear cult may be the oldest religion in existence, featuring in the lore of all the countries of the north and probably far older than the type of shamanism of the cave temple period, which is reflected in the cave paintings of France and Spain. Alpine grottoes have been discovered, dating from around 100,000 BCE, which contain cave bear skulls and ceremonial hearths.[189]

To the Greeks and Romans the bear was the figure of motherly compassion. The Greeks and Romans referred to the bear only in the feminine gender. Ancient writers believed that the mother bear continually licked her little cub until it took shape, from which we derive the saying 'licked into shape'.

The constellation of the Great Bear is known in Wales as 'Arthur's Wain' (Arthur's wagon). The seven main stars of the Great Bear look rather like an old fashioned plough with a crooked handle. The right hand side of the plough has two stars that point to the pole star Polaris, the last star in the tail of the Little Bear, and these are called 'the Pointers'. The Pole Star was used as an aid to navigation by travellers on both sea and land as the nearest star to the celestial 'north pole', around which all the constellations appear to turn. Bears can lumber along on all fours, or stand up on their hind feet and gesture with their front paws. Ursa Major, in its travels throughout the heavens, seems to run along on all fours nearest the horizon and then rises to its hind feet to begin the ascent back into the sky.[190] *"The celestial bear prowls around the pole, performs a seasonal death, and returns to life when the world does…By dying, the celestial bear lives forever."*[191]

To the Norse people the Pole star was a place of secrets and mysterious powers. Many arctic peoples believed that the bear constellation Ursa Major was the point of entry to the Upper world. The Bear stars had guided peoples up north and the Pole star was their still centre of the universe. Ursa Major was seen as a great source of celestial powers. She was the image of the source of life.[192]

Some believed that Ursa Major is the Cosmic Elk cow with Ursa Minor as her calf, and that the Elk ran out of the Heavenly Taiga and carried off the Sun on one of her antlers. These beliefs are rooted in hunting societies of great

189   Joseph Campbell, *The Way of Animal Powers*, Harper and Row, New York, 1988

190   Julius D.W. Staal, *The New Patterns in the Sky* Macdonald and Woodward, 1988

191   Dr E.C.Krupp, *Beyond the Blue Horizon*, Oxford University Press, Oxford, 1991

192   Monica Sjöö, *The Norse Goddess*, Dor Dama Press, 2000.

age in Siberia and elsewhere. Finnish tradition has a story whereby the Bear (or Human-Bear) Hunter chases the Stag that steals the sun in order return it.

Following the Great Bear is the constellation of Boötes, the herdsman, with its brightest star Arcturus meaning 'Bear Keeper', a star held sacred by the Celts. When it first rises over the eastern horizon in January, it is a sign that spring is on its way. Arcturus is known as 'The One who Comes', rising not long after the winter solstice each year, just as Arthur is known as the 'Once and Future King' who sleeps until the day of his promised return. The Celtic goddess Brighid was styled 'daughter of the bear', because her spring festival of Imbolc follows the rebirth of the sun and rising of Arcturus.

BEE

In Scotland, it was believed that on Christmas morning, all bees will leave their hives, swarm, and then return. In the north of England they were said to assemble on Christmas Eve and hum a Christmas hymn.

BOAR

Boars were officially hunted in October, the fall of the year, associating them with dissolution and death, and the turning of the season into winter. In many legends it is a wild boar that kills the summer vegetation god: in Egyptian myth Osiris, lover of the goddess Isis; in Greek myth Adonis, the lover of the goddess Aphrodite; while in Irish myth a boar slew Diarmuid, lover of Grainne.

Though pork or boar was the favourite meat of the Celts it was not part of their everyday diet, but seems to have been reserved for special feasts, especially winter festivals. In Scotland, it was rarely eaten, and some tribes would not eat it at all. This may have been because of its association with death and the underworld; joints of pork were buried with nobles for use in the afterlife. The first herd of pigs was a gift from Arawn, the king of the Underworld. There are many accounts of pork being served at feasts in the Otherworld, with magical beasts being killed, roasted, eaten and found alive the next morning. The 'good god' Dagda carried two pigs, one alive and one roasted, which never decreased in size, no matter how much was eaten. The sea god Mannanan had a whole herd of pigs that could be served in a similar manner. He explained that the meat would not boil in the cauldron until a truth was spoken for each quarter. Whoever ate them gained immortality. Thus, the boar was associated with truth, spiritual sustenance, resurrection and immortality.

In Norse myth, Frey owns a boar called Gullinbursti whose mane glows to illuminate the way for his owner. Frey rode to Balder's funeral in a wagon pulled by Gullinbursti. The boar was created for him by the dwarf smiths Sindri and Brokkr. The radiant bristles of Gullinbursti may symbolise the solar rays, or perhaps the golden grain as the boar, by tearing up the ground with his sharp tusks, is said to have first taught mankind how to plough. At Yule, a boar was consecrated to Frey for prosperity and led it out so everyone present could lay their hand on the boar and swear a solemn oath. One Swedish song and dance game may contain elements of this sacrifice. Several youths, with blackened faces and persons disguised, are the performers. The victim sits clad in a skin, holding in his mouth a wisp of straw cut sharp at the ends and standing out. Some speculate that this is meant to resemble a swine's bristles, and that the man represents a boar sacrificed to Frey.

The popularity of Christmas pork dishes and the boar's head feast may all derive from this annual sacrifice to Frey. The boar's head at the Yule feast traditionally wears a crown. In mediaeval times it was processed into the hall as the first dish to be placed on the lord's table. The custom is maintained in such places as the ceremony of the Boar's Head at Queen's College, Oxford before the master and fellows, where the head is placed on a silver platter dating from 1668, decorated with rosemary and bay and adorned with flags with the college arms. At The Swan Hotel in Bedford morris men accompany the boar's head with the *Boar's Head Carol*, as at Oxford:

The boar's head in hands bear I,
Bedecked with bay and rosemary,
And I pray you, my master, be merry...

CAT
From Iceland comes the legend of the sinister Yule Cat (*Jólakötturinn*). Those who did not help to finish all work on the autumn wool by Yule time missed out on the Yule reward of a new article of clothing, and were threatened with being eaten by the Yule Cat.

The *lussikatter* (Lucy cats) or the golden saffron rolls that are served by the Lucia Bride in Sweden are said to be the devil's cats which Lucia subdued, and the cats were pictured at her feet. Cats were also associated with Freya whose special season was Yule when she dispensed wealth and plenty. The traditional shape of the rolls is a cross shape where the arms are rolled inward and in the curve are bright pieces of fruit or small candles in the form of a solar wheel. [193]

There were horrible sacrifices of dogs and cats in Germany and Bohemia at Christmas. In Lauenburg and Mecklenburg on Christmas morning,

193   Susan Granquist, 1995, http://www.irminsul.org/arc/001sg.html

before the cattle were watered, a dog was thrown into their drinking water, in order that they may not suffer from the mange. In the Uckermark a cat might be substituted for the dog. In Bohemia a black cat was caught, boiled and buried by night under a tree to keep evil spirits from injuring the fields.

GOAT

The sign of the goat (Capricorn) rules the winter solstice, perhaps symbolised by the new born Zeus being nursed by the goat-nymph Amalthea.

The god Thor is one of the candidates for the model of the modern Santa Claus. According to Norse mythology, he has a chariot that is pulled by the goats Tanngrisnir and Tanngnjóstr. At night when he sets up camp, Thor eats the meat of the goats but take care that all bones remain whole. Then he wraps the remains up and in the morning the goats always come back to life to pull the chariot.

Possibly related, the Yule Goat is one of the oldest Scandinavian and Northern European Yule and Christmas symbols and traditions. 'Yule Goat' originally denoted the goat that was slaughtered around Yule, but it may also indicate a goat figure made out of straw. The Gävle Goat is a giant version of the Yule Goat, erected every year in the Swedish city of Gävle. The Julbock or Yule goat from Sweden and Norway, carries the Yule elf when he makes his rounds to deliver presents and receive his offering of porridge.

The custom of going door-to-door singing carols and getting food and drinks in return, is called 'Going Yule Goat'.

HORSE

Many midwinter horsing ceremonies survive in Britain. In Wales the Mari Lwyd custom takes place, when a horses head is carried from house to house where contests take place in singing Welsh verse and there is dancing, food and drink. This custom was once wide spread, but is now seen only in a few locations such as Llangynwyd and Pencoed in Mid Glamorgan. At Hythe and Folkstone in Kent, the ceremony of the Hoodening takes place: the hooden horse goes from pub to pub, accompanied by carol singers and morris dancers. In a variety of locations a death and resurrection mumming play is performed, featuring a horse. On the Isle of Man a similar ceremony took place on Twelfth Day when during the supper the *laare vane,* or white mare, was brought in. This was a horse's head made of wood held by a person concealed by a white sheet. He went round the table snapping the horse's mouth at the guests who finally chased him from the room.[194]

---

194   A.W.Moore, *Folklore of the Isle of Man,* 1891

Horses are symbolic of the sun, moon and the land. They represent virility, fertility, strength and swiftness. Horse cults existed in Britain long before the coming of the Celts and would have been centred on the wild ponies. Horses were sacred. A Stone Age carving found in Derbyshire shows a man in a horse mask. Even today there is a repugnance to eating horseflesh in Britain.

The horse is associated with the ancient mare-goddess who rides between the worlds, sacred since the earliest times. In Greece she was Mare Headed Demeter, and in Crete Leucippe the White Mare. By the Roman era the cult of the Gaulish horse goddess Epona ('Divine Horse') was widespread, and became merged with that of the Welsh Rhiannon and the Irish Macha. Epona is always depicted with a horse, sitting on a horse or with two foals. Her name gives us the word 'pony'.

Rhiannon ('Great Queen') fled from her suitor Pwyll in the form of a white mare. Eventually she allowed him to catch her, and married him. At the winter solstice she gave birth to a son called Pryderi ('Anxiety') who was spirited away. Her jealous maids smeared her with blood and accused her of having eaten him. As a punishment she had to carry visitors to the palace on her back, like a horse. Rhiannon is shown as the white mare rising from the sea (the white horses that are the crest of the waves) surrounded by a cloud of birds. She sent seven blackbirds or maidens to take Arthur to Avalon.

The Irish horse goddess was Macha who, heavily pregnant, entered a foot face against a horse. She won but died giving birth on the finish line, cursing the king of Ulster who had forced her into the race. The curse said that in times of battle the warriors of Ulster would become as weak as women in childbirth. The place of the Kings of Ulster was named 'Emain Macha' after her.

In Many ancient civilisations the sun was thought to be drawn across the sky by celestial horses. Several of these are named in myth including Abraxas, a horse of the dawn goddess Aurora (the letters of his name in Greek make the numerical value 365, the number of days of the year), Aethon ('fiery red'), a sun horse; Eoos ('dawn') another horse of Aurora, and Abakur ('hot one'). Dag, the Norse god of the day, was conveyed across the sky by his white horse Shining Mane, which spread light across the world. Odin possessed an eight legged horse called Sleipnir, who could run across land and water alike (eight is the number of solar increase). It carried Hermod to the Underworld to beg Hel for the return of the slain Baldur.

The black horse was considered unlucky, funerary, heralding death and symbolising chaos. It was said to appear during the twelve days of chaos between the old and new year. White animals were generally associated with sky deities, and black animals with Underworld deities. The Celts believed that souls travelled to the land of the dead on horseback. In the middle ages a bier was called St Michael's horse, he being the archangel for guiding a discarnate human spirit. The horse depicted in catacombs symbolised the swiftness of life. Several horses of the Underworld are named in myth including the horses of the god Pluto – Abaster ('deprived of the light of day') and Abatos ('inaccessible'). Another association of the horse with death and the Underworld is the night mare who nests in rock clefts or the branches of yew trees which are sacred to the death goddess. They are lined with white horse hair and the feathers of prophetic birds, and filled with the jaw bones and entrails of poets. Odin is said to have bound the nightmare.

In Greek myth Poseidon, the sea god, created the horse and it was sacred to him. He also invented horse racing. The month of the winter solstice was sacred to him.

Gods and shamans tether their horses to the World Tree, via which journeys to all the realms are possible. The Norse world tree is *Askr Yggr-drasill* which means 'the ash tree that is the horse of Yggr'. Yggr is one of the titles of Odin. The Altaic shaman's journey begins at his tent, before which a fire burns. A horse is tethered to a post, which represents the cosmic axis or world tree. The world tree has seven branches, which represent the seven stages of heaven. At the top of the post is a line from which the pelt of the sacrificed horse is hung. The horse spirit carries the shaman into other worlds. A shaman's drum is often referred to as his 'horse', since the drum beat is a vehicle which enables him to travel to other realms.

St Stephen took over the horse associations of the season which formerly belonged to Pagan deities such as Poseidon and Epona. His feast day was a day for horse races and hunts, when in England the usual hunting laws were suspended and anyone could catch whatever they liked.

In England and elsewhere it was traditional to bleed horses on St Stephen's Day in the belief that it would benefit them. [195]

If you bleed your nag on St Stephen's day
He'll work your work for ever and aye

In the Tyrol, in addition to bleeding horses, it was the custom to give them consecrated salt and bread or oats and barley. In the churches water and salt were consecrated, and then the water was used to sprinkle food, barns and fields in order to avert the influence of witches and evil spirits, while bread soaked in it is was to the cattle when they were driven out to pasture on Whit

---

195   Clement A. Miles, *Christmas in Ritual and Tradition*, Christian and Pagan, T. Fisher Unwin, 1912

Monday. The salt was also protective and was given to the animals, or taken by people about to set out on long journeys and pilgrimages.[196] In some of the Carinthian valleys where horse-breeding was a speciality, the young men rode into the villages on unsaddled horses and raced four or five times around the church while the priest blessed the animals, and sprinkled them with holy water. The Finns threw a piece of money or a bit of silver into the trough out of which the horses drank, under the notion that it prospered those who did it.[197]

Similar customs existed in parts of Germany. In Munich, for example, more than two hundred men on horseback rode three times round the interior of a church until the practice was abolished in 1876. The horses were decorated with multi-coloured ribbons. At Backnang in Swabia horses were ridden out, as fast as possible, to protect them from the influence of witches.[198] In the Hohenlohe region male servants rode out in companies to neighbouring villages where they indulged in heavy drinking. In Holstein, lads would visit their neighbours in a company, groom the horses, and ride about in the farmyards, making a great noise until the people woke up and treated them to beer and spirits. At the village of Wallsbüll near Flensburg the peasant youths in the early morning held a race, and the winner was called Steffen (Stephen) and entertained at the inn. At Viöl near Bredstadt the child who got up last on December 26th received the name of Steffen and had to ride to a neighbour's house on a hay-fork. In other German districts the festival was called 'the great horse-day' when consecrated food was given to the animals, they were driven round and round the fields until they sweated violently, and at last were ridden to the blacksmith's and bled, to keep them healthy through the year. The blood was preserved as a remedy for various illnesses.[199]

As might be expected, the horse aspects of the festival were more pronounced in Sweden. It was the custom to ride horses into north flowing water at one o'clock in the morning, and then for them to drink 'the cream of the water' which would keep them healthy for the coming year. There was a race to get to the water first, and the man who won was rewarded with a drink. After service on St. Stephen's Day there was a race home on horseback, and it was supposed that he who arrived first would be the first to get his harvest

196   *Ibid*

197   *Hones Everyday Book,* online at
       http://www.uab.edu/english/hone/etexts/edb/home.html

198   Clement A. Miles, *Christmas in Ritual and Tradition,* Christian and Pagan, T. Fisher Unwin, 1912

199   Clement A. Miles, *Christmas in Ritual and Tradition,* Christian and Pagan, T. Fisher Unwin, 1912

158

in. The so-called 'Stephen's Men', companies of peasant youths, raced from village to village to awaken the inhabitants with the folk-song called *Staffansvisa*, expecting to be treated to ale or spirits in return.

REINDEER

Our modern image of Santa Claus is a jolly old elf in a flying sleigh pulled by reindeer – but why reindeer?

Reindeer have a long and close association with shamanism and shamanic flight. There are cave paintings of reindeer from 30,000 years ago. In the Old Stone Age reindeer were buried in moors as sacrificial offerings. In Germany they were topped by cultic poles crowned with anthropomorphic mushrooms with caps. Sometimes reindeer skulls were placed on top of the stakes.

Siberian shamans say that the moon is a man on a sleigh drawn by two reindeer that can fly to earth and back to heaven. It is also said that reindeer live in the World Tree, and shamans ride reindeer spirits to climb it. The shaman beats his drum until he reaches a state of ecstasy. In this altered state his soul travels to the spirit world to converse with the dead. First the drum must be granted life by means of a particular ritual, and possessed by a guardian spirit – most commonly a reindeer. The shaman, with the help of his reindeer guide can make his spiritual journey. On the drum skin are painted (in alder bark mixed with spit) various blood-red symbols that help guide the shaman on his 'reindeer vision' across the cosmic road (Milky Way) to *Jábmeájmoo*, the Land of the Dead. [200] One symbol on the drum is a miniature sleigh pulled by a tiny reindeer. This image is used by the shaman to 'ride into the sky'.[201]

Another association of reindeer and shamanism is the fly agaric (*Amanita muscaria*) mushroom. Reindeer are attracted to the mushrooms and search for them in the snow. The animal's metabolism removes the toxins from the mushrooms but leaves the hallucinogenic properties intact in the urine. The shamans then drink this to achieve spirit flight.

Traditionally, the Saami use reindeer to pull a sleigh (*pulka*). It is said that the Wildman, Snowman, and Bigfoot all consume raw deer flesh. In Sàpmi, at winter solstice, reindeer slaughter celebrations take place – a culling of the herds, since there is not enough fodder to maintain all the animals through the extreme winter. The Saami mythical reindeer Mandash-

200   http://www.forteantimes.com/features/articles/134/lapp_of_the_gods.html
201   *Ibid*

pyrre has golden antlers that shine like the sun.

Possibly, reindeer were chosen to pull Santa's sleigh because they were the most suitable for a Scandinavian ex-god, and symbolic of the snowy wastes of the North. However, it cannot be overlooked that the reindeer or stag was one of the most important cult animals. The reindeer was sacred to the Norse Mother Goddess, as was the stag to the Greek Diana the Huntress, whose chariot was drawn by four stags with golden antlers.

At Stellmoor, a Neolithic site near Hamburg, the bodies of twelve reindeer were found on the floor of a lake together with a pole which once stood on the shore, surmounted by a reindeer skull. In this country, at Chaldon Herring in Dorset, the graves have been discovered of men in a sitting position wearing antlers on their shoulders. It may well be that the wide-spread and long-standing custom of dressing in an animal's skin and head is an identification with the god. Although the wearing of skins and horns in ceremonies and folk festivals was severely condemned by certain Church leaders, the practise has continued to this day, for instance in the Abbots Bromley Horn Dance in Staffordshire, which originally took place at the winter solstice, but is now enacted in September. The horns are six sets of reindeer antlers, three white and three black. They have been carbon dated to around 1065, and must have been imported from Scandinavia.

ROBIN *Erithacus rubecula*
The robin is a member of the thrush family and is one of Britain's best loved birds. It is known in both town and countryside and can become very tame, even perching on the spade of the resting gardener. The bird is easily recognisable as both male and female have a red face and breast,

edged with grey, whitish under parts and brown upper parts and tail. The robin is territorial and the male birds aggressively defend their patches. The robin nests in thick ivy, tree roots and undergrowth, or even old sheds and outbuildings.

In the old rhyme, the sparrow killed the robin with his bow and arrow, and this may relate to its symbolic death or sacrifice at the end of its six month rule over half of the year. The robin is also said to be husband to the wren, another six monthly ruler of the year.

At the winter solstice the robin becomes associated with Robin Hood, the ram or stag horned fertility god, with the burning of the Yule log (the hood) when the spirit of the year, Robin, escapes up the chimney.

In mediaeval times the wassailing ceremony to welcome the New Year involved hanging up gifts of food for the robins who were good spirits and brought luck for the coming year. When you see the first robin of the year it is still the custom to make a wish, for if the bird flies away before you have decided what you want you will have no luck in the coming year.

The robin is said to have burned its breast, making it red, by throwing itself onto the wren to stifle the flames which were burning it when it was bringing fire to mankind. The Welsh for robin '*bronrhuddyn*' means 'scorched breast'. Others say that the robin was part of a relay of birds that brought fire from the sun for mankind. The robin held the brand too close to the flames and burned its breast. In Scotland and Cornwall a game called Robin's Alight was played. It involved passing a burning brand from hand to hand and the person holding it when the flames went out had to pay a forfeit. Robins were associated with fire rituals, and until recently in Wales it was thought that anyone who killed a robin would have his house burned down.

In Norse myth the robin was sacred to Thor, god of lightening and was under his protection. In Germany it was thought the presence of a robin averted lightening.

The lore that surrounds the robin indicates that it was a sacred, protected bird in the past. Legend has it that if a robin finds a dead human body in the woods it will cover it with leaves. Harming a robin is very bad luck and will result in your house being struck by lightening, ills of the hands and legs or even death:

The robin and the lintil, the laverock and the wren,
Them that harries their nests will never thrive again.

The robin is associated with fire, particularly the fire of the sun at the winter solstice. Its red breast marks it as a fire bird in the midst of winter. The French ceremony of spitting the robin on the hazel twig at Imbolc symbolised the banishing of the power of darkness and winter.

STAG

The stag has played an important part in the religion of many parts of the world. The earliest representations of the stag god - or of the shaman wearing stag horns - date from round 12,000 BCE, the most famous being the 'sorcerer' of Les Trois Freres. Stags appear on Old Stone Age paintings and carvings. Antlers have been found buried at Newgrange, Glastonbury, Stonehenge and a set discovered at Star Carr, Pickering, Yorkshire (northern England) were adapted for use as headgear.

The Celts considered all horned beasts to be sacred, counting the horns as powerful emblems of fertility. On a practical level, antlers were amongst the earliest tools used to till the soil, while powdered stag antlers are among the best fertilisers known. On a symbolic level, they represent the potency and strength of the male animal. The aggressive clashes of the stags during the rutting season were much admired by Celtic warriors. Horns were placed on helmets to signify such might, and all sorts of creatures were depicted with horns to imbue them with vigour, including those that did not possess them naturally, such as birds.

Unlike that other influential horned symbol, the bull, stags shed their antlers each year, just as deciduous trees shed their leaves. The stag is a solar animal, with its antlers sometimes shown curving like the rays of the sun. The growth of the antlers represents the sun's increase in summer and the shedding the loss of the sun's 'virility' in the winter. This made the stag a symbol of passing of the seasons, reflected in the life cycle of the stag. They clean their new antlers in August and September, rubbing off the velvety coating on the branches of trees. The rutting season begins from then on, often going on into November, driven to greater ferocity by the frosts. Then, in the early summer at Beltane, the roebuck acquires his new red coloured coat.

King Arthur's knights took part in a yearly hunt of the white stag, and its head would be presented to the fairest lady in the land. This may be a seasonal tale in which the white solar beast is killed. It was once thought that the 'King Stag', the leader of the herd, should be ritually hunted and killed every year to ensure the return of summer. The king or royal stag was a beast with twelve or fourteen points on his horns (a stag would have to have to be seven years old to have twelve points). In Celtic myth, the stag or hind often symbolises the soul, usually the soul of a king or hero. As the stag was considered to be a royal beast, its hunting was often the preserve of the nobles, perhaps originally only the priest-king. In mediaeval times, it was death for anyone but the king to hunt deer.

King Arthur seems to have had several dealings with magical stags. In one Irish story, Arthur and his knights were beguiled into the Otherworld by a deer-woman called Ailleann. She persuaded Arthur's men to take fairy wives, and married Arthur herself. This legend may be derived from an even older tale where Arthur marries the lady who represents the sovereignty of the land, and becomes the stag king.[202] The stag was identified with the sacred king (the god), whose sacrifice was necessary.

WREN

Wren ceremonies were enacted up to the nineteenth century and have been revived in several places. These ceremonies were conducted around the midwinter solstice, when rituals were performed to chase away the powers of darkness. The wren's supposed poverty at this time is parallel to the death of the physical body of the sun. The wren may have represented the death and rebirth of the sun at the winter solstice, or its death may have represented the killing of the old year.

One tale relates how the wren brought fire to mankind, and was scorched by the sun. In gratitude the other birds all gave a feather to renew his plumage, except the owl who refused. This is why the wren is such an untidy looking bird. Birds, flying high, were often regarded as fire bringers. The Bretons say the wren fetched fire not from heaven, but from Hell. Her plumage became scorched as she escaped through the keyhole.

The goldcrested wren has a fiery crest and lives in evergreen trees, though wren customs are now related to the common wren. In ogham its name *druen,* related to *dur* or oak. In Welsh the wren is still called 'druid' as *derw* or *dryw*. Wrens were once thought to roost in caves, and their Latin name means 'cave-dweller' (*Toglodytes troglodytes*). They sometimes shelter in caves in winter but in summer build large round nests, hence their solar symbolism.

The wren appears to be associated with kingship. In several European languages his name means 'king': in French *Reytelet*; in Welsh *Bren*; Teutonic *Konig-Vogel* ('king-bird'); in Dutch *Konije* ('little king'). Some have speculated that the sacrificed wren represented the soul of Arthur at his winter solstice death. The humble wren is known as the king of the birds. According

202   Marion Davies, *Sacred Celtic Animals,* Capall Bann, Chieveley

to one folk tale all the birds gathered to see who would be king. It was decided that the one that flew highest would gain the title. The eagle was sure of victory and soon flew higher than the others. The wren however, hid amongst his feathers and when the eagle was at his last gasp flew even higher.

The wren was an attribute of Bran, a Celtic death and resurrection god who was said to have assumed the form of a wren and hidden in an ivy bush to escape pursuit. The wren hunters search for the wren in the ivy bush and beat it with birch branches. Sometimes then wren is described as being caught in the furze, a totem of the spring equinox.

It is often paired with the robin, sometimes being seen as the female to the robin's male. They are sometimes thought to battle for rulership of the year. The rhyme 'who killed cock robin' may be la later version of a very old story.

The wren was doubtlessly a sacred bird, and the prohibition on killing it only lifted at the winter solstice. In France anyone who killed a wren could expect his house to be destroyed by fire, or his fingers would shrivel and drop off. In England anyone who harms a wren will suffer a broken bone shortly afterwards.

In Somerset the wren was carried about as 'the King' in a glass box, surmounted by a wheel on which there were various coloured ribbons. He was symbolically so big he had to be carried on a cart pulled by six horses, which may represent the six months of his rule. Seven cooks then boiled the wren in a huge pan.

On the Isle of Man, wren customs took place on Christmas Eve. Towards evening, people waited until the bells rang out at midnight, and then went to hunt a wren. Having found one they killed it and laid it on a bier, and went from house to house with it, asking for contributions, and reciting:

We hunted the wren for Robin the Bobbin,
We hunted the wren for Jack of the Can,
We hunted the wren for Robin the Bobbin,
We hunted the wren for every one.

Afterwards they took it to the parish church and buried it with great solemnity, singing dirges over it in the Manx language. Only then could Christmas begin. Another account, from the mid-nineteenth century, describes how on St. Stephen's Day Manx boys went from door to door with a wren suspended by the legs in the centre of two hoops crossing one another at right angles and decorated with evergreens and ribbons. In exchange for a small coin they would give a feather of the wren, which was carefully kept as a preservative against shipwreck during the year. [203]

The Wren-boys in Ireland, who are also called *Droleens*, went from house to house, for the purpose of levying contributions, carrying one or more dead wrens in the midst of a bush of holly, gaily decorated with coloured ribbons:

The wren, the wren, the king of all birds,
St. Stephen's day was caught in the furze,
Although he is little, his family's great,
I pray you, good landlady, give us a treat.
My box would speak, if it had but a tongue,
And two or three shillings would do it no wrong;
Sing holly, sing ivy—sing ivy, sing holly,
A drop just to drink, it would drown melancholy.
And if you draw it of the best,
I hope, in heaven your soul will rest;
But if you draw it of the small,
It won't agree with these Wren-boys at all."

If money or drink was not forthcoming, the following verses were added:
"*Last Christmas-day, I turned the spit,*
I burned my "fingers (I feel it yet),
A cock sparrow flew over the table,
The dish began to fight with the ladle.
The spit got up like a naked man,
And swore he'd fight with the dripping pan;
The pan got up and cocked his tail,
And swore he'd send them all to jail."

In parts of Pembrokeshire, wren customs were enacted on Twelfth Night. The wren was secured in a small house made of wood, with door and glazed windows and decorated with ribbons. Sometimes several wrens were placed in the same cage. The bier of the wren was called the 'Cutty Wren'. It was then

203   Clement A. Miles, *Christmas in Ritual and Tradition*, Christian and Pagan, T. Fisher Unwin, 1912

taken around principal houses in the neighbourhood, where the *Song of the Wren* was sung:

Joy health, love, and peace
Be to you in this place,
By your leave we will sing
Concerning our King:
Our King is well drest,
In silks of the best;
With his ribbons so rare,
No King can compare.
In his coach he does ride,
With a great deal of pride;
And with four footmen
To wait upon him.

We four were at watch,
And all nigh of a match;
With powder and ball,
We fired at his hall.
We have travelled many miles
Over hedges and stiles,
To find you this King,
Which we now to you bring.
Now Christmas is past,
Twelfth day is the last,
Th' Old Year bids adieu;
Great joy to the New.

The wren boys were then rewarded with drinks and a gift of money. There were many regional variations on the song. In Tenby, the wren was placed in a box and the men would carry it on four poles, groaning under the supposed weight, singing:

O where are you going? Says Milder to Melder,
O where are you going? Says younger to elder
O I cannot tell you, says Festel to Fose,
We're going to the woods, says John the red nose.
O what will you do there? Shoot the Cutty Wren.
O what will you shoot her with? With bows and with arrows.
O that will not do. With great guns and cannons.

O what will you bring her home in? on four men's string shoulders.
O that will not do. On big carts and wagons.
What will you cut her up with? With knives and with forks.
O that will not do. With hatchets and cleavers.
O what will you boil her in? in pots and kettles.
O that will not do. In brass pans and kettles.[204]

---

204   Trefor M. Owen, *Welsh Folk Customs*, Gomer Press, Llandysul, 1994

Whittlesey Staw Bear

Chapter 11
YULE RITUALS

THEMES OF YULE
- Rebirth of light, hope, renewal, regeneration
- The Child of Promise
- Light and hope in the time of greatest darkness
- Encouraging the sun with fire, light, spherical (sun-shaped) decorations on the tree
- Evergreen life persisting in the time of death
- Order rescued from chaos, time and the cosmos renewed
- Death of the old, birth of the new
- A time apart, a pause, a breath before the cycle continues
- Cessation of hostilities, peace and goodwill
- The levelling of social barriers, a reversal of social order, misrule
- Reward and punishment for the deeds of the year- a time of reckoning
- What rebirth do you seek?
- What ending do you seek, what do you need to leave behind?

THE FIRST RITUAL OF YULE - THE YULE LOG
13th December – Little Yule

Our own first ritual of Yule is the bringing in of the Yule log on Little Yule, or December 13th. The Yule log is carefully lit with a piece of the old log from the previous year and given offerings of mead or cider.

THE SECOND RITUAL OF YULE- SOLSTICE

Cast the circle in the usual manner.

Priestess: *Arianrhod, starry Queen of the Northern skies, Lady of Night, Lady of barren woodlands, Lady of the crystal snows we call upon you. Mistress* *of Life, Mistress of Death, Keeper of the Spiral Castle; you who guards the gateway to mysteries of rebirth, we call upon you. Mother of the Light, we beseech thee, be with us in this circle."*

Priest: *In this the season of the Dark Time, shrouded in the frosted cloak of the Crone, we celebrate the festival of Yule, the rebirth of the sun, and the life of the coming year.*

Priestess:
In the coldness of winter we hunger
In the stillness of winter we are silent
In the ice of winter we are caught in the north wind's blast
In the depths of winter the world is wrapped in sleep

We need the fire in our hearts to love
We need the fire in the hearth to eat
We need the fire in the head to make
We need the fire in the heavens to live

Priest: *The year has reached its lowest ebb, all is darkness and death. Yet in this darkness we must find hope. In this darkness we must find light. The sun must be reborn!*

He then leads the dance and chant which everyone joins in:

Water, air, fire and earth
Bring the Sun God to rebirth

Each person then takes a token, usually the remains of last year's mistletoe, or an object that symbolises something they wish to be rid of, or a piece of paper on which they have written all the things they wish to be consigned to the past (such as bad habits, illness, old ties, destructive relationships and so on). This is then consigned to the fire.

The Hearth Witch smudges each person with juniper smoke. *"May we be purified, ready to greet the Sun as he is reborn, carrying with him all our hopes for the coming year"*

South:
At the threshold of the Underworld, the Dark God waits,

As death moves to life and dark turns to light
The Lord of the Dead, he stalks the land,
The Bringer of Chaos, he stalks the land,
The Keeper of Mysteries, he stalks the land.
The year ebbs and the wheel spins as
Dark turns to light
At the threshold of the Underworld, the Dark God waits.

Through the underworld the God has passed
Open the gate and let him in.

West:
At the threshold of the year, the Stag Lord waits,
Hunter and the hunted; red blood on white snow,
Antlered God of winter stillness, waiting
Our sacrifice of flesh for life, waiting
On the edge of the forest, the Lord is waiting,
He knows the ancient secret of
Red blood on white snow,
At the threshold of the year, the Stag Lord waits.

Through the underworld the God has passed
Open the gate and let him in.

North:
At the threshold of life, the Green Man waits,
Ivy clad, scarlet berries, dark green leaves,
Ever green and ever growing, pauses,
The moment nears and yet he pauses,
The light will come, till then he pauses,
In the holly and the ivy,
Scarlet berries, dark green leaves,
At the threshold of life, the Green Man waits.

Our God has passed through the underworld
Open the gate and let him in.

East:
On the threshold of dawn, the Sun King waits,
The light of the world, gold light in black sky.

On the rim of the world, the Sun King dances,
Our child of promise, the Sun King dances,
At his moment of birth, the Sun King dances,
The light of our hope,
Gold light in black sky.
On the threshold of dawn, the Sun King waits.

Our God has passed through the underworld
Open the gate and let him in.

Queen of Heaven and Queen of Earth
Queen of death and Queen of birth
Queen of sadness, grieving, bane
Grant our God returns again,
Grieving wife and widowed Mother
Awaken now thy son, thy lover.
Give him birth from womb of night
Renew the world with the power of light.
Give to us the promised One
The shining, radiant, beautiful Sun.

On the threshold of dawn, the Sun King waits,
The light of the world, gold light in black sky.
On the rim of the world, the Sun King dances,
Our child of promise, the Sun King dances,
At his moment of birth, the Sun King dances,
The light of our hope,
Gold light in black sky.
On the threshold of dawn, the Sun King waits.

Our God has passed through the underworld
Open the gate and let him in.

The Sun God, played by the Year King, is reborn from the cloak of the Priestess who represents the Virgin Mother. The Sun King passes round the circle from North to East, South and West to North again, saluting each quarter of the circle in turn.

North: (giving him a lit beacon) *The light is reborn!*

East: (giving him the staff) *Be thou armed to conquer the dark.*

South: (draping him with a red sash) *May the year grow with you.*

West: (crowning him with mistletoe bound with red thread). *May you grow in strength.*

The Sun King: (plants the beacon in the North of the circle) *The light is reborn!*

Priest: *"With the sun we are each reborn. Blessed Be!"*

All : *"Blessed Be."*

Each person in turn lights a candle from the North beacon to symbolise their hopes for the coming year and places it in the part of the circle most suitable- west for emotional matters and love, north for practical matters, health and work, east for mental efforts and study, south for energy and creativity. Candles for friends and families may also be lit.

Meditation, magic etc is performed.

Bread and wine follows.

The circle is broken.

THE THIRD RITUAL OF YULE – WASSAILING
Twelfth Night or New Year's Day

The wassailers should wear garlands of ivy and mistletoe, or ivy and mistletoe around their hats. The Year King should be finely arrayed, and the Priestess and Maiden dressed in green. The Priestess carries the wassail bowl and the Maiden the cake.

The King taps the trunk of the tree to 'wake it up' and says:
Apples and pears with right good corn,
Come in plenty to every one.
Eat and drink good cake and hot ale,
Give Earth to drink and she'll not fail"

The Maiden places the cake in the main fork of the tree. The wassail drink is thrown three times at the roots of the tree and all chant:
"Here's to thee, old apple tree!
Whence thou may'st bud,
And whence thou may'st blow
Hats full! Caps full! Bushel-bags full!
And my pockets full too!"

The wassail bowl is recharged and all drink the health of the orchard with the word 'wassail'.

Drums and musical instruments are played to wake up the spirits of vegetation and drive away the spirits of winter and bane.

The Year King takes a burning brand and carries it around the property to infuse the spirit of warmth and fire into the earth, to purify it and bring luck for the coming year.

Everyone gathers around the fire and recharges the wassail bowl for a final toast of 'wassail'.

MIDWINTER RITUAL

Candles and robes are blue, white and silver. Decorate the circle with snowflake shapes, glittering tinsel etc. Unlit on the altar are three white and blue candles. The circle is cast.

Priestess: *This is the season of the Cailleach, the Crone.*

All: *Cailleach be welcome!*

All perform the chant and circle dance:
Earth is frozen, hard as stone,
Welcome Goddess, winter crone.

Priestess: *The face of the Cailleach is blue with cold, her hair white as ice, her cloak the snow that covers the bare earth. She snaps her fingers and the bare black branches of the trees crack with frost. In her wake is winter and death.*

Priest: *Yet hers is the face of wisdom. The wheel turns and winter follows summer, night follows day and death follows life.*

Priestess: *The secret wisdom of the Crone is that the wheel shall turn once more. Night shall melt into day as the ice of winter melts into spring.*

Priest: *In death the Goddess shall wrap us in her dark cloak, but we shall see another dawn. Rebirth follows on the heels of death, just as spring follows on the heels of winter.*

Priestess: *Let the candles be lit in token of our hope.*

The three altar candles are lit. Poetry dedicated to the season may be read, spells performed, divination etc. pursued. When everything is finished the priestess breaks the circle and says:

Priestess: *We have met together tonight to celebrate the Season of the Crone and her dark wisdom. Let us depart now from this place, but carry her hope in our hearts for all our days, safe in the knowledge that the wheel shall turn. Blessed Be.*

All: *Blessed Be.*

THE OAK KING AND THE HOLLY KING

LORD OF MISRULE:
In comes I, the Lord of Misrule
And now you all will play the fool.
Yuletide comes but once a year
And when it comes, it brings good cheer.
But here comes two who want to fight
Whether I say 'tis wrong or right.

HOLLY KING:
In comes I, the Holly King
Fierce and brave with winter's sting
If you come with hot blood bold
My sword shall shortly draw it cold

OAK KING:

In comes I, the new Oak King
Crowned with leaf and acorn ring
Let Holly quake and shake with fear
For I am come to close this year.

HOLLY KING:

Listen fool and you shall hear
How Holly rules the waning year
The light has gone, the sun is old
And winter's grasp is cold, so cold.
My leaves are green, my berries red
While yours are withered, blasted, dead.
Though you have journeyed west to east
You shall die like any beast.
I shall fell thee like a hornéd bull
With blows upon your naked skull.

OAK KING:

So strike if you're a valiant knight,
As solstice comes we both must fight.
Strike, then, strike my boy,
Or I will strike if you are coy,
For I journeyed lately from the west
Where the dying sun came down to rest,
I fought dim shadows in bloody wars
Beyond the grave, among the stars,
The restless ghosts and what you know
Shall flee this dawn when the cock doth crow;
I'll send them back to dismal Hel
And I'll delight to hear them yell.
Let darkness go through winter's door
Back to chaos' infernal shore.
If you, my boy, this year would keep
You first must send me back to sleep.

They fight and the Oak King falls.

LORD OF MISRULE:

Holly King what hast thou done

For you have slain the rising sun!
Oh where is healing to be found
To save this knight upon the ground?

IVY GIRL:
Here is healing to be found
To cure this knight upon the ground

LORD OF MISRULE:
What can you cure?

IVY GIRL:
Oh, I can cure the winter death
My leaves stay green 'neath icy breath
And I can cure the waning light
With spiral growth make day from night.

LORD OF MISRULE:
I think more healing must be found
To cure this knight upon the ground

MISTLETOE BULL:
Here is healing to be found
To cure the knight upon the ground.

LORD OF MISRULE:
What can you cure?

MISTLETOE BULL:
These white berries can heal all
From man to beast and things that crawl
With my magic I can raise the dead
And draw Oak back on Wyrd's fast thread.
A little to the eye,
A little to the thigh,
A little to the string bone of the heart,
Rise up, thou noble knight, and try to stand.

The Oak King jumps up again.

OAK KING:
Now see, Old King, I've risen again.
And now I shall begin my reign

GARDNERIAN RITE FOR YULE

Form circle in usual manner, invoking the Mighty Ones.

The Cauldron of Cerridwen is placed in the circle at the south wreathed with holly, ivy and mistletoe, with fire lighted within it. There should be no other light except for the candles on the altar and about the circle.After all are purified, the Moon should be drawn down.

Then the High Priestess stands behind the Cauldron in pentacle position, symbolizing the rebirth of the sun. The people, man and woman alternately, stand round the circle. The Magus stands facing the High Priestess with a bundle of torches, or candles, and the book of words of the incantation. One of the officers stands beside him with a lighted candle, so that he may have light to read by.

The people begin to slowly move round the circle sunwise. As each passes him the Magus lights his candle or torch from the fire in the Cauldron, which may be simply a candle, till all have lighted candles or torches. Then the people dance round slowly as he reads the incantation. (A real fire must now be kindled in the Cauldron.)

Queen of the Moon,
Queen of the Sun.
Queen of the Heavens,
Queen of the Stars.
Queen of the Waters,
Queen of the Earth.
Who ordained to us the child of promise:
It is the Great Mother who gives birth to him,
He is the Lord of Life who is born again,
Darkness and tears are set behind,
And the star of guidance comes up early.
Golden sun of hill and mountain
Illumine the land, illumine the world,
Illumine the seas, illumine the rivers,

Grief be laid, and joy be raised.
Blessed be the Great Mother,
Without beginning, without ending,
To everlasting, to eternity,
I O. Evohe, Blessed be.

The dance commences slowly, in rhythm with the chant, all taking up the call "I. O. Blessed be." The Priestess joins dance and leads them with a quicker rhythm. The cauldron with burning fire is pushed so that the dancers leap or step over it, in couples. Whichever couple is passing it as it goes out, should be well-purified, three times each, and may pay any amusing forfeit as the High Priestess may ordain. Sometimes the cauldron is relighted several times for this purpose.

SOLO RITE FOR YULE

Prepare a sacred place, preferably outdoors, but if the ritual is to be indoors clean the room thoroughly, then sweep through it with a broom to the door, visualising all negativity being swept away. Set up candles in the four quarters – a red candle in the south, a blue candle in the west, a green candle in the north and a yellow candle in the east. Place a large flat stone or a small table in the north for the altar. Place on it three candles (red or green) in holders, a jug of wine, fruit juice or water and a plate of cakes or bread. A Yule log may be decorated with candles, corn and holly and placed on the altar. Decorate the space with holly, ivy and mistletoe. Also prepare a paper token which represents a fear or problem which you would like to be rid of. Place an unlit candle in the centre of the circle, either in a holder or in the cauldron if you have one.

Bathe in salt water and put on clean clothes or a robe and a chaplet of evergreens. Light the incense and the altar candles and say: *I call upon the guardians of the North* (light the north candle), *the guardians of the east* (light the east candle), *the guardians of the south* (light the south candle), *the guardians of the west* (light the west candle). *And the guardians of above and below to witness that this becomes for a while a time between times and a place between places.*

Sit before the altar for a while and meditate on the season. When you are ready say:

Goddess of Death and Rebirth
Be with me here for a time.
Tonight at the winter solstice
The waning year comes to its end
The Sun God returns to us from the Spiral Castle
The place of the Silver Wheel.
Return to us the One
The Child of Light, our Lord.
And light return to us again.
Blessed is the Virgin Mother
Queen of Dark and Queen of Day.

Light the candle in the cauldron (if you are indoors you can also put on the lights on the Yule tree) and say: *The sun is reborn!*

In this season of the dark time, shrouded in the cloak of the Crone we celebrate the festival of Yule, the rebirth of the sun and of life for the coming year. At dawn the sun is reborn and the days will grow longer. All changes as the new replaces the old in a never ending cycle as the wheel of the year spins on.

Take the paper token of the things you wish to leave behind and burn it in the candle flame of the cauldron. *The Dark God has passed through the underworld and has been reborn as the Sun Child from the womb of the Mother. With him we are each reborn. Blessed Be!*

Take the wine: *Goddess, bless the wine in this cup in token of the cauldron which contained three drops of wisdom for all the world.* Drink the wine.

Take the cakes and say: *Let these cakes, the gift of the Earth Mother be blessed.* Eat the cakes.

When you are ready to close the rite say: *I thank the Guardians of the North, the east, the south, the west and the guardians of above and below for this sacred space, created for a while that we may worship our Lord and Lady in the ancient ways. Let this circle be dissolved, the candles put out.* (Put out the quarter candles). *I thank the Lord and Lady for their presence here tonight. Let all that I have learned be with me. May the gods light my path, now and for all time. The rite is ended.* (Put out the altar candles.) *Blessed Be.*
Let the cauldron candle burn itself out.

Chapter 12
THE YULE FEAST

SAVOURY DISHES

White Stilton Soup
8 oz white stilton cheese, crumbled
1 leek, well rinsed and finely chopped
2 tbs. flour
1 pt vegetable stock
1 pt milk
Salt to taste
White pepper
2 sticks celery, grated
½ parsnip, grated
Method
Fry the leek in the butter without browning until tender. Add the milk, stock, flour and cheese. Bring to the boil, stirring constantly and add the vegetables. Simmer for 15 - 20 minutes until the vegetables are tender. For an extra special soup, stir in a tablespoon of sherry.

Chestnut Pie
2 lbs mushrooms
8 oz dried chestnuts
12 oz stoned prunes
4 cloves garlic
2 red onions
2 strong white onions
Bunch of fresh sage
½ bottle red wine
Pinch of sugar
2 oz margarine

For the pastry:
1 egg
1 lb plain flour
6 oz margarine
200 ml water
Salt and black pepper
Method
Soak the chestnuts overnight in some water, drain and place in a casserole dish with half the wine, a pinch of sugar, salt and pepper. Cover and cook in a slow oven until soft. Chop coarsely. Stew the prunes in some water until plump, drain and chop. Slice the mushrooms. Chop the garlic. Melt 1 oz of the margarine, add half the garlic and cook for two minutes. Add the mushrooms. Cover and slow cook for 15 minutes. Slice the red onions and sweat with the remaining garlic in 1 oz of margarine. Add the sage and the rest of the wine. Simmer for 10 minutes.

To make the pastry, melt 6 oz margarine in 200 ml of boiling water. Meanwhile, sift the flour with a tsp of salt. Make a well in the middle and pour in the weather and margarine. Line an 8 inch spring-form tin with the pastry, reserving some for the lid.

Layer in the mushrooms, chestnuts, onions, prunes etc, ending with a layer of mushrooms. Cover with the rest of the pastry and brush with beaten egg. Cut a cross in the centre and fold back the edges. Bake at 200° C for 60 minutes. Brush with more beaten egg and cook for a further 15 minutes.

Vegetable Pie
2 large onions, chopped
2 potatoes, peeled and chopped
2 sticks celery, chopped
4 oz broccoli, chopped
2 oz cauliflower, cut into florets
2 oz mushrooms, chopped
2 oz swede, chopped
12 oz shortcrust pastry
Seasoning to taste
2 tbs. chopped mixed herbs
¼ pint vegetable stock
1 tbs. made mustard
1 oz grated cheese
Method
Fill a 2 pint baking dish with the vegetables, herbs and seasoning and pour the

stock over them. Stir in the mustard. Roll out the pastry and cover the dish. Scatter the grated cheese over the top and bake at 200°C/400°F/ gas mark 6 for 15 minutes, reduce the heat to 170°C/325°F/gas mark 3 and bake for a further 45 minutes.

Roast Potatoes with Chestnuts

1 lb. potatoes, peeled
Salt
Oil
4 oz peeled chestnuts
Method
Cut the potatoes in half and par boil in salted water for four minutes. Put them in a roasting tin, sprinkle with salt, coat with oil and cook in a hot oven for 30 minutes. Add the chestnuts and continue cooking until the potatoes are done.

Roast Parsnips

Parsnips
Vegetable oil
Method
Peel the parsnips and cut them in half, lengthways. Place them on a baking tray and pour enough oil over them to coat thoroughly. Roast in a hot oven at 220°C /gas mark 7 for around 30 minutes or until lovely and crispy.

Laufabrauð – Leaf Bread

2 lbs flour
¼ teaspoon cream of tartar
1 teaspoon salt
3 pints milk
Fat for deep frying
Method
Heat the milk just to the boiling point. Sift the flour together with the cream of tartar and the salt. The milk is stirred into the flour mixture and the whole is kneaded into a glistening, rather tough dough, then formed into a long roll. Cut the roll into pieces and roll out very thin. This is best done on a well-floured pastry cloth. The bread is formed with a round dish and then decorated. As each piece is completed, place between linen towels to prevent drying. Just before cooking, prick with a fork, being careful not to disturb the design. Deep fry on high heat, decorated side down, until golden-brown. Serve with butter.

The Laufabrauð, or Leaf Bread, is a work of art in itself, the designs often accompanying families through generations. The Laufabrauð started as a speciality food in Northern Iceland but is now served all over the country.

SWEET DISHES

Yule Log
3 eggs
3 oz sugar
3 oz self raising flour
¼ pt double cream
1 tbs. finely chopped poached fruit
4oz plain chocolate
Method
Place the eggs in a bowl and stand this in hand hot water. Whisk the eggs for two minutes. Add the sugar and continue to whisk until the eggs have doubled their volume (around ten minutes). Remove the bowl from the water and continue whisking until the mixture is cool. Carefully fold in the flour. Turn into a greased and lightly floured Swiss roll tin lined with grease proof paper and bake at 200°C/400°F/gas mark 6 for 10 minutes until well risen and firm to touch. Place a clean tea towel on your work surface and a sheet of grease proof paper over it. Turn out the cake onto this and cut away the hard edges. Roll up loosely and cover with a damp tea towel. Allow to go completely cold. Meanwhile, whisk the cream until it forms peaks. Fold in the fruit. Carefully unroll the cake and remove the paper from the underside. Fill with cream mixture and re-roll. Hold the roll in position for a minute or so to set. Melt the chocolate by breaking it into a bowl and heating this over a pan of hot water. Pour the melted chocolate over the log. Chill to set the chocolate. When cold, decorate your Yule log with holly leaves etc. Serve.

Twelfth Night Cake
2 ¼ lb. mixed dried sultanas, raisins and currants
2 oz mixed peel
2 oz glace cherries
2 oz chopped walnuts
¼ pint whisky
¼ pint milk
12 oz muscavado sugar
12 oz butter
4 eggs

1 lb. 4 oz plain flour
1 level tbs. baking powder
2 level tsp. mixed spice

Method

Place the dried fruit and peel in a bowl. Stir in the whisky and milk, cover and leave overnight. Heat the oven to 140°C /gas mark 1. Oil a large tin [approx. 12 inch x 10 inch] and line the base and sides with grease proof paper. Brush the paper with oil. Cream the butter and sugar, add the beaten eggs a little at a time. If the mixture curdles add a little flour. Sift the flour, baking powder and spice and fold into to the creamed mixture. Add the fruit, nuts and whisky. Stir well. Turn into the tin. Bake in the centre of the oven for 2 ¼ to 2 ½ hours. Leave to cool in the tin. Turn out and remove the paper. If you really must, you can sprinkle more whisky. The cake can be iced and decorate with stars, ribbons, wheat ears, nuts and glace fruit.

Yule Cake

9 oz plain flour
1 tsp. ground mixed spice
½ tsp. ground cinnamon
2 ½ lb. mixed fruit
2 oz chopped blanched almonds
3 oz glace cherries
8 oz Demerara sugar
8 oz butter
4 beaten eggs
1 ½ tbs. Black treacle
3 tbs. rum

Sieve together flour and mixed spice in a large bowl. In a separate bowl cream together the butter and sugar until very pale and fluffy. Beat in the eggs, a little at a time, adding a little of the flour to prevent the eggs from curdling. Stir in the treacle and add this to the flour, together with the mixed fruit, peel, cherries and nuts. Stir until well combined. Double line the base and sides of an 8 inch cake tin with grease proof paper. To insulate the tin and prevent the cake burning, tie a band of doubled brown paper around the outside, so that it comes 1 inch above the side of the tin. Turn the cake mixture into the tin and bake in a cool oven at 150°C gas mark 2 for 3 hours. Reduce the heat to 140°C gas mark 1 and continue cooking for a further 50 minutes or until a skewer inserted comes out clean. Leave the cake in the tin for 10 minutes, during which time it will shrink away from the sides and can then be turned out onto a wire cooling rack. When cool, but not cold, turn the cake upside down and make holes in the bottom with a skewer. Spoon the rum over and allow it to soak in. Leave until cold and wrap and store in an airtight tin. When required, drizzle the cake with a little more rum, over the top this time, coat with marzipan and ice as desired, perhaps with fondant decorations in the shapes of violets, apples, acorns, holly leaves and mistletoe. Alternatively, decorate with bundles of cinnamon sticks, sprigs of holly and mistletoe.

The cake should be made six weeks to a month before Yule and iced one week before.

King's Cake
18 oz flour
1 ½ oz yeast
100 ml water
Pinch of salt
Zest of a lemon
3 egg yolks
5 fl oz sparkling wine
3 ½ oz melted margarine
1 dried bean
5 ½ oz glacé fruit
1 beaten egg
7 oz glacé fruit for decoration
Icing sugar
Jelly to taste
Method
Pour 12 oz flour into a large bowl. Blend the yeast with the remaining flour and add to the lukewarm water. Add the mixture to the bowl containing the flour, combine well and shape the dough into a ball. Add the salt, lemon zest, egg yolk, sparkling wine and the melted margarine. Knead the dough well (it should have the consistency of a bread dough).Then add the diced glacé fruit to the dough and knead again. Cover the dough and leave to rest in a warm spot until double in size. Knead the dough once again and shape into a ring. Place the ring of dough onto a baking sheet dusted with flour. Now insert a small coin wrapped into tissue paper and the dried bean into the dough. Cover the holes. Allow the cake to rise once again. Brush the cake with beaten egg and decorate with glacé fruit. Bake in an oven at 160 °C for approx. 1 hour until golden brown. Once the cake has cooled, brush the candied fruit with jelly and dust with icing sugar.

Fortune Cake of St. Basilius
2 lb 3 oz flour
7 oz sugar
5 oz melted butter
8 fl oz warm milk
1 oz fresh yeast
6 eggs
½ tsp salt
1 large pinch of ground cinnamon
1 large pinch of coriander
Grated zest of 1 orange
Grated zest of 1 lemon
Coating:
1 egg yolk blended with 2 fl oz cream
Decoration:
5 oz icing sugar
2 oz sliced roasted almonds
Lemon and orange juice
Method
Blend the flour with the salt in a bowl. Crumble the yeast, add and prepare a
first dough with half of the milk, a spoonful of sugar and some flour. Cover
and allow to rise in a warm place for 20 minutes. Combine with the remaining
ingredients into a smooth dough and beat until the dough separates from the
base of the bowl. Cover and allow to rise in a warm place for around 1 hour.
Line a round cake tin (approx. 30 cm in diameter)with buttered non-stick
paper. Place dough into the cake tin, leaving sufficient space to "spread".
Insert a small coin into the cake! Then cover the cake again and leave in a
warm spot until double in
size. Brush the surface with the beaten egg yolk and cream mixture. Bake in
a pre-heated oven for around one hour at 180 °C until the surface is golden
brown. In the meantime, prepare the icing: Heat 150 g sugar with 90 ml of a
mixture made from orange juice, lemon juice and water until the sugar has
molten and runs off the spoon like honey. Remove the fortune cake from the
oven and brush while hot with the icing. Sprinkle the almonds on top. Allow
to cool and remove from the cake tin.

Jólagrautur - Yule Porridge
½ pint water
3 pints milk
6 oz rice

186

1 teaspoon salt
2 ½ oz raisins
Cinnamon and sugar
Milk
1 almond
When the water comes to a boil, stir in the rice and cook for 10 minutes. Add the milk to the pot and cook over a low heat for 1 hour. Add the raisins in the last 10 minutes. Add salt to taste. Add milk, sugar, and cinnamon to taste. The skinned almond is added and the porridge poured into a bowl. The housewife deals portions out and whoever finds the almond receives a small gift.

Yule Pudding
8 oz fresh breadcrumbs
1 ½ lb. mixed fruit
4 oz chopped mixed peel
3 fl oz stout
1 oz acorns, peeled and chopped
Juice and rind of 1 lemon
1 tsp. ground mixed spice
¼ tsp. cinnamon
1 tsp. grated nutmeg
6 oz butter
8 oz demerara sugar
2 oz sloes from sloe gin, stoned (optional)
Small silver coin or favour
Method
Combine the fruit, ale and lemon juice and rind. Cover and stand over night. In a bowl, cream together the butter and sugar. Beat in the eggs. Add all the other ingredients, including the coin or favour and mix well. Everyone who helps to stir the pudding can have a wish, so share this chore with as many as possible. Grease a large pudding bowl and press the mixture in, tying a cloth or grease proof paper over the top, making a pleat in the middle to allow for expansion. Stand the bowl in a large pan of hot water and boil for 4 hours, topping up the water as necessary. Turn out whilst still hot and pour over 1 or 2 tbs. whisky and light the pudding in the traditional way. *Don't forget to warn everyone to check their dish for the coin or favour.*

Plum pudding was originally a soup made by boiling beef & mutton with dried plums (prunes), wines and spices. The prunes & meats were later removed, raisins added and the pudding was thickened with eggs & breadcrumbs to be more like a steamed or broiled cake. So "plum pudding" is not a pudding and contains no plums. In the 17th century the word "plum" was commonly used to refer to any dried fruit.

Mincemeat
1 lb currants
1 lb raisins
1 lb sultanas
1 lb cooking apples, peeled, cored and finely chopped or coarsely grated
1 lb chopped beef suet, or vegetarian suet
3 ½ oz blanched almonds, roughly chopped
1 lb light muscovado sugar
1 tsp cinnamon
1 pinches grated nutmeg
1.5 tsp mixed spice
1 lemons, grated rind and juice
1 oranges, grated rind and juice
7 oz mixed candied peel, chopped
7 fl oz dark rum
9 fl oz dry sherry

Mix everything together in a really large bowl. It's a good idea to get stuck in and use your hands for this. Cover the bowl and leave on one side for a day so that the flavours can develop. Give it a good stir now and again. Pack the mincemeat into sterilised jars, seal with greaseproof paper jam pot covers and tight-fitting lids. Store in a cool place - if you have the time, let the mincemeat mature for 2-3 weeks before using it for mince pies. (For those who don't know, mince pies are small shortcrust pastry pies or tartlets filled with sweet mincemeat.)

Mincemeat pie was originally mainly minced meat preserved with sugar & spices. Fruits were often used as a less expensive preservative and flavouring agent than sugar. Meat was increasingly omitted (except for beef fat) and additional fruits were included.

RECIPES FOR GIFTS

Brandied Apricots
16 oz dried apricots
8 oz sugar
¼ pint brandy

Method

Soak the fruit in cold water overnight. Place the fruit and water in a pan and bring to the boil. Cover and simmer for 15 minutes. Strain the liquor into a measuring jug and return the fruit with ¼ pt. of liquor to the pan. Stir in half the sugar and bring to the boil. Simmer without stirring for a couple of minutes. Using a slotted spoon, remove the fruit and pack it into jars. Add the remaining sugar to the pan and stir until dissolved. Boil for four minutes and remove it from the heat. Cool the syrup and measure it. Add an equal amount of brandy. Pour the mixture into the jars, covering the fruit. Seal. This will keep for up to 6 months.

Decorated Biscuits

4 oz margarine
3 oz butter
2 oz icing sugar
5 oz plain flour
4 oz self raising flour
1 tbs. cornflour

Method

Cream together the butter and margarine, fold in the icing sugar, then the flours and cornflour. Knead lightly to make a smooth dough. Wrap in cling film and chill in the fridge for half and hour. Roll out the dough on a floured board to ¼ inch thick. Bake at 180°C/350°F/gas mark 4 for 15 minutes. Transfer to a cooling rack. In Germany these biscuits are traditionally cut into tile shapes and decorated and hung on the tree. Before baking, extra dough can be cut out or piped onto the biscuits to make raised patterns and a hole for hanging can be made with a clean drinking straw. After cooling the biscuits can be iced with royal icing and painted with food colourings, threaded on ribbons and hung on the tree.

Brandy Snaps

3 oz butter
2 oz sugar
3 fl oz golden syrup
2 oz flour
1 tsp. ground ginger
Juice of ½ lemon
6 fl oz double cream
2 tbs. brandy

Method

Heat the oven to 180°C/350°F/gas mark 4. Grease a baking sheet. In a pan melt the butter, sugar and golden syrup over a low heat. Remove from the heat and add the flour, ginger and lemon juice. Beat until the mixture is smooth. Drop spoonfuls onto a baking sheet and bake for 10 minutes. Turn off the oven and leave the biscuits in there to keep warm- if they cool they won't be malleable. One by one remove them from the baking sheet with a palette knife and curl them round the handle of a greased wooden spoon. Ease them off and put them on a cooling rack. When you are ready to serve them, beat up the cream until thick and add the brandy. Whisk up again until stiff and pipe into the brandy snaps.

Mint Humbugs

1 lb. soft brown sugar
3 tbs. butter
5 fl oz water
1 tbs. golden syrup
¼ tsp. cream of tartar
4 drops peppermint oil
2 tbs. icing sugar

Method

Put the butter, sugar, water, syrup and cream of tartar on a pan and stir over a low heat to dissolve the sugar. Increase the heat slightly and cover the pan. Cook for three minutes. Turn up the heat and bring to the boil. Continue to boil until a drop of the mixture, dropped into cold water, sets into a brittle thread which will bend and break. When this happens, remove from the head and pour the mixture onto an oiled board. Sprinkle with the peppermint oil and work the mixture with a palette knife until it it cool enough to handle. Oil your hands and stretch out the mixture into a rope and then fold back again. Continue to do this repeatedly until the mixture becomes elastic and shiny. Dust a surface with icing sugar and roll the mixture into a long rope. Snip with scissors into humbugs. Store them in an airtight jar.

Chocolate Fudge

2 oz butter
1 lb. sugar
5 fl oz milk
2 oz dark chocolate

Method

Put the milk, sugar and chocolate on a pan and stir over a low heat until the sugar has dissolved. Bring to the boil and continue boiling [do not stir] until a little of the fudge dropped into cold water forms a soft ball. Remove from the heat and cool for 5 minutes. Cut the butter into pieces and beat into the fudge, continue to beat until the fudge is smooth and thick. Pour the fudge into a well greased tin and allow to cool before cutting into squares.

Peppermint Creams

1 lb. icing sugar
1 tsp. lemon juice
1 egg white
4 drops peppermint essence

Method

Combine all the ingredients in a large bowl. Sprinkle a board with icing sugar and roll out the peppermint mixture to ¼ inch thick. Cut the mixture into shapes.

Rum Truffles

8 oz dark chocolate
2 tbs. icing sugar
1 ½ tsp. rum essence
2 oz chocolate sprinkles

Method

Melt the chocolate in a bowl over a pan of hot water, or in the microwave. Combine with the sugar and rum essence, stirring with a wooden spoon until well blended. Cool for 15 minutes and shape into small balls with your hands. Roll them in the chocolate sprinkles or cocoa powder.

DRINKS

Ginger Punch

1 pint tea made with two tea bags
1 pint apple juice
1 pint ginger beer
4 tbs. lemon juice

To decorate:

Lemon slices
Maraschino cherries

Method

Make the tea and remove the tea bags. Add the other liquids, transfer to a punch bowl and decorate with the fruit.

Irish Coffee

1 ½ oz. Irish whisky

1 ½ tsp. sugar

Black coffee

Whipped cream

Method

Pour the whisky into a coffee cup. Add the sugar and fill with hot, black coffee. Stir to dissolve sugar. Float whipped cream on top, do not stir. Add a straw if desired.

Seasonal Spice

2 fl. oz. rum

1 sugar cube

1 tbs. lemon juice

3 cloves

Cinnamon stick

Boiling water

Method

Combine all of the ingredients in a cup or mug. Add the boiling water. Stir with the cinnamon stick until the sugar dissolves. You may prefer to remove the cloves before drinking.

Hot Buttered Rum

1 ½ oz. rum

1 tsp. sugar

1 pat of butter

2 cloves

Boiling water

Method

Place the sugar, rum, and cloves in a cup or mug. Fill with boiling water. Add the pat of butter and stir.

Wassail (wine recipe)

½ lb. honey

2 pints red wine

1 pint water

Juice of 2 oranges

Juice of 1 lemon

Cinnamon stick

4 cloves

1 very small piece ginger root
1 handful of raisins
Method
Boil the water with the spices. Add the honey and raisins and stir until dissolved. Simmer for 5 minutes. Add the fruit juice. Remove from the heat and add the wine. Pour into a stew pot or deep casserole dish with a lid. Place in a low oven at 140°C/275°F/gas mark 1 for 40 minutes. Do not remove the lid whilst the wassail is in the oven, or the alcohol will evaporate. Serve hot.

Wassail (cider recipe)
2 ¼ pt cider
3 apples, grated
2 oz brown sugar
½ tsp. ground ginger
Grated nutmeg
Method
Put a ¼ pint of cider in a pan and add the grated apples. Cook until the apple is soft and add the brown sugar, ginger and the other 2 pints of cider. Heat through but do not allow to boil. Add some grated nutmeg and pour into a large cup or bowl. This is passed from one person to another with the blessing *"Waes haelinch"* or 'good health'.
The wassail cup is a traditional Yuletide drink. Formerly it was mulled mead, to which whole fruits and seasonings were added. The exotic spices are a more modern addition.

Negus
2 pints elderberry wine
6 cloves
Juice of 2 oranges
¼ pint water
¼ pint rum
Pinch grated nutmeg
Method
Heat all the ingredients together gently, but do not boil. Serve warm.

Atholbrose
1 tsp. clear honey
1 measure whisky

Method
Stir the honey into the whisky and drink. Quantities can be adjusted to taste.
In Scotland, this is considered an ideal breakfast drink!

Mulled Wine
½ lb. brown sugar
½ pint water
12 cloves
Cinnamon stick
½ tsp. ginger powder
1 lemon
1 orange
2 oz raisins
2 bottles red wine
To decorate:
Orange and lemon slices
Method
Put the sugar and water in a pan and heat slowly to dissolve, add the juice of the lemon and orange and their grated rinds and the spices. Boil for five minutes and leave to infuse for an hour. Strain into a large pan, add the raisins and bring to the boil. Add the wine, but do not allow it to boil [all the alcohol disappears!], just warm it through. Serve hot in glasses decorated with orange and lemon slices.

Mulled Mead
1 pt mead
½ oz bruised ginger
4 cloves
1 cinnamon stick
Method
Heat the mead to no hotter than 60° C with the bruised ginger, cloves cinnamon.

Mulled Ale
2 pt Ale
2 tsp. Demerara sugar
2 oz raisins
Grated nutmeg

Method
Heat all the ingredients together to 60°C . Serve hot.

Egg Nog with Brandy
4 fl oz. brandy
2 tsp. sugar
2 eggs
Milk
Pinch nutmeg
Method
Shake the brandy, sugar and eggs with the crushed ice and strain into 2 tall glasses. Fill with milk and sprinkle nutmeg on top.

THE CALENDAR OF YULE AND THE NEW YEAR

30th November

St Andrew's Day – Andrew seems to have taken over many of the functions of the god Frey. In parts of Germany, Austria and the Slavonic countries, there is a belief that the eve of St. Andrew's Day is suitable for magic and especially divinations concerning future lovers and marriage. In some areas in Austria, young women would drink wine and then perform a spell, called *Andreasgebet* (Saint Andrew's prayer), while nude and kicking a straw bed. This was magic supposed to attract a future husband. Yet another custom was to throw a clog over the shoulder: if it landed pointing to the door, the woman would get married in the same year.

1st December

Kalends of December (Roman) - To propitiate the spirits and ensure enough food for winter, on the first day of December Romans laid tables with food for the *Parcae* ('To Produce'), the three sisters of fate, and goddesses of abundance and motherhood. Nona spun the thread of life, Decima measured it, and Morta cut it. In the fifth century and again in the eleventh, German theologians condemned the custom of putting out food, drink and three knives for "those three Sisters whom the ancients in their folly called *Parcae*."

Day of Poseidon (moveable) (Greek) - In ancient Greece the lunar month in honour of Poseidon began with the new moon nearest to the end of the year. However, when the lunar calendar was changed into a fixed solar calendar by the Romans, the new moon of December was set aside on honour of Poseidon (Latin Neptune), the sea god who created the horse. The month of *Poseideôn* (roughly late December and early January) was dedicated to Poseidon and the eighth day was especially sacred to him. Poseidon's name seems to mean 'Husband of Earth' and he is sometimes described as married to Demeter, just as Saturn was the husband of Rhea.

St Eligius Day – The patron saint of jewellers, silversmiths and all metal workers. He is also the patron saint of horses and vets, and his symbol is the horseshoe. This seems to have been a Christian attempt to replace the day of Poseidon, who created the horse.

According to the legend, Eligius was a blacksmith and goldsmith who created a golden throne for King Clotaire and another throne from the gold left over. It was said that he possessed a magical horse and could rejuvenate himself by means of the fire from his forge. A popular song stated that Saint Eligius restored everything to its place. [205] Here we may possibly glimpse a fragment of an ancient theme concerning the part the divine blacksmith and his fire play in the restoring of the cosmos after the time of chaos. St Eligius has another festival near the summer solstice.

2nd December

3rd December

Marry on December third
For all the grief you ever heard

St Birinus' Day – A seventh century missionary from Dorchester-on-Thames, Oxfordshire, St Birinus tried to convert the Pagan Midlanders, but after several fruitless efforts he decided to stay put and became the first bishop of Dorchester. He was bitten by an adder and died in 650 CE. As he died he declared that all people of Dorchester would be safe from snake bite as long as they stayed in earshot of church bells. It is believed that snakes continue to by-pass the village as long as the bells are rung regularly.

4th December

Festival of Bona Dea ('Good Goddess') (Roman) – Bona Dea, sometimes called Fauna, was a goddess of fertility (of both women and the earth), healing, virginity and women, variously described as the daughter or wife of the god Faunus. She was very popular amongst women who sought her aid with their problems, with slaves who petitioned her for freedom, and with the poor and the sick, who were tended with herbs in her temple garden. Her temple was on the Aventine Hill, but special secret rites were performed

---

205   Prof. Philippe Walter, *Christianity, the Origins of a Pagan Religion,* Inner Traditions, Vermont, 2006

on this day by the wife of the *pontifex maximus* in her own home, assisted
by Vestal Virgins, and attended by women only, by special invitation, this
contrasted with her May festival at the temple which was open to all women,
whether patrician, free or slave. According to Plutarch's *Life of Caesar*:

> *"The Romans have a goddess whom they call Bona, the same whom
> the Greeks call Gynaecea. The Phrygians, who claim a peculiar title
> to her, say she was mother to Midas. The Romans profess she was one
> of the Dryads, and married to Faunus. The Grecians affirm that she is
> that mother of Bacchus whose name is not to be uttered, and, for this
> reason, the women who celebrate her festival, cover the tents with vine-
> branches, and, in accordance with the fable, a consecrated serpent
> is placed by the goddess. It is not lawful for a man to be by, nor so
> much as in the house, whilst the rites are celebrated, but the women by
> themselves perform the sacred offices, which are said to be much the
> same with those used in the solemnities of Orpheus. When the festival
> comes, the husband, who is either consul or praetor; and with him every
> male creature, quits the house. The wife then taking it under her care,
> sets it in order, and the principal ceremonies are performed during the
> night, the women playing together amongst themselves as they keep
> watch, and music of various kinds going on."*

For a man to see the ceremony was sacrilege and there was a notorious
incident when Publius Clodius Pulcher was prosecuted for infiltrating the
rite dressed as a woman. Though he managed to bribe his way out of the
conviction, it led to a life long enmity with Cicero who prosecuted him,
and to Julius Caesar divorcing his wife who had been hosting the ceremony
commenting, "Caesar's wife must be above suspicion".

Even paintings or other representations of men and male animals were
banned, along with the word 'wine' and myrtle because Bona Dea had once
been beaten by Faunus with a myrtle stick after she got drunk. The women
drank wine at the ceremony, but since wine was officially taboo, they called
it 'milk' and the jar from which it was served a 'honey-pot'. Very little is
known about the ceremony, but the worship seems to have been an agricultural
mystery cult in nature.

Her image frequently occurred on ancient Roman coins, and Bona
Dea was sometimes depicted with a sceptre, vine leaves, wine and a serpent
usually curled around her arm. Consecrated snakes were kept in her temple at
Rome. Sometimes she was depicted seated, holding a cornucopia.

Her other major festival is May 1st, the day of the dedication of her
temple, which was also run only by women, and during which a pregnant sow
was sacrificed. The temple to Bona Dea in Rome stood over an overhanging

198

rock, or cave, and both serpents and healing herbs were associated with the cave. Some men did bring offerings to Bona Dea at this festival.

She was also called Damia and her priestess *damiatrix*. These names are Greek and it is probable that the Greek cult of Damia was grafted onto the original cult of Bona Dea.

Carlo Ginzburg describes an early shamanic cult centred around the 'Good Goddess' (also called Herodiade, Diana, Habondia ['Abundance'] and Richessa) whose followers flew through the night skies with her to enter the homes of the rich and feast there.[206] She seems to have been a goddess of the dead and fertility, both of which come from the Underworld. It is possible that she was the origin of many of the winter/hag beliefs associated with this time of year.

Day of Barbet (Dutch) – In Dutch Pagan tradition there were three main goddesses, Anbet the earth, Wilbert the moon and Barbet the sun. In Germanic lore, there were three sister goddesses, Einbet, Barbet and Wilbet, and one of their shrines existed at the spot where Speyer Cathedral now stands.[207] In other areas of Germany the Nornes were called 'the three eternal ones' and their names were Einbet (Urd), Barbet (Verdandi), and Wilbet (Skuld). Barbet was Christianised as St Barbara.

Barbale (Georgian) – Barbale, also known as Babari, Babale and Barboli, was associated with fertility and the harvest, and some say a sun goddess. The origin of the Christian St Barbara may lie in the cult of the sun-goddess Barbale practiced by the Svans (a North Georgian tribe). She may be associated the Sumerian sun deity Babar.

St Barbara's Day – The Christian church replaced the Pagan goddesses Barbale and Barbet with St Barbara but abolished her in 1969, finding no credible evidence of her existence since her legends lie in the myths of those earlier Pagan goddesses. Slavonic art portrays both St Barbara and St Catherine with the solar haloes which are usually reserved for important male saints. St Catherine is associated with the fiery wheel and Barbara with lightning, and both may originally have been solar maidens. Some legends place Barbara inside a mountain, like the Venusberg or the Horselberg, the mountain of the fairy queen.

---

206   Carlo Ginzburg, *Ecstasies*, Hutchinson Radius, London, 1990

207   Nigel Pennick, *The Goddess Year*, Capall Bann, Chieveley

The Christian version of the legend recounts that Barbara was imprisoned in a high tower by her father to discourage her many suitors, but when he found out she had converted to Christianity, he handed her over to his henchmen for torture and eventually beheaded her himself, whereupon he was immediately struck dead by lightning. Therefore she is invoked against lightning, tempests and explosions and is the patron of artillerymen, miners, architects, builders and stonemasons. Another legend says that she was running through the mountains to get away from her father who wanted her to marry the son of a wealthy family. As she ran, she called out, "Mountains, take my body's elegance, and forests my thick tresses, and you, oleander trees, take my face's loveliness."

In many places, the Christmas season begins with her feast and it is especially associated with wheat. In the Lebanon a special dish of grain called *kahmie* is served. The head of the household tells the story of St Barbara while the wheat cooks. In southern France, especially in Provence, wheat grains are soaked in water, placed in dishes and set to germinate in the warm chimney corner or a sunny window. If it grows fast, crops will do well in the coming year. Another folk divination performed on her day is the gathering of cherry branches which are brought into the house and placed in water. They bring good luck in the coming year if they bloom by solstice. In Germany it was also the custom to cut Barbara twigs from fruit or nut trees and to place them in a warm place so that they will flower on Christmas Day. The Greeks invoked her for protection against smallpox and left her offerings of honey-cakes, *kollyva* (boiled wheat sprinkled with cinnamon and almonds) or *varvara* (boiled wheat broth), at crossroads.

In the Voudun tradition, she is associated with Shango, the fire-god, whose colours – like hers – are red and white. [208]

Old St Clement's Day- A sheep fair was held at Lambourn in Berks where stallholders sold sweets and Clementy Cake, spiced fruit buns made in Wantage and delivered to the fair.

5th December

Faunus (Roman) – A Roman festival was held on this day in honour of Faunus, the consort of Fauna. He is the rustic god of woods and flocks – a Roman Pan – the son of Picus, whom Circe turned into a woodpecker for spurning her love. According to Robert Graves, the tomb of Faunus on Crete

208   http://www.schooloftheseasons.com/decdays1.html

bore the inscription "Here lies the woodpecker who was also Zeus." Pan, the Greek god of the wild woods, and Hermes were also both associated with woodpeckers.

St Justinian's Day – St Justinian was a Breton hermit, a student of St David, who went to live on Ramsey Island, off the coast of Wales. He asked his fellow holy man Honorious to banish his sister and her maid so that they wouldn't be distracted by the company of women. Honorious complied, and Justinian gained a reputation for purity and chastity. One day two sailors came to tell Justinian that St David was dying and offered to row him across the water. He accepted but half way across realised that the sailors were demons in disguise and sang *Psalm 79*. The sailors changed into their true demonic forms, then into crows which flew away. David wasn't ill at all. Later the demons possessed Justinian's servants. When he told them to get to work, they tossed him in the air and chopped off his head. Justinian picked up his head and carried it to a part of the island where he was buried. The head formed a healing spring and a church was raised over the saint's body.

Eve of St Nicholas – St Nicholas, or more correctly Nikolaos ('victory of the people') was said to be the bishop of Lycia (part of modern day Turkey) who died on 6th December 346 CE, though there is no historical evidence of his existence. He is the patron saint of sailors, merchants, archers, thieves, children and students.

He is associated with many miracles, both before and after his death. In one tale, during a famine a butcher lured three young children (or three clerks) to his house, where he killed and butchered them with the intention of selling the meat. St Nicholas resurrected them with his prayers.

His most famous legend concerns three poor girls whose father could not afford to supply them with dowries, which meant that they would be unable to marry and would be forced to turn to prostitution. Nicholas secretly went to their house and threw three purses of gold through their window. In some versions he threw in purses for three nights, in others over a period of three years. Learning that the father lay in wait to find out the identity of the mysterious benefactor, St Nicholas dropped the last purse down the chimney, where it landed in a stocking left hanging by the hearth to dry. In his honour, medieval nuns are said to have gone about on St Nicholas' Eve leaving baskets of food and clothes at the doorsteps of the needy. [209]

He had a great reputation for gift-giving, and took over the legends

209   http://en.wikipedia.org/wiki/Saint_Nicholas

and functions of the gift giving spirits of the season (such as Woden and Befana etc.), even being identified as Santa Claus. In the Netherlands, children put their wooden clogs (or sometimes baskets) by the hearth on the Eve of St. Nicholas, hoping that St Nicholas, riding through the air on his white horse, will pause, come down the chimney and fill them with sweets. Carrots and hay are left out for his white horse. This is plainly a Christianisation of the legend of Woden flying through the air on his eight legged horse around the winter solstice. In some cases, children spread a white sheet on the floor and sing special songs welcoming St Nicholas. The door suddenly opens and a shower of treats falls upon the sheet. Then St Nicholas (or rather, the man playing him) appears, dressed in his bishop's robes, and questions the children about their behaviour. He is accompanied by Zwarte Piet ('Black Peter'), who carries a thick rod and a sack and threatens to carry the children off if they have been naughty. After the children are sent to bed, adults exchange gifts and feast on hot punch, chocolate and boiled chestnuts served hot with butter and sugar.[210]

In Czechoslovakia, children believe that St Nicholas comes down a golden cord carrying a basket of apples, nuts and sweets. In Hungary, shoes are left outside the window to be filled by the passing saint. In France, children hang stockings near the fire saying:

Saint Nicholas, mon bon patron,
Envoyez-moi quelque chose de bon.[211]

In the Tyrol children prayed to the saint on his Eve and left out hay for his white horse and a glass of *schnaps* for his servant. He appeared dressed in bishop's robes, and tested children on their catechism, and rewarded the good children with sweets, while bad children were shown his servant, the hideous Klaubauf, a shaggy monster with horns, black face, fiery eyes, long red tongue, and chains that clanked as he moved.[212] In Lower Austria the saint is followed by a similar figure called Krampus or Grampus, in Styria by a horrible attendant called Bartel. Sometimes St. Nicholas himself appears in a non-churchly form like Pelzmärte, with a bell or with a sack of ashes which gains him the name of Aschenklas. Sometimes, however, he is accompanied by St Peter, an angel and even Jesus Christ. These are represented by children, who perform a kind of mumming play, during which the children in the

---

210   http://www.schooloftheseasons.com/decdays1.html

211   *Ibid*

212   Clement A. Miles, *Christmas in Ritual and Tradition*, Christian and Pagan, T. Fisher Unwin, 1912

202

audience are accused of various misdeeds, and are defended by the *Heiliger Christ* who eventually rewards them with nuts.

The protestant reformer Martin Luther tried to get rid of Catholic elements of Christmas, and replaced Nicolas with *das Christkindl* (an angel-like Christ Child) who brought Christmas gifts. This figure later evolved *der Weihnachtsmann* (Father Christmas) and in America into Kris Kringle.[213]

In Germany, St Nicholas' Eve is called *Nikolausta* and in the Catholic regions a man dressed as Nicholas goes from house to house taking gifts to children, carrying a book which is supposed to list all their naughty and good behaviour. He is accompanied by scary figures like Krampus, who jokily frightens the children, threatening them with a switch. In other regions, Krampus is called Knecht Ruprecht, who sometimes brings the gifts in place of Nicholas. Sometimes they don't make a personal appearance, and in this case children leave their shoes by the window or door on December 5th in the hope that they will be filled with treats. In past times, naughty children would have had a switch left instead, though this aspect has faded away. In parts of France and Luxembourg, he is accompanied by Père Fouettard, a hairy wildman figure with a red beard.

Like other saints and gods of this time of year, St Nicholas is associated with grain and with plenty. During a famine, he asked for some wheat for the hungry from a ship which lay in the harbour, loaded with grain for the Emperor of Byzantium. The sailors were worried that they would be punished for anything missing by the emperor, but Nicholas assured them they would be safe. Nicholas took enough wheat for two years with enough left for sowing. To the sailors' amazement, when they arrived at the capital, their holds were as full as before they left.

As the patron saint of sailors, he remains a favourite among the Greek and Italian sailors and fishermen, and is the patron saint of many harbour towns. In Greek folklore he is described as 'Lord of the Sea' and took over many of the functions and attributes of Poseidon. This may come simply from the similarity of his name to the Scandinavian sea god Hold Nickar, whose name remains as Old Nick, a term for the devil.

There is a story that Saint Nicholas had a run in with the Pagan goddess Diana. After he destroyed her statue, the goddess disguised herself as a nun and gave returning sailors a flammable oil, designed to destroy the sanctuary where the saint preached. Nicholas miraculously appeared to the

---

213   http://german.about.com/library/blnikolaus.htm

sailors while they were still at sea, and had them burn the oil upon the waters, showing that Christian magic was stronger than Pagan magic. [214]

Amongst Albanians, Saint Nicholas or Shen'Kollë is widely venerated. His feast is celebrated on 5th December, and is known *Shen'Kolli i Dimnit* (Saint Nicholas of Winter). On the eve of the feast day, Albanians light a candle and abstain from meat, preparing a feast of roasted lamb and pork to be served to guests after midnight. Guests will greet each other, saying, *"Nata e Shen'Kollit ju nihmoftë!"* ("May the Night of Saint Nicholas help you").

The three purses he left for the three impoverished virgins are said to be the origin of the pawnbroker's sign, making him the patron saint of pawnbrokers. The Low Countries interpret the three gold balls as oranges or other fruits, which were imported seasonally from Spain, giving rose to the idea that the saint lived in Spain and visited each winter, bringing oranges and other winter delicacies. [215]

6th December

St Nicholas Day – St Nicholas's Day was particularly popular in Belgium and the Netherlands, with shops stocking special biscuits, gingerbread images of the saint, toys and little gifts. A church service would be held which would be attended by seafarers in particular, looking for the blessing of their patron saint.

Boy Bishop – In the Middle Ages in England a 'Boy Bishop' was elected to rule from St Nicholas Day St Innocent's day (December 28th) officiating in all the bishop's duties except the mass. If he died in office he was buried with all the ceremony of a real bishop. (See December 28th.)

Christkindlmärkte – This is the traditional date when local Christmas markets open in the main square of almost every town in Austria and Germany.

St Leonard's Ride – In Bavaria, people dress up in native costume and decorate their horses in preparation for a festive procession in honour of St Leonard, the patron of cattle. They march with their cattle in the procession, led by white horses, while singing and cracking whips. It is possible this date was once associated with a cattle sacrifice. St Leonard is also the patron of

214   Prof. Philippe Walter, *Christianity, the Origins of a Pagan Religion*, Inner Traditions, Vermont, 2006
215   http://en.wikipedia.org/wiki/Saint_Nicholas

204

women in childbirth, because it was said that when the wife of the King went into labour suddenly while hunting in the woods, St Leonard came out of his hermit's cell to pray for her and she was safely delivered. He is also the patron of prisoners, and when invoked by those who have been unjustly imprisoned, he brings about their freedom.

7th December

8th December

Immaculate Conception (Christian) – In the seventh century this date was chosen to mark the date of the Immaculate Conception because it is nine months before Mary's birthday (but obviously not nine months before December 25th). On this day in Madeira, women begin baking the *bolo de mel* cake which is served at Christmas. This honey cake contains walnuts, almonds and candied peel. It is traditional to leaven the cake with a piece of dough from bread-baking. Also any honey cakes left from the previous year must be eaten up on this day. In Sicily, it is traditional to have a cylindrical, hard biscuit called *pietrafendola*, which means 'rock splitter'.

9th December

Conception of St Anne – In the Orthodox Church, this is considered the day when St Anne conceived the Virgin Mary (Mary's birthday is September 8th). On a seventeenth century Scandinavian calendar, this day is marked with a pitcher for "it is time to pour water on the barley in order to brew the beer for Christmas cheer."

10th December

St Obert's Day –A play was once held at Perth on Tayside commemorating St Obert, a local hero and patron of bakers. The bakers wore outlandish costumes and paraded the streets, and performed a mumming play with one of them taking the part of Obert. The Protestants banned it after the Reformation.

11th December

Agonalia of Sol Indiges – Agonalia was a festival celebrated several times a year in honour of various deities on January 9th, May 21st, and December 11th (and probably March 17th when the *Liberalia* or *Agonia Martiale* was celebrated). The word is derived either from *agonia,* 'a victim' or from *agonium* 'a festival'. A ram was sacrificed by the *rex sacrificulus.*

Sol was the sun god in ancient Rome. In the early days, when Rome was stilled ruled by kings, Sol came to be identified with Janus. Janus and Jana were worshipped as sun and moon, the highest of the gods who received their sacrifices before all the others. Sol Indiges ('the native sun' or 'the invoked sun') represents the earlier, more agrarian form in which the Roman god Sol was worshipped.

Septimontium – Roman festival celebrating the Seven Hills of Rome, originally held in September, but later on 11th December.

Old St Andrew's Day – At Kirton-in-Lindsey in Lincolnshire the T'Andra Fair used to be held. Locals drank from the Ash-well, which ensured they would never want to leave the village. In Northamptonshire the day was the lace maker's holiday when people cross-dressed and drank copiously.

12th December

Virgin of Guadalupe – This festival commemorates a sixteenth century sighting of the Virgin Mary by peasant by a hill called Tepeyac situated outside Mexico City. She appeared with dark skin and dressed in the robes of an Aztec princess, speaking Nahuatl, the Aztec language, and saying she was the Mother of God. A chapel was built on the spot, an ancient shrine of the ancient Aztec goddess, Tonantzin, a mother-goddess honoured on the winter solstice. She was portrayed by a woman dressed entirely in white and covered with shells and eagle feathers, who danced through the crowd, weeping and singing, until she was ritually killed.

Hari No Kuyo – A Japanese festival when men and women reverse roles, reminiscent of the Roman Saturnalia.

St Lucy's Eve – Saint Lucy or Lucia ('Light') was a Christian martyr of the early fourth century CE and is one of seven women, aside from the Blessed Virgin Mary, commemorated by name in the Canon of the Mass. She is said to have lived during the Diocletian persecution, and to have consecrated her virginity to God, refusing to marry a Pagan, giving her dowry to the poor. Her suitor denounced her as a Christian to the governor of Syracuse in Sicily. The story was first recorded in the fifth-century, and had become widespread the sixth century. A later version of the tale has her sentenced to be defiled in a brothel, to which she replied that God would bless her with a twofold purity, since it was done against her will. Tradition has it that she was so filled with the Holy Spirit that it needed a team of oxen to cart her away. A fifteenth century addition to the story has her having her eyes pricked out by her guards, prior to execution. She is often pictured with her eyes on a plate or cup beside her, and became patron saint of the blind. In another version, her suitor praised her beautiful eyes and she plucked them out and sent them to him. In this version, God restored her sight.

St Lucy's Eve was a mysterious and dangerous time in many parts of Europe, a time when witches were thought to be especially powerful. In Britain, witches and fairies would kidnap anyone who went to bed without any supper. In Lower Austria witchcraft was feared and had to be averted by prayer and incense. A procession was made through each house to cense every room. On this evening, too, girls were afraid to spin lest in the morning they should find their distaffs twisted, the threads broken, and the yarn in confusion. On St Lucy's Eve, candles are lit and all electrical lights are turned off, and on the Sunday closest to December 13th Danes traditionally attend church.

It was also a time when the future could be divined. In Austria a mysterious light called *Luzieschein* ('the Lucy-shining') was observed by boys outdoors at midnight, and the future could be foretold from its appearance. Meanwhile, at midnight the girls would go to a willow-bordered brook, cut the bark of a tree partly away, without detaching it, make with a knife a cross on the inner side of the cut bark, moisten it with water, and carefully close up the opening. On New Year's Day the cutting would be opened, and the future augured from the markings found. Danish maids prayed "Sweet St. Lucy let me know: whose cloth I shall lay, whose bed I shall make, whose child I shall bear, whose darling I shall be, whose arms I shall sleep in".

St. Lucia is the patron saint of the city of Sicily, where she is said to have been born. Children are asked to leave some food for Lucia and for the flying donkey that helps her carry gifts but they must not see Santa Lucia delivering gifts, or she will throw ashes in their eyes, temporarily blinding them. An old tradition on the village Montedoro, after sunset on the Eve, was for a procession of men, youths and children, each flourishing a thick bunch of long straws all afire, to rush wildly down the streets. "The darkness of the night," said an eye-witness, "was lighted up by this savage procession of dancing, flaming torches, whilst bonfires in all the side streets gave the illusion that the whole village was burning." [216] At the end of the procession was the

---

216   Clement A. Miles, *Christmas in Ritual and Tradition*, Christian and Pagan, T. Fisher Unwin, 1912

image of Santa Lucia, holding a dish which contained her eyes. In the midst of the piazza a great mountain of straw had been prepared onto which everyone threw their burning torches, and the saint was placed in a spot from which she could survey the vast bonfire.[217]

Lucy had a bit of a mixed reputation. In central Europe she had another aspect entirely. In the Böhmerwald she was said to go around the village in the form of a nanny-goat with horns, giving fruit to the good children, and threatening to rip open the belly of the naughty. In one classic Scandinavian tale, she was said to have been the first wife of Adam and the mother of the *vittra* (fairy) people who lived underground. In a similar story Eve, was said to be the mother of the *huldufolk* (fairies). Again in Scandinavia, Lussi rode through the air with her followers, called *Lussiferda* in a similar manner to the Wild Hunt. Between Lussi Night and Yule, trolls, ghosts and evil spirits were thought to be active. It was particularly dangerous to be out during Lussi Night. Children who had been naughty had to take special care, since Lussi would fly down the chimney and take them away. Certain tasks to be finished, or else Lussi would punish the household.

Whether an actual person called Lucia ever existed or not, the saint seems to have taken her mythology and characteristics from local Pagan deities, and is such is seen differently in different regions. In Italy it is likely that she is derived from the Roman goddess Juno Lucina or Lucetia, the Mother of Light who also carried a tray and a lamp, bestowing the gifts of light, enlightenment and sight, who as also known as the opener of the eyes of newborn children. [218] In Scandinavia she seems to have taken on attributes of the goddess Freya who was known as the *Vanadis*, or the shining bride of the gods. [219] The *lussikatter* (Lucy cats) or the golden saffron rolls that are served by the Lucia Bride are said to be the devil's cats which Lucia subdued, and the cats were pictured at her feet. Cats were also associated with Freya. Freya's special season was Yule when she dispensed wealth and plenty. The traditional shape of the rolls is a crossed shape where the arms are rolled inward and in the curve are bright pieces of fruit or small candles in the form of a solar wheel.[220] Lucia may also have some aspects of the Norse sun-goddess Sunna, whose emblem is the fiery wheel.

---

217   *Ibid*

218   Susan Granquist, 1995, http://www.irminsul.org/arc/001sg.html

219   *Ibid*

220   *Ibid*

13ᵗʰ December

St Lucy's Day- In Sweden the Christmas season begins with St. Lucia's Day, and as such, is sometimes referred to as 'little Yule'. It is thought that to celebrate the day with vigour will help a person live through the winter days with enough light. Lucy's is one of the few saints days celebrated in Scandinavian countries, and is also observed in Norway, Denmark, Iceland, Latvia, Estonia and Finland, as well as Malta, Italy, Bosnia, Bavaria, Croatia and Slovakia.

In Scandinavian celebrations, it is a festival of light when Saint Lucy comes as a young woman with lights and sweets. Processions of young women are traditional, often holding candles and singing Lucia songs to the tune of the Neapolitan *Santa Lucia,* but with different lyrics according to the locality, such as *Natten går tunga fjät* ('The Night walks with heavy steps'), or *Santa Lucia, ljusklara hägring* ('Saint Lucy, bright mirage') and *Ute är mörkt och kallt* ('Outside it's dark and cold'). Sometimes, the procession is headed by a girl wearing a red sash and a crown of lingonberry (*Vaccinium vitis-idaea*) twigs and candles. In the past, young women went from farm to farm all through the night, carrying torches to light their way and offering food at each farm they visited, returning home at dawn. [221]

In the home, the oldest daughter rises first and wakes the rest of the family. She is dressed in white with a red sash, and wears the nine-candle wreath, though her younger sisters will just dress in white and carry a single candle as they take breakfast to their parents, with hot coffee and *lussekatter* ('Lucy cats' i.e. yeast rolls). For the day, the girl is called *Lussi* (Lucy) or *Lussibruden* (Lucy bride). The family then eats breakfast in a room lighted with candles.

In the Scandinavian countries, threshing was supposed to be finished by Lucia's Day so sometimes people worked all night and were rewarded for their efforts with food and drink.

In Christian times it became the day for butchering the Christmas pig. Traditionally the butcher would be given the *lussesup* ('cup of light') which was brandy or other spirit. This may relate to the earlier Pagan *bragarfull* or holy cup that oaths were sworn on which were associated with the *sonargolt* or holy boar at Yule. [222] The *bragarfull* 'promise-cup' or *bragafull* 'best cup' or 'chieftain's cup' was in Norse culture a particular drinking from a cup or

---

221   Susan Granquist, 1995, http://www.irminsul.org/arc/001sg.html

222   *Ibid*

drinking horn on ceremonial occasions, often involving the swearing of oaths when the cup or horn was drunk by a chieftain or passed around and drunk by those assembled.[223] According to a passage in the eddic poem *Helgakviða Hjǫrvarþssonar*:

> *Hedin was coming home alone from the forest one Yule-eve, and found a troll-woman; she rode on a wolf, and had snakes in place of a bridle. She asked Hedin for his company. "Nay," said he. She said, "Thou shalt pay for this at the bragarfull." That evening the great vows were taken; the sacred boar was brought in, the men laid their hands thereon, and took their vows at the bragarfull. Hedin vowed that he would have Sváva, Eylimi's daughter, the beloved of his brother Helgi; then such great grief seized him that he went forth on wild paths southward over the land, and found Helgi, his brother.[224]*

The tradition of the maiden with candles in her wreath is a relatively modern one, started in the in the area around Lake Vänern and spreading slowly to other parts of the country during the 1800s. Some trace it to the white-clad Christkind, or the tradition of the star boys and white dressed angels singing carols during the festive season. The public processions started in 1927 when a newspaper in Stockholm elected an official Lucia for Stockholm. Other regions followed suit and schools elect a Lucia and her maids. In West Gothland Lussi went round the village preceded by torchbearers, and in one parish she was represented by a cow with a crown of lights on her head.

There are now also boys in the procession, some dressed in the same kind of white robe, but with a cone-shaped hat decorated with golden stars, and these are called *stjärngossar* ('star boys'). Others may be dressed up as *tomtenissar* (fairies) carrying lanterns and others may be dressed up as gingerbread men. They sing songs, usually *Staffan Stalledräng*, which tells the story of Saint Stephen and his five horses. The *stjarngossar* may be a legacy of the young men who previously went from door to door frightening people, singing songs and begging money. The figures have parallels with the guisers and mummers in Britain and elsewhere at this time of year.[225] The Star Boys were originally, like the wildman, dressed in furs with blackened faces. In other Scandinavian areas, St Lussi is a man dressed in goat skins with a

---

223   http://www.statemaster.com/encyclopedia/Bragarfull

224   *Ibid*

225   Susan Granquist, 1995, http://www.irminsul.org/arc/001sg.html

devil mask and horns. Lussi threatens to disembowel children who have been naughty.[226]

Influenced by Swedish culture, Finland is recorded as having a Lucy celebration in 1898, and larger celebrations since 1930. In Finland today, one girl is chosen to serve as the national Lucia and she is honoured in a parade in which she is surrounded by torchbearers. Following on, Denmark began celebrating in 1944, importing the traditions from Sweden. After World War II, the Swedish customs were imported into Norway, though it was a secular event, rather than a religious one. Boys take part in the procession, dressed as magi with tall hats and star-staffs or sometimes as *nisses* (fairies).

14th December

Halcyon Days begin – The Halcyon Days are the seven days before and the seven days after (or some say the seven days surrounding) the winter solstice, when the weather is supposed to be calm and storms never occur. The name comes from Greek myth, reported by both Ovid and Hyginus.

Alcyone was the daughter of Aeolus, and married Ceyx, son of Eosphorus, the Morning Star. They were very happy together but made the mistake of blasphemously calling each other Zeus and Hera. Not surprisingly, this made Zeus very angry and he threw a thunderbolt at Ceyx's ship, as he was sailing to consult an oracle. Ceyx appeared to Alcyone as a ghost, and in grief, she threw herself into the sea. Out of compassion, the gods changed them into halcyon birds (kingfishers). During the Halcyon Days, Alcyone the kingfisher lays her eggs, and her father, the god of winds, ensures that they are safe. The Mediterranean is typically calm around the time of the winter solstice. The dried body of a kingfisher was used as a talisman against lightning.

Ember Days (moveable) – The Wednesday, Friday and Saturday after December 13th are Ember Days, when Catholics say special prayers for the clergy.

Rural Dionysion – The ancient Greeks celebrated this holiday around the time of the full moon in the month of Poseidon. Plutarch complained that the rustic festival he remembered from his youth, featuring a jar of wine, a vine, a goat, a basket of raisins and a depiction of a phallus had been replaced with

226   http://www.forteantimes.com/features/articles/134/lapp_of_the_gods.html

an elaborate procession featuring gold vessels, decorated horses and people wearing costumes and masks. This was a time for revelry including bawdy songs and raucous game.

15ᵗʰ December

Consualia or Consuales Ludi (Roman) – This was the festival of Consus, god of the grain stores and councils, who also had festivals on July 7ᵗʰ and August 21ˢᵗ. (His consort Opalia was honoured on December 19ᵗʰ and his August festival followed by the Opiconsivia in her honour on August 25ᵗʰ). His name seems to be Etruscan or Sabine in origin and relate to 'crops/ seeding' (*conserere* = 'to sow'). He may have become the god of secret councils from a misinterpretation of his name, from *consilium* ('councils/ assemblies), not to be confused with counsel ('advice').

At this time of year, the harvest was in stored vaults underground. The temple of Consus was also underground, near the Circus Maximus, with an altar covered with earth which was only uncovered for this festival. He was represented by a grain seed.

During the celebration horses, mules, and asses were exempted from work, and were led through the streets adorned with garlands and flowers. Chariot races were held this day in the Circus Maximus, which included an unusual race in which chariots were pulled by mules. Consus was often called Neptunus Equestris ('Equestrian Neptune') and seems to be connected with Neptune (Poseidon), the sea god who created horses.

Mars, as a protector of the harvest, was also honoured on this day, as were the *lares*, the individual household gods.

16ᵗʰ December

Las Posadas ('Inn/ Shelter') (Mexico) – During the nine nights before Christmas, children dress up and process from house to house, looking for shelter in intimation of Mary and Joseph. The procession is led by a child dressed as an angel, followed by two clad as Mary and Joseph. The others carry lighted candles. They sing a carol at each house and beg for shelter, but they are always told to move on until they reach a house where the family sing "Let the chosen one enter". On entering, they place their candles around the nativity scene and say a prayer and a blessing for their hosts.

Pastorelas (shepherd's plays) are also performed. In them, a group of shepherds travel towards Bethlehem, but are tempted by devils. Angels rush in to rescue the shepherds and drive off the devils. These plays feature singing, dancing and satire, similar to medieval English mummer's plays which were often performed during this season. [227]

Official start of the mince pie season.

17th December

Saturnalia begins – Saturn was a major Roman god of the seasons, the calendar, agriculture and the harvest. He was depicted holding a sickle in his left hand and a bundle of wheat in his right. In Roman mythology after Jupiter defeated him, Saturn fled to Rome and established a Golden Age there as an earthly king, a time of perfect peace and harmony. When the era was over, Saturn departed to lie asleep on a magical island, but will one day return and bring back another golden age. His friend Janus instituted the Feast of Saturnalia in memory of him every year in the winter at the winter solstice, and its customs were meant to recapture something of this perfect time - no taxes could be collected, no wars declared and no prisoners executed. Presents were given and feasts and merrymaking were the order of the day.

The meal normally prepared only for the masters was prepared and served first to the slaves by the masters. All people were equal and, because Saturn ruled before the current cosmic order, Misrule, with its lord (*Saturnalia Princeps*), was the order of the day. According to Macrobius' *Saturnalia*, the holiday was originally probably only one day, although he notes an Atellan playwright, Novius, described it as being seven days. With Caesar's changing of the calendar, the festival lengthened.

The spirit of the season may be judged from the legislation which Lucian attributes to Cronosolon, priest and prophet of Cronus, including:

* All business, be it public or private, is forbidden during the feast days, save such as tends to sport and solace and delight. Let none follow their avocations saving cooks and bakers.
* All men shall be equal, slave and free, rich and poor, one with another.
* Anger, resentment, and threats are contrary to law.
* No discourse shall be either composed or delivered, except it be witty and lusty, conducing to mirth and jollity.
* Every man shall take place as chance may direct; dignities and birth and wealth shall give no precedence.

---

227   http://www.schooloftheseasons.com/decdays1.html

- All shall be served with the same wine.... Every man's portion of meat shall be alike.
- When the rich man shall feast his slaves, let his friends serve with him.

Sow Day – In Orkney, a sow was killed on this day, probably a custom that derived from the islanders' Viking ancestry. The pig has long been a significant animal at this time of year, a symbol of abundance, especially in the north. Every family that kept swine would slaughter a sow for Yule. Pork is a traditional Yule dish in Norway - probably a reminder of the time when the boar, an animal sacred to Frey, the Norse god of Yule and fertility, was sacrificed at Yule and its flesh eaten as part of the feast.

18th December

Eponalia (Roman/ Celtic) – The Romans readily adopted the Celtic goddess Epona, and she was the only Celtic deity actually worshipped in Rome itself. Her veneration was widespread throughout the empire between the first and third centuries CE. She was incorporated into the Imperial cult by being invoked on behalf of the Emperor, as Epona Augusta or Epona Regina. She was the protector of horses and donkeys, and under Rome became the patron goddess of the cavalry, especially the Imperial Horse. Small images of Epona have been found in Roman sites of stables and barns over a wide geographical area, suggesting that her worship took place in stables. On her feast day, grooms decorated her shrine in the stable and draft animals like horses, mules and oxen were given the day off.

Her name means 'Great Mare' and is from the Gaulish language, probably derived from the inferred proto-Celtic *ekwos* meaning 'horse', which gives rise to modern Welsh *ebol* 'foal'. She is always shown riding on a horse, or seated with horses around her or with foals eating out of her lap and as a goddess of fertility with a *patera,* cornucopia and ears of grain.

The key to the Underworld is one of her symbols, and the goddess and her horses were leaders of the soul in the after-life ride, like the Brythonic Rhiannon.

Other fertility and earth goddesses were also associated with the horse. The early form of the Greek goddess Demeter, for example, had also been a Great Mare. She was mounted by Poseidon (in the form of a stallion) and then gave birth to Arion and the daughter who was unnamed outside the

Arcadian mysteries. Demeter was venerated as a mare in Lycosoura in Arcadia into the historical period.

Some have suggested that the seasonal hobby horse, pantomime horse and Mari Llwyd customs may derive from the earlier worship of Epona.

Nuestra Senora de la Soledad – Our Lady of Solitude (Mexico) – In the cathedral in Oaxaca, the Virgin's statue is dressed in black satin and ornamented with pearls and gold thread and lilies. Processions are held in her honour for several nights previous to and on December 18th, with people carrying lanterns, candles and figures of birds, a boat along with banners displaying the sun and the moon and other objects made of flowers, leaves and coloured paper. Offerings of nuts, fruits and flowers are laid at the feet of the Virgin. Booths around the cathedral sell *bonuelos*, big crisp pancakes fried in lard and eaten with syrup. After eating them, it is customary to break the plate.

19th December

Opalia, 3rd day of Saturnalia (Roman) – Ops or Opis means 'abundance, plenty, riches' and gives us our word 'opulent'. The name may also relate to *opus* or work, in the sense of working the land. She was an underworld goddess, the earth mother who made the crops grow, the giver of all the riches of the earth. She was invoked by her worshipers while sitting, with their hands touching the ground, according to Macrobius' *Saturnalia*. Her consort is Consus, who may be an aspect of Saturn with Ops an aspect of Rhea.

20th December

Midwinter's Eve

St Thomas' Eve – Saint Thomas is the apostle who didn't believe that Christ had risen until he saw him in the flesh, and is therefore sometimes called 'doubting Thomas'.

His feast day on solstice eve accumulated all the earlier traditions of the festival, and is accounted one of the uncanniest nights of the year. In some Bohemian villages the saint was believed to drive about at midnight in a chariot of fire (doubtless derived from an earlier solar myth) and went to the churchyard, where all the dead men called Thomas had risen from their graves to help him out of his chariot and accompany him to the churchyard cross, which glowed red with supernatural radiance. There he prayed and blessed the Thomasses who returned to their coffins. People listened for the passing of his chariot and prayed to him for protection. Before going to bed, the man of the house would go to the cow byre and sprinkle it with holy water and consecrated salt, and then sprinkle every cow with a prayer that Saint Thomas would preserve them from sickness. In the Böhmerwald the cattle were fed with consecrated bayberries, bread and salt to avert disease.[228] In Upper and Lower Austria St. Thomas's Eve was reckoned as one of the *Rauchnächte* (smoke-nights) when houses and farm-buildings were sanctified with incense and holy water.

This was one of the prime nights of the year for forecasting the future. In Germany shoes were thrown backwards over the shoulder. If the points were found turned towards the door the thrower was destined to leave the house during the year. In England there was divination by means of the 'St. Thomas's onion'. Girls used to peel an onion, wrap it in a handkerchief and put it under their heads at night, with a prayer to the saint to show them their true love in a dream.

Byanna's Sunday (moveable) – In Shetland the Sunday before Yule was called Byanna's Sunday, and a special meal was eaten in which half a cow's head was boiled and eaten. The skull was saved and cleaned, and a candle inserted into its eye sockets on Yule morning.

21st December

Date of winter solstice in most years.

Compitalia – In ancient Rome, the spirits of the hearth and home were honoured at the *Compitalia*, celebrated soon after the solstice, when merrymaking accompanied the performance of theatrical farces. Slaves and freedmen especially venerated the *Lares* (household gods) as it was one of the few state cults to which people of all stations were admitted. The *Compitalia* called for the use of artificial light, and the *Lares* traditional sacrificial victim was the pig.[229]

---

228   Clement A. Miles, *Christmas in Ritual and Tradition*, Christian and Pagan, T. Fisher Unwin, 1912

229   In many traditions pig meat was taboo, associated with the underworld and only acceptable food at certain festivals. Boars were sacrificed to the Norse Frey at the winter solstice and the ceremony of bringing in the boar's head at the Yuletide feast arose from this. The heroes of Valhalla daily killed and ate the boar Saehrimnir who regrew every night, echoing the solar boar which rises, crosses the sky, sinks into the underworld to renew itself to rise once again in the morning. In ancient Egypt the boar was also associated with the midwinter solstice, when the taboo on eating pig flesh was annually broken at the feast of the boar's head.

Brumalia – In Rome, this was the celebration of the solstice - *bruma* means 'shortest day'. The festival of Saturnalia immediately preceded Brumalia.

Dong Zhi ('Extreme of Winter') (Chinese) – The festival marks the time when positive yang energy returns with lengthening daylight hours. The winter is the season of the Yin and summer the season of the Yang. Dong Zhi is marked by optimism and celebrated with merriment, family gatherings, gifts and feasting. It is believed the oldest of ancestors return to be with the family. Rituals are carried out to ensure future prosperity and both house and stables are thoroughly cleaned to prepare them for the new season.

Soya'la (Hopi) - The Hopis of the American south west hold a winter solstice ceremony timed by their sun watchers. Its name means 'they come out' referring to the *kachinas*, the guardian cosmic spirits who guard and protect the Hopi though their seasons of life, symbolising the beginning and renewal of life and growth. The *kachinas* are messengers between men and the gods. At midsummer they leave the Hopi villages to return to their homes in the mountains for half the year, where they are believed to visit the dead underground and hold ceremonies for them. They awake and begin to emerge from the *Kivas* (the underground ceremonial chamber believed to be a gateway to the underworld) at the winter solstice.

Shalako - The Zuñi celebrated *Shalako* on midwinter's day in a ceremony that extended through the night. The *Pekwin* ('Sun Priest'), having fasted and watched the rising and setting of the sun for several days, announced the exact moment of the rebirth of the sun with a low, mournful call. This signalled general rejoicing and the appearance of twelve *Katchina* clowns in masks, accompanied by twelve-foot bird headed effigies representing the messengers of the gods. Many Zuni houses contained plates fixed to the walls that were lit by the rays of the sun passing through a small window at the winter solstice.[230]

Touji Taisai - In the Japanese Shinto calendar this day is sacred to the sun goddess Amaterasu-no-Mikuni. When her brother, the raucous storm trickster Susanoo-no-Mikuni insulted and ridiculed her, she withdrew into a cave and caused the Earth to suffer in such cold and darkness that the other gods came to sing and dance outside her cave until the goddess relented and came back out.

---

230   John Matthews, *The Winter Solstice*, Godsfield Press, Arlesford, 2003

The Divalia (Roman) - This festival was held on December 21ˢᵗ in honour of the goddess Angerona, giving it is alternative name of the *Angeronalia*.

Angerona or Angeronia was an old Roman goddess, whose name and functions are variously explained. She is sometimes identified with the goddess Feronia and was worshipped as Ancharia at Faesulae. She was depicted with a bandaged mouth and a finger pressed to her lips, demanding silence. She was a goddess who relieved men from pain and sorrow, and was a protecting goddess of Rome and the keeper of the sacred name of the city, which might not be pronounced lest it should be revealed to her enemies.

The priests offered sacrifice in the temple of Volupia, the goddess of pleasure, in which stood a statue of Angerona, with a finger on her mouth, which was bound and closed.

Day of Frey - In the Germanic tradition, Frey ('Lord') presides over the winter solstice period. He is the chief god of the Vanir, and a god of fertility, sexuality, animal husbandry and agriculture, as well as sacred kingship. In Icelandic tradition he was called 'God of the World'. He is the male counterpart of Freya ('Lady'). His sacred animals are the horse and the boar. His boar was called Gullinbursti ('Golden-bristles'), whose bristles shone in the dark and which could outrun any horse, on which he rode to Balder's funeral. At Yule, oaths were sworn on the finest boar of the herd, which was then sacrificed to Frey and Freya and eaten. His Yuletide festivities included feasts and mumming, with mummers wearing bells.

Hertha - According to Hottes, the early Germans considered the Norse goddess Hertha or Bertha, the goddess of domesticity and the home. They baked yeast cakes shaped like slippers, which were called the slippers of Hertha, and filled with gifts. Hottes wrote:

During the Winter Solstice houses were decked with fir and evergreens to welcome her coming. When the family and serfs were gathered to dine, a great altar of flat stones was erected and here a fire of fir boughs was laid. Hertha descended through the smoke, guiding those who were wise in saga lore to foretell the fortunes of those persons at the feast. Hertha's altar stones became the hearthstones of the home. We learn from this story why Santa Claus comes down the chimney instead of at the door. It is a survival of the coming of Hertha…[231]

---

231   Alfred Carl Hottes, *1001 Christmas Facts and Fancies*, De La Mare, New York, 1937

218

St Thomas Day – Saint Thomas is the patron saint of carpenters, masons and architects since he was a carpenter. According to the old saying:

St Thomas grey, St Thomas grey
The longest night and the shortest day

Or because this was the time to prepare for the Christmas feast:

St Thomas divine,
Brewing, baking, and killing of fat swine

On this day in England, the poor went about begging. This was called going 'a-Thomassing' and donors were presented with sprigs of palm and bunches of primroses. In Warwickshire the poor on St. Thomas's day went go with a bag to beg corn of the farmers, which they called going 'a corning'. [232] In Kent Saint Thomas' Day was called Doleing Day, and women went 'a gooding', begging for money, and benefactors were presented with sprigs of evergreen and Christmas flowers in return. In Herefordshire, a similar custom existed where the day was called 'mumping day' i.e. 'begging day'.

On the Isle of Man it was *Laa'l Thomase* or Thomas's Feast-day' also called *Laa'l Fingan* or 'Fingan's Feast-day' after St. Fingan, an Irish scholar devoted to the study and exposition of Scripture. It was said on this day "A large turf for Eve of Fingan's Feast", meaning it was necessary to have an extra large turf for cooking as Christmas was coming.

In Denmark it was formerly a great children's day, when the schools broke up. Children used to take their master an offering of candles and money, and in return he gave them a feast. In the neighbourhood of Antwerp children went early to school on St. Thomas's Day, and locked the teacher out, until he promised to treat them with ale. Then they would buy a cock and hen, which were set free and had to be caught. The girl who caught the hen was called the queen, and the boy that caught the cock was called the king. In England it was also the custom to lock the teacher out, and in some places if the master managed to gain entry, he could set penalties for the pupils, but if failed the pupils could make the terms.

Beiwe (Saami) – Beiwe is the sun-goddess worshipped by the Saami, the indigenous people of Finland. She travels with her daughter, Beiwe-Neia, through the sky in an enclosure of reindeer bones, bringing back the green plants for the reindeer to feed upon. On the winter solstice, her worshippers sacrifice white female animals and thread the meat on sticks which they bend into rings and tied with bright ribbons. They also smear their doorposts with butter so Beiwe can eat the rich food and begin her recovery.

_____

232   *Hones Everyday Book*

Rozhanitsa (Russian) - Another winter goddess of the north is the Russian goddess, Rozhnitsa. In the twelfth century, the eastern Slavs worshipped her as an ancestor, offering her honey, bread and cheese — all bloodless sacrifices, like those offered at the Haloa. In the nineteenth and early twentieth centuries, Russian women still embroidered and wove bright linens, usually red on white, which depict the goddesses of the seasons.

Winter embroideries were made to honour the feast of Rohanitsa, the Mother Goddess, held in late December. These cloths depict (her) together with her daughter goddess, or with children who may or may not be divine. She was often shown with deer horns sprouting from her head or headdress…. The horns are a sign that in ancient times the Mother Goddess gave birth to deer as well as children. For her feast, small, white-iced biscuits shaped like deer were given as presents or good luck tokens.

Birth of Osiris/ Horus (Egyptian) – According to Plutarch, Osiris was born on the 361st day of the year, was betrayed by Typhon (Set), the power of darkness, killed dismembered on the 17th day of Athyr when the sun enters the sign of the scorpion (i.e. when winter begins in the sign of Scorpio). Osiris was reborn as Horus at the winter solstice, unfinished and infant-like "amid plants that burgeoned and sprouted before their season" according to Plutarch. Three centuries later the Latin writer Macrobius (395–423 CE) wrote:

"…at the winter solstice the sun would seem to be a little child, like that which the Egyptians bring forth from a shrine on an appointed day, since the day is then at its shortest and the god is accordingly shown as a tiny infant". In the temple of Neith and Isis at Sais was an ancient inscription "The present and the future and the past, I am. My undergarment no one has uncovered. The fruit I brought forth, the sun came into being".

The Temple of Luxor show images of Thoth announcing to Isis that she will conceive Horus and then the virgin birth and the adoration. The pictures and statues of Isis suckling her son Horus are the prototype of the Virgin Mary and her Child. Horus is shown in the inscriptions as sailing forth from the underworld at dawn, piercing the great python, born of night, as he advances. They set the length of the festival at twelve days.

The Greek philosopher Plutarch (c.46-119 CE) was initiated into the mysteries of Isis and Osiris and wrote:

"Around the time of the winter solstice, they carry a cow seven times around the sun temple, and this walk is called the visit of Osiris…One had to walk seven times around the temple, because the sun finishes

220

> *its walk from the winter to the summer solstice in the seventh month.
> Horus, the son of isis, is supposed to have made a sacrifice to Helios on
> the fourth day of the month, as in the book called Birthday of Horus. To
> make an incense offering to Helios three times a day, offer resin at dusk,
> myrrh at midday and so-called kyphi at dawn... These are believed to
> show favour to Helios and to serve him."*

He compared the Egyptian cult of Isis and Osiris to Hesiod's concept of
creation out of chaos:

> *"It might appear that Hesiod, in making the very first things of all to
> be Chaos and Earth and Tartarus and Love, did not accept any other
> origins but only these, if we transfer the names somewhat and assign to
> Isis the name of Earth and to Osiris the name of Love and to Typhon the
> name of Tartarus; for the poet seems to place Chaos at the bottom as a
> sort of region that serves as a resting-place for the Universe."* [233]

Yalda ('Birth') (Persian) – Winter solstice celebration which remains a social
occasion in present-day Islamic Iran.

Inti Raymi – The Incas celebrated *Inti Raymi* ('Resurrection of the Sun')
at the time of the winter solstice when Inti, the son of the creator/sun god
Viracocha, was honoured. Preparations began with a fast of three days,
during which no fire lit and the people refrained from sexual intercourse. This
festival itself then lasted nine days with feasting and drinking. Ceremonies
were banned by the Roman Catholic conquistadores in 1572. A local group of
Quecia Indians in Cusco, Peru revived the festival in 1944.

Quetzalcoatl – According to Frazer, at the festival of the winter solstice the
Aztecs 'killed' their god Huitzilopochtli and ate him. An image of the deity was
fashioned out of seeds of various sorts, which were kneaded into dough with the
blood of children. The bones of the god were represented by pieces of acacia
wood. This image was placed on the chief altar of the temple and on the day of
the festival the king offered incense to it. Early next day it was taken down and
set on its feet in a great hall. Then a priest, who bore the name and acted the
part of the god Quetzalcoatl, took a flint-tipped dart and hurled it into the breast
of the dough-image, piercing it through and through. One of the priests cut out
the heart of the image and gave it to the king to eat. The rest of the image was
divided into minute pieces so that every man and male child could get one to eat.
The ceremony was called *teoqualo*, that is, 'god is eaten'.[234]

233   Plutarch, *Moralia*
234   James Frazer, *The Golden Bough*, Macmillan Press, London, 1976

Quetzalcoatl, the Aztec fiery Feathered Serpent, was also born at the winter solstice, the son of the virgin goddess Coatlicue. He seems to have been a god of vegetational renewal, part of a triad of agricultural deities with the Goddess of the Cave symbolizing motherhood, reproduction and life, and Tlaloc, god of rain, lightning and thunder. He was connected with the planet Venus, a herald of the rainy season and associated with warfare. As god of the morning star he was called *Tlahuizcalpantecuhtli*, meaning 'lord of the star of the dawn' while his twin brother Xolotl was the evening star.

He was the inventor of books and the calendar, the giver of maize and sometimes a symbol of death and resurrection. In Aztec lore, we are now living in the age of the fifth sun, the previous four having been destroyed. When the last one was obliterated Quetzalcoatl went to Mictlan (the underworld) and created fifth-world mankind from the bones of the previous races and imbued them with life using the blood from a wound in his own penis.

Choimus or Chaomos (Pakistan) - The Kalash is the only tribe in the area which never converted to Islam. Choimus honours the demigod Balomain, who once had lived among the Kalash and is remembered for his giving spirit and epic deeds. At Choimus, Balomain's spirit wanders the country of the Kalash and counts the people and collects their prayers on behalf of Dezao, the creator God. The rites of Choimus begin with purification. One the first day, *Shishaou Sucheck,* is the purification of women and girls with a ritual bath. They then braid their hairs and dress in elaborate costumes and headdresses and many paint their faces. After chanting the hymns to Balomain, water is then poured over their hands and each is given five loaves of a bread, *jaou* or choimus bread, that had been made earlier in the day by the men only. A branch of burning juniper is whirled three times over each woman's head to the words, *"Sooch Be pure".* On the next day then men and boys are purified, they bathe and are forbidden to sit on chairs or beds until the evening, when the blood of a goat is sprinkled on their faces. The men's hats are adorned with holly, oak and juniper as well as feathers and beads. During Choimus long, edible, apricot kernels necklaces are given as gifts. Ancestral spirits are offered seasonal foods and then a torch for the ancestors, a *kotik*, is lit. The torches are carried in a procession then are thrown into a large bonfire. People then circle the fire singing, dancing and leaping.

22ⁿᵈ December

Hanukkah - Jews celebrate the eight day festival of Hanukkah (Feast of Lights) during December. According to legend, Antiochus, the king of Syria, conquered Judea in the second century BCE, putting a stop to worship in the Temple and stealing the sacred lamp, the menorah, from before the altar. Three years later Judah the Maccabee led a band of rebels who succeeding in retaking Jerusalem and restored the temple. They lit the menorah, thinking that they only had enough oil to last for a day but the flames burned steadily for eight days.

Modern Jews celebrate Hanukkah by lighting one candle for each of the eight days of the festival. There is a fifteen hundred year old commentary on the Babylonian Talmud that relates how Adam, after his expulsion from paradise, noticed the days of the winter shortening and prayed and fasted for eight days in the hope of restoring the lost light. Thereafter, the days grew longer again, and Adam repeated the ritual every year.

Tulya's E'en - Mrs Jessie Saxby, a nineteenth century Shetlander, had no doubts as to when Yule began. She declared that the festivities began on Tulya's E'en. [235] But the date of Tulya's E'en, or even what it marked, remains unclear. The folklorist Ernest Marwick suggested it may be a corruption of Tolyigi's E'en, itself a corruption of St Thorlak's Eve. St Thorlak was an Icelandic saint, whose feast day was celebrated on December 23ʳᵈ. Sigurd Towrie [236] wonders whether it is a corruption of the dialect word *tulye* or *tulyo*, meaning 'a battle' or 'struggle in combat' as this was the night the trows left the underworld and came to earth.

23rd December

Poseidea The month of *Poseideôn* was dedicated to Poseidon and the eighth day was especially sacred to him (as was the seventh to Apollo and the sixth to Artemis). (In general the summer months are assigned to Apollo and the winter months to other gods, since that is when he is in Hyperborea and Dionysos takes His place at Delphi.) Poseidon's name seems to mean "Lord of the Earth" or "Husband of Earth," which reminds us of Saturn, husband of Rhea.

---

235   http://www.orkneyjar.com/tradition/yule/index.html
236   *Ibid*

Larentalia or **Acca Laurentia** - In Roman mythology, Dea Tacita ('the silent goddess') was a goddess of the dead. She was worshipped at a festival called *Larentalia* on December 23ʳᵈ, though the Emperor Augustus ordered that it should be held twice a year. Others have attributed this feast in honour of Acca Larentia, the wolf nurse of Romulus and Remus, and wife of Faustulus. Others say she was a lover of Heracles or after spending a night in the temple of Heracles, she was told to give herself to the first man she met. He happened to be a rich man who married her. After his death, she inherited his fortune, which she gave to Rome, a generosity which the Romans celebrated with a rowdy feast. These legends might derive from the fact that *lupa* means both 'she-wolf' and 'prostitute'.

In later times, she was equated with the earth goddess Larunda (also Larunde, Laranda, Lara) who was the daughter of the river Almo. In Ovid's *Fasti* she is described as beautiful but a gossip who betrayed Jupiter's affair with the nymph Juturna to his wife Juno. Jupiter responded by cutting out her tongue, and she thus became Muta ('speechless') and exiled her from the land of the living, ordering Mercury to conduct her to the Underworld realm of the dead (*manes*), a place of silence (*tacita*) However, Mercury fell for Larunda and made love to her on the way (or some say he raped her). She gave birth to two children, the Lares. Some say the festival was held in honour of the Lares, the domestic gods who were worshipped in houses and thought to be the guardians and protectors of families, who were supposed to reside in the hearth. Varro (116 BCE – 27 BCE) believed that she and her children were originally Sabine and named her as Mania, a name which later Roman authors used in the general sense of an evil spirit. Macrobius applied it to the woollen figurines (*maniae*) hung at crossroad shrines during Compitalia. These were, according to him, substitutions for ancient human sacrifice once held at the same festival and suppressed by Rome's first consul.

A sacred meal was offered to the Mother of the Lares in the temple of Dea Dia, with prayers recited over a sacred, sun-dried earthenware pot of porridge, which was then thrown from the temple doorway, towards the earth.

24th December

The Mothers – The Venerable Bede, writing about the customs of the Pagan Anglo Saxons in England, mentioned their practice of celebrating a holiday he called *Modranicht* or *Modresnacht* on the eve of Christmas. In his account of the Pagan calendar in 725 CE, he said:

"And the very night that is sacrosanct to us, these people call modranect, that is, the mothers' night, a name bestowed, I suspect, on account of the ceremonies which they performed while watching this night through."

This 'night of the Mothers' was evidently a sacred night devoted to a group of feminine divinities, like those pictured on carvings and statues all over Celtic France and Britain which show three women together, holding children and fruit, fish, grain and other bounties of the earth.

In Shetland, into recent times, it was called Helya's Night when each child was committed into the protection of Mother Mary. Helya may be a corruption of the Old Norse *heilagr*, meaning holy. This is probably Mother's Night overlaid with a Christian veneer. [237] An account written in the nineteenth century says that, once the children were in bed, the old woman (the reporter's grandmother) rose from her place by the peat fire and made her way over to the cradle where the youngest lay. Raising her hands over the slumbering infant, she spoke aloud:

Mary Midder had de haund
Ower aboot for sleepin-baund
Had da lass an' had da wife,
Had da bairn a' its life.
Mary Midder had de haund.
Roond da infants o' wur land.

This procedure was repeated over all the children, while the grandfather sat raking the peats in the hearth. The old man was also thought to have been reciting something but, unfortunately, his softly spoken words were inaudible.

Christmas Eve – In folk belief there is a sense of the nearness of the supernatural on Christmas Eve with visiting spirits and the return of the dead. It was also a time for divination.

It was a widespread idea that at midnight on Christmas Eve all water turns to wine. In Sark the superstition is that the water in streams and wells turns into blood, and if you go to look you will die within the year. In Russia all sorts of buried treasures are supposed to be revealed on the evenings between Christmas and the Epiphany, and on the eves of these festivals the heavens are opened, and the waters of springs and rivers turn into wine, a tradition left over from the worship of Dionysus who is said to have turned water to wine at the Epiphany.

---

237   http://www.orkneyjar.com/tradition/yule/yule3.htm

225

In Sweden the Trolls were believed to celebrate Christmas Eve with dancing and revelry.

In Scandinavian folk-belief it was the time when the dead revisited their old homes. When the Christmas Eve festivities were over, and everyone has gone to bed, the parlour was left tidy and adorned, with a great fire burning, candles lighted, the table covered with a festive cloth and plentifully spread with food, and a jug of Yule ale ready.

In one part of Norway it used to be believed that on Christmas Eve, at rare intervals, the old Norse gods made war on Christians, coming down from the mountains with great blasts of wind and wild shouts, and carrying off any human being who might be about. The sign of the cross was often used as a protection against uncanny visitors. The cross (probably originally Thor's hammer) was marked with chalk or tar or fire upon doors and gates, or formed of straw or other material and put in stables and cow byres.

In Sussex the wassailing of fruit-trees took place on Christmas Eve, and was accompanied by a trumpeter blowing on a cow's horn.

Adam and Eve's Day – In the fourteenth and fifteenth century, miracle plays depicting the expulsion of Adam and Eve from Paradise were performed in churches on the Eve of Christmas. As part of the scenery, apples were tied on evergreen trees, one of the possible sources of the Christmas tree.

25th December

Dies Natalis Solis Invicti ('the birthday of the unconquered sun') (Roman) - The title Sol Invictus had been applied to a number of solar deities. Many Oriental cults were practised informally among the Roman legions from the mid-second century, but only that of Sol Invictus was officially accepted. Sol Invictus was identified with the earlier Roman sun god Sol. This is the traditional birth date of sun gods and gods with solar attributes such as Pryderi, Frey, Saturn, Dionysus, Adonis, Attis, Tammuz, Baalim, Quetzalcoatl, Mithra and Zeus.

Juvenalia – After the Saturnalia, the Romans celebrated the birth of new life with a festival honouring children, who were given talismans (like bells, shoes, warm clothes and toys) for good luck in the coming year.

Yule – Yule is the modern English version of the Old English words *ġeól* or *ġeóhol* (the festival of Yule) and *ġeóla* or *ġeóli* (the month of in which

Yule occurs i.e. December). The etymology is uncertain. According to *The Barnhart Concise Dictionary of Etymology*, Yule is derived into modern English from *Jól* deriving from Old Norse *hjól*, meaning 'wheel', perhaps related to an ancient Indo-European root meaning 'to go around'. Many scholars deny it has any connection with 'wheel'. Both words are thought to be derived from Common Germanic **jexwla*. Adolf Spamer (*Christmas in Old and New Times*) reported that in the early eighteenth century the word *Jól* carried the connotations of 'shout for joy'. It was associated with the Old Nordic *êl* (snow flurry) and *jek* (to speak) as well as a middle German word for 'invocation to the sun'. Some have suggested that it refer to Odin as one of his many epithets was *Jólnir* or 'Yule Man'. Whatever Yule means, it referred to a period of time, and not a single day. Bede mentions two months, 'early Yule' and 'later Yule'; *ærra ġeóla* referred to the period before the Yule festival and *æftera ġeóla* referred to the period after Yule. Yule is attested early in the history of the Germanic peoples; from the fourth century Gothic language it appears in the month name *fruma jiuleis*.

Yule was the time that marked the death of Balder, the sun-god, the result of the jealousy of the trickster Loki (fire). Loki knew that everything in nature had promised not to injure Balder except the mistletoe which was considered to be too insignificant to worry about. He searched for the mistletoe until he found it growing on an oak tree on the eastern slope of Valhalla. He cut it off and fashioned a dart from it, returning to find the gods engaged in the amusement of tossing spears, axes and stones at Balder and watching them bounce off him harmlessly. Then Loki handed the twig of mistletoe to the blind god of darkness, Höder, directing his hand and encouraging him to throw it. When the mistletoe struck Balder it he fell lifeless to the ground, his spirit sinking into Hel. Great consternation swept through the hall, and the gods would have slain Höder had it not been for the fact it was the season of peace and goodwill which was never to be desecrated by acts of violence. Gifts from the gods and goddesses were laid on Balder's bier and he, in turn, sent gifts back from the realm of darkness into which he had fallen.

Yule was also the festival of Frey, god of rain, sunshine and the fruits of the earth. Frey possessed a magical gold boar named *Gullinbursti* ('Golden Bristles'). This boar was a remarkable animal; he could run faster than a horse, through the air and over water. Darkness could not overtake him, for he was symbolical of the sun, his golden bristles typifying the sun's rays. At one time the boar was believed to be emblematical of golden grain, as he was the first to teach mankind the art of ploughing. This creature was able to run as fast as any steed and glowed with a golden light that could drive away shadow and turn night into day. The solar attributes of this incredible beast, created by the dwarfs Brokk and Eitri, are clear. The midwinter sacrifice of a boar could also be seen to symbolise the death of the old sun, and the rebirth of the new. The boar also had a role in the swearing of sacred oaths. On Yule Eve, the best boar in the herd was brought into the hall where the assembled company laid their hands upon the animal and made their unbreakable oaths. Heard by the boar, these oaths were thought to go straight to the ears of Frey himself. Once the oaths had been sworn, the boar was sacrificed in the name of Frey and the feast of boar flesh began.

The *Saga of Hákon the Good* concerns King Haakon I who was instrumental in Christianising Norway and who moved the date of Yule, which had been celebrated at midwinter for three nights, to coincide with the Nativity. According to the saga, the previous Heathen customs included much drinking of ale, the sacrifices of livestock and horses for fertility, with the blood being sprinkled on the idols and men present. Afterwards, the meat of the animals was boiled and served as food at the feast. A fire was lit in the middle of the temple floor and the sacrificial beaker and meat were blessed by the chieftain presiding. Afterwards toasts were drunk to Odin "for victory and power to the king", then to the gods Njörðr and Freyr "for good harvests and for peace", and then a beaker was drunk to the king himself, and afterwards to departed kinsfolk. It was a festival of peace and goodwill when no fights were allowed, and one of great rejoicing and mirth. [238]

Christmas – Birthday of Jesus of Nazareth, originally celebrated at various times of year, but transposed to coincide with Pagan celebrations of the winter solstice (see Chapter 8, Christmas).

Saint Anastasia's Day – Yet another Christian virgin whose chastity was threatened by a Roman Pagan. This time the Roman prefect thought he was embracing Anastasia, when in fact he was making love to the cooking pots and kitchen utensils. When he emerged from his imaginary amorous encounter he was covered with soot, and his servants thought him a demon, and chased him away with blows.

---

238   http://en.wikipedia.org/wiki/Yule

26th December

First Day of Christmas (see Chapter 5)

27th December

Second Day of Christmas (see Chapter 5)

28th December

Third Day of Christmas (see Chapter 5)

29th December

Fourth Day of Christmas (see Chapter 5)

30th December

Fifth Day of Christmas (see Chapter 5)

31st December

Sixth Day of Christmas (see Chapter 5)

1st January

Seventh Day of Christmas (see Chapter 5)

2nd January

Eighth Day of Christmas (see Chapter 5)

3rd January

Ninth Day of Christmas (see Chapter 5)

4th January

Tenth Day of Christmas (see Chapter 5)

<h2 style="text-align:center">5th January</h2>

Eleventh Day of Christmas (see Chapter 5)

<h2 style="text-align:center">6th January</h2>

Twelfth Day of Christmas (see Chapter 5)

<h2 style="text-align:center">7th January</h2>

Christmas Day (Coptic) – In Egypt Christians belonging to the Orthodox
Coptic Church constitute about 7% of the population. Religious holidays
are determined by the Coptic calendar, which puts Christmas at January 7th.
Christmas is preceded by a forty-three day Advent fasting period which
prohibits eating between midnight and 3 pm, and in which meals are
vegetarian or fish. Advent ends at Midnight Mass at Christmas.

St Distaff's Day or Rock Day – In the past, women returned to their spinning
duties on the first day after the Twelve Days of Christmas. It was a sign that
the festive period was over and things were back to normal. It is also called
'Rock Day' with rock being an alternative name for the spindle or distaff from
the German *rocken* meaning a distaff. St Distaff is not a saint. From a poem
of Herrick's (*Hespirides*) it appears that the men, in jest, tried to burn the
women's flax, and the women in return poured water on the men:

> *Partly work, and partly play*
> *You must on St. Distaff's day:*
> *From the plough soon free your team,*
> *Then come home and fother them;*
> *If the maids a-spinning go,*
> *Burn the flax and fire the tow.*
>
> *Bring in pails of water then,*
> *Let the maids bewash the men;*
> *Give St. Distaff all the right,*
> *Then bid Christmas sport good night;*
> *And next morrow, every one*
> *To his own vocation.*

January 8th

Plough Monday (moveable) – Whereas women went back to work on Distaff's Day, the men did not return to work until after Plough Monday, the traditional start of the agricultural year falling the first Monday after Twelfth Night. References to Plough Monday date back to the late fifteenth century.

In some areas, particularly in northern England and East Anglia, a plough was dragged from house to house in a procession, with the ploughmen collecting money. They were often accompanied by musicians, an old woman or a boy dressed as an old woman called the Bessy, and a man in the role of the fool, who wore animal skins, a hairy cap and had an animal tail hanging from his back, in the manner of our friend the wildman.

In the Isles of Scilly, locals would cross-dress and then visit their neighbours to joke about local occurrences. There would be 'goose dancing' and considerable drinking and revelry. [239]

It was a day for mumming plays. In Derbyshire:

"On Plough Monday the 'Plough bullocks' are occasionally seen; they consist of a number of young men from various farmhouses, who are dressed up in ribbons.... These young men yoke themselves to a plough, which they draw about, preceded by a band of music, from house to house, collecting money. They are accompanied by the Fool and Bessy; the fool being dressed in the skin of a calf, with the tail hanging down behind, and Bessy generally a young man in female attire. The fool carries an inflated bladder tied to the end of a long stick, by way of whip, which he does not fail to apply pretty soundly to the heads and shoulders of his team. When anything is given a cry of 'Largess!' is raised, and a dance performed round the plough. If a refusal to their application for money is made they not unfrequently plough up the pathway, door-stone, or any other portion of the premises they happen to be near." [240]

'Plough Pudding', a boiled suet pudding containing meat and onions was eaten in Norfolk on Plough Monday.

Plough Monday customs declined in the nineteenth century but have now been revived in many places, and celebrated with a plough procession, morris and molly dancing.

---

239   http://en.wikipedia.org/wiki/Plough_Monday

240   Clement A. Miles, *Christmas in Ritual and Tradition*, Christian and Pagan, T. Fisher Unwin, 1912

January 9th

The Argonium of Janus

Country Dionysia (Greek) – Plutarch described the Country Dionysia in which everyone participated. On the first day there was a procession with participants carrying a jar of wine and a vine, someone leading a he-goat, the *Kanêphoros* (basket-bearer) carrying a basket of raisins, then the carriers of a wooden phallus, decorated with ivy, and finally the singer of the *Phallikon* (Phallic Song). On *Askôlia*, the second day of the festival were silly games including a contest to see who can balance longest on top of a greased, inflated wine-skin, one-legged races, hopping on one leg and so on. *Askôliazô* may refer to standing on one leg. There were also dramatic contests. [241]

January 10th

Halôa (Greek) – In honour of Dionysus and Demeter this festival seems to have been a celebration of the pruning of the vines and the tasting of the wine after its first fermentation, or perhaps to encourage the growth of corn from the seed. It is named after the *halôs* (the circular threshing-floor). In the earliest times the first part of the festival was restricted to married women, but later to prostitutes. The Eleusinian Magistrates prepared a banquet including phallic and pudenda-shaped cakes, but excluding those foods forbidden in the Mysteries (pomegranates, apples, eggs, fowls and some types of fish).[242] The magistrates then left to leave the women to eat and drink and behave in a decadent manner. Afterwards, the women would carry clay models of phalluses and pudendas and go to the threshing floor, where they would dance around a giant phallus which was decorated with corn leaves, and engage in ritual obscenity. Afterwards men were admitted, and a priest and priestess with torches representing Dionysus and Demeter sat on closed chests to preside over the ensuing revels.

January 11th

Carmentalia – Carmenta ('Magic Spell') was the Roman goddess of childbirth and prophecy, the protectress of mothers and children. Her festival the *Carmentalia* was held from January 11th to January 15th, and mainly

---

241   *Bruma* http://www.cs.utk.edu/~mclennan/BA/SF/WinSol.html
242   *Ibid*

celebrated by women. She was invoked as *Postvorta* and *Antevorta*, epithets which had reference to her power of looking back into the past and forward into the future.

January 12th

This day is sacred to goddesses of wisdom such as Minerva, Sophia and Athene.

January 13th

St. Knut's Day – The twentieth after Christmas. It was said that:
Twentieth day Knut
Driveth Yule out
On this day a mock fight used to take place, the master and servants of the house pretending to drive away the guests with axe, broom, knife, spoon, and other implements. The name, "St. Knut's Day," is apparently due to the fact that in the laws of Canute the Great (1017-36) it is commanded that there is to be no fasting from Christmas to the Octave of the Epiphany.

Midvintersblöt (Norse) – This is one of the most important festivals in the Northern tradition, falling twenty days after Yule.

Tiugunde Day (Norse) – Tiugunde is the sky god variously called Tiwaz, Tiu, Ziu and Tyr. It is particularly powerful when it falls on a Tuesday. According to Nigel Pennick (*The God Year*) the Plough Monday celebrations and the Whittlesea Straw Bear Festivals may be a continuation of this festival.

As sky-father, Tiwaz was the most important deity in earlier times but in the Viking Age his position was taken over by Odin, the All-father. He is the god of justice and order, and master of the *Thing* (people's assembly place), and is described as 'ruler of the temple' in the Old Icelandic Rune poem. He was worshipped at mountains, moot and *Thing* places. [243]

---

243   Nigel Pennick, *The God Year*, Capall Bann, Chieveley

SEASONAL STORIES, POEMS AND SONGS

SIR GAWAIN AND THE GREEN KNIGHT

As Arthur and his court were celebrating Yule the great doors of the feasting hall flew open and in rode a knight, entirely green from head to foot. In a loud voice he issued a challenge to the company - was anyone brave enough to take the axe he carried and chop off his head, which compliment he would return in a year's time?

Puzzled by his request the knights merely stared and the mysterious Green Knight chided them as cowards. Stung by this Sir Gawain leaped up, seized the axe and cut off the knight's head. To everyone's amazement the Green Knight merely picked up his head and bid Gawain to meet him in a year's time at the Green Chapel.

A year passed and Gawain rode off with a heavy heart in search of the Green Chapel. He travelled far and wide, but was unable to find anyone who had even heard of it. Eventually he came to a castle which was preparing to celebrate the Yuletide season. The Lord of the manor, a big, jovial, red headed man, made him welcome and admitted he knew where the chapel was, a short ride from his estate. However, as there were still three days to go to the appointment, he invited the knight to remain with his wife and himself until the time should come, and Gawain readily agreed.

Each day Gawain hunted with the Red Lord, but each night the Lord's wife came to his room to try to seduce him. Being an honourable knight Gawain refused, but on the last night the lady came to him with a magic green garter, which she said she would exchange for a kiss. She claimed the garter had the quality of protecting its wearer from any kind of weapon. Seeing a chance to save his life for no more than a kiss, the bargain was made, the lady kissed and the garter taken.

The next day Gawain set off to the Green Chapel, a cave in the woodlands. The Green Knight stepped out to meet him and asked if he was ready to lose his head. Gawain meekly kneeled before him and bowed his

234

head. The Green Knight raised the axe high and brought it down, but just stopped short of the neck of Gawain, who couldn't help flinching. Ashamed of his cowardice he apologised and bid the knight strike again. Once again the axe came down and stopped short, but Gawain held himself steady. Raising the axe once more the Knight struck, merely nicking Gawain's neck.

Gawain looked up and instead of the Green Knight, there stood his host, the Red Lord. The Lord praised his courage in meeting the challenge and said that the two blows that didn't touch him were in reward for his constancy in refusing the seductions of the Lady of the castle. The third blow which cut him was for giving in to temptation and kissing the lady. Embracing each other they returned to the castle to celebrate the Twelve Days of Yule, and it was a strange tale that Gawain had to tell when he returned to Arthur's court.

THE TWELVE DAYS OF YULE

On the first day of Yuletide, my true love sent to me
Mistletoe upon an oak tree

On the second day of Yuletide, my true love sent to me
Two robins red,

On the third day of Yuletide, my true love sent to me
Three ivy boughs,

On the fourth day of Yuletide, my true love sent to me
Four calling wrens,

On the fifth day of Yuletide, my true love sent to me
Five wassail bowls,

On the sixth day of Yuletide, my true love sent to me
Six wrens a-singing,

On the seventh day of Yuletide, my true love sent to me
Seven stars a-turning,

On the eighth day of Yuletide, my true love sent to me
Eight stags a-leaping,

On the ninth day of Yuletide, my true love sent to me
Nine stones a-dancing,

On the tenth day of Yuletide, my true love sent to me
Ten fools a-prancing,

On the eleventh day of Yuletide, my true love sent to me
Eleven boys a-chanting,

On the twelfth day of Yuletide, my true love sent to me
Twelve beasts a-leaping.

DECEMBER
Last of the months, severest of them all.
For lo! The fiery horses of the Sun
Through the twelve signs their rapid course have run;
Time, like a serpent, bites his forked tail,
And Winter, on a goat, bestrides the gale;
Rough blows the North-wind near Arcturus' star,
And sweeps, unreigned, across the polar bear.

Unaccredited poem reproduced in *The Book of Christmas*, The Folklore Society, 1888, and published in *The Zodiac*, 1835, also unaccredited.

DEATH OF THE OLD YEAR
Full knee-deep lies the winter snow,
And the winter winds are wearily sighing:
Toll ye the church bell sad and slow,
And tread softly and speak low,
For the old year lies a-dying.
Old year you must not die;
You came to us so readily,
You lived with us so steadily,
Old year you shall not die.

He lieth still: he doth not move:
He will not see the dawn of day.
He hath no other life above.
He gave me a friend and a true truelove
And the New-year will take 'em away.
Old year you must not go;
So long you have been with us,
Such joy as you have seen with us,

Old year, you shall not go.
He froth'd his bumpers to the brim;
A jollier year we shall not see.
But tho' his eyes are waxing dim,
And tho' his foes speak ill of him,
He was a friend to me.
Old year, you shall not die;
We did so laugh and cry with you,
I've half a mind to die with you,
Old year, if you must die.

He was full of joke and jest,
But all his merry quips are o'er.
To see him die across the waste
His son and heir doth ride post-haste,
But he'll be dead before.
Every one for his own.
The night is starry and cold, my
friend,
And the New-year blithe and bold,
my friend,
Comes up to take his own.

How hard he breathes! over the snow
I heard just now the crowing cock.
The shadows flicker to and fro:
The cricket chirps: the light burns
low:
'Tis nearly twelve o'clock.
Shake hands, before you die.
Old year, we'll dearly rue for you:
What is it we can do for you?
Speak out before you die.

His face is growing sharp and thin.
Alack! our friend is gone,
Close up his eyes: tie up his chin:
Step from the corpse, and let him in
That standeth there alone,
And waiteth at the door.

There's a new foot on the floor, my
friend,
And a new face at the door, my
friend,
A new face at the door.
Alfred Lord Tennyson

**TWELFE NIGHT, OR KING
AND QUEENE.**
Now, now the mirth comes
With the cake full of plums,
Where Beane's the King of the
sport here;
Besides, we must know
The Pea also
Must revell, as Queene, in the
Court here.

Begin, then, to chuse
(This night, as ye use),
Who shall for the present delight
here,
Be a King by the lot,
And who shall not
Be Twelfe-day Queene for the
night here.

Which knowne, let us make
Joy-sops with the cake;
And let not a man then be seen
here
Who un-urg'd will not drinke
To the base, from the brink,
A health to the King and the
Queene here.

Next, crowne the bowle full
With gentle lamb's-wooll;
Adde sugar, nutmeg, and ginger,
With store of ale too;

237

And thus ye must doe
To make the wassaile a swinger.

Give then to the King
And Queene wassailing;
And though, with ale, ye be whet
here,
Yet part ye from hence
As free from offence
As when ye innocent met here.
Herrick

THE WREN SONG
The wren, the wren, the king of all
birds,
St. Stephen's day was caught in the
furze,
Although he was little his honour was
great
Jump up, me lads, and give him a
treat.

Chorus:
Up with the kettle and down with the
pan
And give us a penny to bury the
wren.

As I was gone to Killenaule
I met a wren upon a wall,
Up with me wattle and knocked him
down
And brought him into Carrick town.

Droolin, droolin, where's your nest?
'Tis in the bush that I love best
In the tree, the holly tree
Where all the boys do follow me.

We followed the wren three miles
or more
Three miles or more, three miles or
more,
Followed the wren three miles or
more
At six o'clock in the morning.

We have a little box under me hand
(arm),
Under me hand, under me hand,
We have a little box under me
hand,
A penny a tuppence will do it no
harm.

Missus Clancy's a very good
woman
A very good woman, a very good
woman
Missus Clancy's a very good
woman
She gave us a penny to bury the
wren.

THE HOLLY AND THE IVY
The holly and the ivy,
When they are both full grown
Of all the trees that are in the wood
The holly bears the crown
O the rising of the sun
And the running of the deer
The playing of the merry organ
Sweet singing of the choir
The holly bears a blossom
As white as lily flower
The Lady bore the Son of Light
To be our sweet Saviour
O the rising of the sun

And the running of the deer
The playing of the merry organ
Sweet singing of the choir

The holly bears a berry
As red as any blood
The Lady bore the Son of Light
To do poor sinners good
O the rising of the sun
And the running of the deer
The playing of the merry organ
Sweet singing of the choir

The holly bears a prickle
As sharp as any thorn;
The Lady bore the Son of Light
On Christmas Day in the morn.
O the rising of the sun
And the running of the deer
The playing of the merry organ
Sweet singing of the choir

The holly bears a bark
As bitter as any gall;
The Lady bore the Son of Light
For to redeem us all.
O the rising of the sun
And the running of the deer
The playing of the merry organ
Sweet singing of the choir

The holly and the ivy
Now both are full well grown,
Of all the trees that are in the wood,
The holly bears the crown.
O the rising of the sun
And the running of the deer
The playing of the merry organ
Sweet singing of the choir

WASSAILING SONG
Here We Come A-Wassailing
Here we come a-wassailing
Among the leaves so green;
Here we come a-wand'ring
So fair to be seen.

Love and joy come to you,
And to you your wassail too;
And God bless you and send you
a Happy New Year
And God send you a Happy New
Year.

We're not daily beggars
That beg from door to door;
But we are neighbours' children,
Whom you have seen before.

Love and joy come to you,
And to you your wassail too;
And God bless you and send you
A Happy New Year
And God send you a Happy New
Year.

Good master and good mistress,
Are sitting by the fire,
Pray think of us poor children
Who wander in the mire.

Love and joy come to you,
And to you your wassail too;
And God bless you and send you
A Happy New Year
And God send you a Happy New
Year.

God bless the master of this house
Likewise the mistress too!

And all the little children
That 'round the table go

Love and joy come to you,
And to you your wassail too;
And God bless you and send you
A Happy New Year
And God send you a Happy New
Year

Ohhhh, Happy New Year!!

**CORNWORTHY WASSAIL
SONG**
Huzza, Huzza, in our good town
The bread shall be white, and the
liquor be brown
So here my old fellow I drink to thee
And the very health of each other
tree.
Well may ye blow, well may ye bear
Blossom and fruit both apple and
pear.
So that every bough and every twig
May bend with a burden both fair and
big
May ye bear us and yield us fruit
such a store
That the bags and chambers and
house run o'er.

FROM DEVON recorded 1791
Here's to thee, old apple tree,
Whence thou mayst bud
And whence thou mayst blow!
And whence thou mayst bear apples
enow!
Hats full! Caps full!
Bushel--bushel--sacks full,
And my pockets full too! Huzza!

FROM SOMERSET
Good luck to the hoof and horn
Good luck to the flock and fleece
Good luck to the growers of corn
With blessings of plenty and peace

Appendix 3
HERBAL CORRESPONDENCES OF YULE

SAGITTARIUS
Anise
Bergamot [citrus]
Calendula
Carnation
Cedar
Clove
Copal
Dandelion
Dragonsblood
Fir
Frankincense
Ginger
Honeysuckle
Hyssop
Juniper
Lemon balm
Mace
Mallow
Marshmallow
Nutmeg
Oakmoss
Orange
Rose
Rosemary
Saffron
Sage
Sassafras
Ylang ylang

CAPRICORN:
Comfrey
Cypress
Honeysuckle
Lilac
Magnolia
Mimosa
Moss
Myrrh
Patchouli
Tonka
Tulip
Vertivert
Vervain

SATURN
The planet Saturn presides over the winter solstice.
Aconite
Asafoetida
Belladonna
Bindweed
Bistort
Blackthorn
Comfrey
Cornflower
Cypress
Datura
Elm

Fern
Fumitory
Hellebore
Hemlock
Hemp
Henbane
Holly
Indigo
Ivy
Mimosa
Mullein
Myrrh
Patchouli
Scullcap
Woad
Yew

YULE
Apple
Ash
Bayberry
Blackthorn
Calendula
Cinnamon
Cypress
Fern
Frankincense
Holly
Hop
Ivy
Juniper
Mistletoe
Oak
Violet

CORNISH MUMMING PLAY

Enter the Turkish Knight:
Open your doors, and let me in,
I hope your favours I shall win;
Whether I rise or whether I fall,
I'll do my best to please you all.
St. George is here, and swears he will come in,
And if he does, I know he'll pierce my skin.
If you will not believe what I do say,
Let Father Christmas come in—clear the way!

Enter Father Christmas.
Here come I, old Father Christmas,
Welcome, or welcome not,
I hope old Father Christmas
Will never be forgot.
I am not come here to laugh or to jeer,
But for a pocketful of money, and a skinful of beer.
If you will not believe what I do say,
Come in the King of Egypt—clear the way!

Enter the King of Egypt.
Here I, the King of Egypt,
Boldly do appear, St. George!
St. George! Walk in, my only son and heir!
Walk in, my son, St. George, and boldly act thy part,
That all the people here may see thy wond'rous art.

Enter St. George.
Here come I, St. George,—from Britain did I spring,
I'll fight the Dragon bold, my wonders to begin.
I'll clip his wings, he shall not fly;
I'll cut him down, or else I die.

Enter the Dragon.
Who's he that seeks the Dragon's blood,
And calls so angry, and so loud?
That English dog, will he before me stand?
I'll cut him down with my courageous hand.
With my long teeth and scurvy jaw,
Of such I'd break up half a score,
And stay my stomach, till I'd more.

St. George and the Dragon fight—the latter is killed.

Father Christmas.
Is there a doctor to be found
All ready, near at hand,
To cure a deep and deadly wound,
And make the champion stand?

Enter Doctor.
Oh yes, there is a doctor to be found
All ready, near at hand,
To cure a deep and deadly wound,
And make the champion stand?

Father Christmas:
What can you cure?

Doctor.
All sorts of diseases,
Whatever you pleases,
The phthisic, the palsy, and the gout;
If the devil's in, I'll blow him out.

Father Christmas:
What is your fee?

Doctor.
Fifteen pound, it is my fee,
The money to lay down
But, as 'tis such a rogue as thee,
I cure for ten pound.
I carry a little bottle of elecampane,
Here, Jack, take a little of my flip flop,
Pour it down thy tip top,
Rise up and fight again.

[The Doctor performs his cure, the fight is renewed, and the Dragon again killed.

Saint George.
Here am I, St. George,
That worthy champion bold!
And with my sword and spear
I won three crowns of gold!
I fought the fiery dragon,
And brought him to the slaughter;
By that I won fair Sabra,
The King of Egypt's daughter.
Where is the man, that now me will defy?
I'll cut his giblets full of holes, and make his buttons fly.

The Turkish Knight advances.
Here come I, the Turkish Knight,
Here come the Turkish land to fight!
I'll fight Saint George, who is my foe,
I'll make him yield, before I go;
He brags to such a high degree,
He thinks there's none can do the like of he.

Saint George.
Where is the Turk, that will before me stand?
I'll cut him down with my courageous hand.

They fight; the Knight is overcome, and falls on one knee.

Turkish Knight.
Oh pardon me, St. George! Pardon of thee I crave,
Oh pardon me, this night, and I will be thy slave

Saint George.
No pardon shalt thou have, while I have foot to stand,
So rise thee up again, and fight out sword in hand.

They fight again, and the Knight is killed; Father Christmas calls for the Doctor, with whom the same dialogue occurs as before, and the cure is performed.

Enter the Giant Turpin.
Here come I, the Giant! Bold Turpin is my name,
And all the nations round do tremble at my fame.
Where'er I go, they tremble at my sight,
No lord or champion long with me would fight.

Saint George.
Here's one that dares to look thee in the face,
And soon will send thee to another place.

They fight, and the Giant is killed; medical aid is called in, as before, and the cure performed by the Doctor—who then, according to the stage direction, is given a basin of girdy grout, and a kick, and driven out.

Father Christmas.
Now, ladies and gentlemen, your sport is most ended.
So prepare for the hat, which is highly commended.
The hat it would speak, if it had but a tongue.
Come throw in your money, and think it no wrong.

YULE INCENSE

There are many types of incense available in shops, from the joss sticks and cones you can buy in supermarkets to the loose incense obtained from occult shops which is burned on charcoal or thrown straight onto the ritual bonfire. However, there are several reasons why it is better to make your own incenses for magical purposes. Commercial joss and cones are made with a compound base and often synthetic mineral-derived oils, and have no magical value. Commercially prepared incenses are usually just made to look attractive and smell nice- even if you buy them from an occult shop. A careful examination of the contents will often reveal inexplicable ingredients, besides which, they are made in bulk at any old time. Make your own and you will be sure that they contain the correct ingredients and are blended in the proper manner at the right magically empowering time.

THE INGREDIENTS
Every plant has its own magical vibration which is utilised in incenses, and we will be looking at this in the next chapter. When it comes to blending incenses, plants can be used in many forms. Traditional Craft incenses are composed largely of flowers and herbs (leaves and stems), but incenses that contain resins, essential oils and aesthetically pleasing shapes like star anise have become popular in recent years. Any herbs, flowers, berries or barks used should be dried.

BLENDING LOOSE INCENSE
Loose incense is probably the easiest type of incense to make, and the most useful kind for magical ritual. The recipes in this book are all for loose incense. First of all assemble your ingredients, your pestle and mortar, your mixing spoons and your jars and labels ready for the finished product. All the measurements in this book are by volume, not weight, and I use a spoon to measure out small quantities when I am making a single jar of incense, or

a cup for large quantities and big batches. Therefore when the recipe says 3 parts frankincense, ½ part thyme and 1 part myrrh, this means three spoons of frankincense, half a spoon of thyme and 1 spoon of myrrh. When using resins and essential oils, these should be combined together first, stirring lightly with the pestle and left to go a little sticky before you add any woods, barks and crushed berries. Next add any herbs and powders and lastly any flowers.

CHARGING THE INCENSE

As you blend the incense concentrate on the purpose for which the incense will be used, and 'project' this into the blend. If you like you can make a whole ritual of the event, perhaps even picking and drying your own herbs, then laying out the tools and ingredients on the altar, lighting a candle and asking the god and goddess for help:

"God and Goddess, deign to bless this incense which I would consecrate in your names. Let it obtain the necessary virtues for acts of love and beauty in your honour. Let Blessing Be".

The incenses should then be stored in screw topped glass jars.

BURNING INCENSES

Loose incense is burned on individual self-igniting charcoal blocks, or thrown directly onto the bonfire. To use your incenses, take a self-igniting charcoal block (available from occult and church suppliers) and apply a match to it. It will begin to spark across its surface, and eventually to glow red. Place it on a flame-proof dish with a mat underneath (it will get very hot). When the charcoal block is glowing, sprinkle a pinch of the incense on top- a little goes a long way. Alternatively, if you are celebrating outdoors and have a bonfire, you can throw much larger quantities of incense directly onto the flames. I have also sprinkled it on the hot plate of my Rayburn, and this smoulders away quite nicely, though it would really mess up a gas or electric hob! A useful tip is when a packet of charcoal blocks has been opened they will quickly start to absorb moisture from the air. This makes them difficult to ignite. Pop them in the oven for ten minutes on a low heat to dry them out, and they will light easily.

MIDWINTER SOLSTICE

3 parts frankincense
½ part mistletoe
1 part crushed juniper berries

Few drops cypress oil
½ part holly leaves and berries
2 parts oak bark
½ part cypress needles
½ part ivy leaves and wood

YULE SUN INCENSE
3 parts frankincense
A few drops orange oil
A few drops juniper oil
1 part crushed juniper berries
½ part mistletoe

SPICY YULE INCENSE
3 parts frankincense
1 part crushed juniper berries
½ part cinnamon bark
Few drops cinnamon oil

YULE EVERGREEN INCENSE
1 part cedar wood
1 part pine wood
1 part crushed juniper berries
Few drops of cypress oil
3 parts frankincense

YULE PURIFICATION INCENSE
1 part juniper leaves
1 part juniper berries
½ part rosemary leaves
4 parts frankincense

SATURN PLANETARY INCENSE
1 part willow bark
Pinch of crushed mace
2 parts white sandalwood
3 parts myrrh
½ part dittany of Crete
½ part cypress
A few drops cypress oil

SUN GOD
½ part fennel
½ part rue
½ part thyme
½ part chervil seed
½ part pennyroyal
1 part camomile flowers
3 parts frankincense

SOLAR INCREASE
2 parts red sandalwood
½ part clove
½ part orange peel
½ part orris root
Few drops orange oil

ARIANRHOD (Welsh goddess of the moon, initiation and rebirth)
½ part ivy leaves and stems
2 parts oak bark
½ part flax flower
1 part hazel wood

BALDER (Scandinavian sun god)
½ part mistletoe,
½ part St. John's wort,
2 parts oak bark

AMUN RA (Egyptian sun god):
1/2 part olive leaves
1 part cedar wood
Pinch of saffron
1/2 part reed stems
Few drops cedar oil
2 parts frankincense

APOLLO (Greek and Roman god of the sun, poetry and medicine):
1/2 part bay laurel leaves
1/2 part peony flowers

2 parts aspen wood
2 parts frankincense
1/2 part cypress needles
1/2 part fennel seeds
2 parts acacia
Few drops bay oil

BACCHUS (Roman god of wine):
½ part ivy leaves
½ part fir needles
½ part vine leaves
¼ part thistle leaves
1 part rose petals
3 parts myrrh
Few drops rose oil (optional)

BEL (Sumerian sun god):
2 parts frankincense
½ part bistort root
Few drops frankincense oil (optional)

BELINOS (Celtic sun god):
2 parts willow bark
½ part daisy flowers
½ part celandine flowers
2 parts frankincense (optional)

DIONYSUS (Thracian/Greek god of vegetation/wine/fertility):
1 part apple blossom
½ part ivy leaves
1 part pine resin
Few drops pine oil
½ part fir needles
½ part fennel leaves
½ part vine leaves
2 parts myrrh
Very few drops of red wine

FREYA (Teutonic moon/love goddess):
½ part primrose flowers
½ part cowslip flowers
½ part cypress needles
1 part mistletoe twigs and leaves
½ part rose petals
½ part daisy petals
½ part strawberry leaves
½ part myrtle
½ part red clover flowers
5 parts myrrh
2 parts benzoin
3 parts red sandalwood
Few drops rose oil (optional)
Few drops sandalwood oil

HELIOS (Greek sun god):
½ part bay laurel leaves
½ part heliotrope (optional)
4 parts frankincense
Few drops cinnamon oil
½ part bistort root

ISIS (Egyptian Queen of Heaven):
½ part heather
5 parts myrrh
½ part rose petals
¼ part vervain
¼ part wormwood
¼ part orris root powder
½ part ivy leaves
Few drops geranium oil
¼ part horehound
¼ part olive leaves
½ part white willow bark
2 parts cedar wood
Few drops cedar oil
½ part cypress needles

¼ part poppy seeds or petals
¼ part dragon's blood powder

JANUS (Roman god of doorways):
1 part oak
1 part amaranth

MITHRAS (Persian god of light/
purity, later god of sun/victory):
1 part cypress needles
Few drops cypress oil
2 parts myrrh
2 parts frankincense

ODIN (Scandinavian chief god):
2 parts ash wood
½ part mistletoe
1 part oak wood
½ part amaranth (optional)
½ part storax
1 part elm wood

ODIN #2
½ part mistletoe
1 part oak bark
½ part mugwort
¼ part valerian root
3 parts frankincense

SATURN (Roman, originally a god
of plenty and harvest):
Few drops cypress oil
Few drops lavender oil
½ part lavender flowers
½ part mandrake root
4 parts myrrh
¼ part holly leaves or wood
2 parts ash wood
¼ part asafoetida

¼ part indigo
½ part ivy leaves

THOR (Scandinavian god of the
sky/thunder):
2 parts ash wood
½ part holly leaves
1 part hazel wood
2 parts oak wood
½ part ox-eye daisy flowers
1 part dried rowan berries
½ part vervain
½ part birch wood
Few drops marjoram oil
1 part gorse flowers
¼ part nettle
¼ part thistle
½ part hawthorn flowers

SUN #1
2 parts acacia resin
3 parts frankincense
½ part orange peel
1 part myrrh
2 parts red sandalwood
½ part rosemary
¼ part cinnamon bark
1 part benzoin
Few drops cedar oil

SUN #2
3 parts frankincense
Few drops orange oil
Few drops cinnamon oil

SAGITTARIUS #1
1 part myrrh
¼ part clove
3 parts frankincense
1 part rose petals

½ part orange peel
Few drops cedar oil
1 part crushed juniper berries
1 part oak bark
½ part copal

SAGITTARIUS #2
2 parts frankincense
Few drops ylang ylang oil
Few drops orange oil

CAPRICORN #1
2 parts sandalwood
1 part benzoin
Few drops cypress oil
½ part willow bark
½ part mistletoe
½ part mugwort

CAPRICORN #2
3 parts frankincense
Few drops patchouli oil
Few drops cypress oil

For more Lear books and
special offers visit
www.learbooks.co.uk